Culture, Place, and Nature
STUDIES IN ANTHROPOLOGY AND ENVIRONMENT

Devon Peña and K. Sivaramakrishnan, Series Editors

Culture, Place, and Nature
STUDIES IN ANTHROPOLOGY AND ENVIRONMENT

Centered in anthropology, the Culture, Place, and Nature series encompasses new interdisciplinary social science research on environmental issues, focusing on the intersection of culture, ecology, and politics in global, national, and local contexts. Contributors to the series view environmental knowledge and issues from the multiple and often conflicting perspectives of various cultural systems.

The Kuhls of Kangra:
Community-Managed Irrigation in the Western Himalaya
BY MARK BAKER

The Earth's Blanket:
Traditional Teachings for Sustainable Living
BY NANCY TURNER

NANCY J. TURNER

THE
EARTH'S
Blanket

TRADITIONAL TEACHINGS FOR
SUSTAINABLE LIVING

UNIVERSITY OF WASHINGTON PRESS
Seattle

*This book is published in memory of
Marsha J. Landolt (1948–2004), Dean of the
Graduate School and Vice Provost,
University of Washington, with the support
of the University of Washington Press Endowment.*

University of Washington Press
P.O. Box 50096
Seattle, WA 98145–5096, U.S.A.
www.washington.edu/uwpress

Library of Congress Cataloging-in-Publication Data
Turner, Nancy J., 1947–
The earth's blanket : traditional teachings for sustainable living /
Nancy J. Turner.
p. cm. _ (Culture, place, and nature)
Includes bibliographical references and index.

ISBN 13: 978-0-295-98474-2 (cloth) · ISBN 10: 0-295-98474-0 (cloth)
ISBN 13: 978-0-295-98739-2 (paper) · ISBN 10: 0-295-98739-1 (paper)

1. Human ecology—Philosophy. 2. Indigenous peoples—Ecology.
3. Philosophy of nature. 4. Conservation of natural resources.
5. Environmental protection. I. Title. II. Series.
GF21.T87 2004   304.2—dc22   2004026122

Editing by Lucy Kenward
Copy-editing by Wendy Fitzgibbons
Cover and text design by Jessica Sullivan
Cover photographs: BACKGROUND: firstlight.ca.
PORTRAITS: Nancy J. Turner and Robert D. Turner
Interior photos by Nancy Turner unless otherwise noted
Printed and bound in Canada by Friesens
Printed on acid-free paper that is forest-friendly (100% post-consumer
recycled paper) and has been processed chlorine-free.

CONTENTS

Preface AND
Acknowledgements

THIS IS A BOOK ABOUT IDEAS—ideas that have been shared with me by my aboriginal friends and teachers, read about in books and papers, and brought together from my own lifetime experiences and observations. These are ideas that I believe all human beings need to consider more widely, because they pertain to the impacts we have on the Earth and, especially, on each other and the other life forms whose habitats we share. Despite the tremendous scientific and technological advances we have made since the Industrial Revolution, humans have not successfully protected our environments or cared for the Earth's other species. Much of today's environmental damage is a direct result of poorly considered use of technology and the impacts of this technological mindset. Our scientific sophistication has not been matched by our caring for the Earth—our environmental ethic.

In writing this book I have not set out to provide "the final word" on sustainable living and resource use. Rather, I hope to highlight the depth and richness of indigenous knowledge and of other ways of relating to the environment. Although much of this knowledge has not been "proven" by western science, I believe there are many ideas and approaches we can look to to help us in our search for better, less harmful ways to live, while maintaining healthy, fulfilling and satisfying lives.

I grew up surrounded by conventional western scientific thinking. My father and my grandfather were both entomologists, studying the biology and ecology of insects. In particular, I remember my father applying the scientific method to his research on the problems of bark beetle infestations in forests. To him, if something could not be verified by experimentation or conclusively demonstrated, it was problematic. I remember trying to quiz him about "water witching," or "dowsing," a method for finding underground water courses using a green willow wand or a stick. I'd watched my friend Freeman "Skipper" King help people determine where to dig wells by walking over the area with a forked willow stick, holding an arm of the Y in each hand and allowing the free central stem to pull itself towards any major water source. As a child I watched, on occasion, when the tip of the Y stick bent downwards and eventually the wand broke, so hard was its pull in Skipper's hands. Of course, I went home and asked my father how such a device could work. Although my father completely dismissed water witching as divination that had no scientific basis, he nonetheless found a way to impart this view without diminishing his, or my, respect for Skipper. He reminded me that there are many things in the world for which we have not yet achieved an understanding.

I learned from my father always to keep my mind open to new ideas and new concepts, always to try to understand other perspectives even if they do not make sense to me at the time. Without knowing it, he started me on a path of learning that has led to endless wonder and fascination as I strive to weave together my two major interests: Nature and human nature.

I began my formal education in other ways of knowing and thinking about the world in 1967 and 1968, as I was completing my undergraduate degree. I was working with Christopher Paul of the Tsartlip Band (W̱JOȽEȽP) on the Saanich Peninsula, my first teacher in ethnobotany— the study of the relationships between plants and people. Since then I have spent some thirty years working with and learning from aboriginal elders and cultural specialists here in British Columbia, through my research in ethnobotany. None of them has been financially wealthy, in the western concept of the word, but all of them have been rich in understanding and wisdom, and all have found immense satisfaction in knowing and living in their home places. Some of them, and their families, are still living in the same locations where their grandparents, great-grandparents and ancestors of many generations past have spent their lives. For those of us who are relative newcomers to the places where we reside, the implications of this extended timeline into the distant past are difficult even to comprehend.

Documenting botanical knowledge, including which species of plants are named and used by different cultures and groups, is a large part of my work. It has led me to understand that what might be just interesting, vague stories to outsiders have a much more profound meaning to people who have intimate knowledge of the places and the characters mentioned. Each story has its own context, its own situation. Not only do narratives and conversation convey essential cultural knowledge and information, they reveal lessons and ethical approaches to relationships with other people and to the environment. They are a way to share culturally sanctioned rules and protocols that have helped some societies to exist and sustain themselves within their local environments for many generations. Part of their traditional ecological knowledge and wisdom, these teachings are thoroughly linked and interwoven with practices and techniques for sustainable resource use, and with ways of learning and communicating both specific practices and ethical and moral principles. By studying and understanding the foundations of some of these ideas with appreciation and respect, people of all cultural backgrounds may be able to live more gently on the Earth.

Over the years I have become more and more aware of the important ties between ethnobotany and conservation, as well as the links between ethnobotany and ecological restoration—the art and science of recovering species and habitats that have been damaged by human activity. I experienced first-hand, working as an ethnobotanist on the provincially established Scientific Panel for Sustainable Forest Practices in Clayoquot Sound on the west coast of Vancouver Island, how traditional knowledge, including respect for the land and the living beings on it, can change the way environmental decisions are made. This independent group of about twenty specialists, including scientists and Nuu-Chah-Nulth elders, worked together from 1993 to 1995 to recommend to the government of British Columbia and to forest managers better ways of looking after the temperate rain forests of Clayoquot Sound. The panel was founded on recognizing and affirming both western science and the knowledge, interests and practices of long-resident First Nations.

In the past, and often still in the present, managers and officials from outside a region have imposed policies and regulations in forestry, fisheries and other activities that have major impacts on the environment and on communities at the local level. Decisions are made with little consideration of local knowledge and perspectives. For example, in Clayoquot Sound, many areas that were sacred to the Nuu-Chah-Nulth, and therefore critical to their well-being and identity, were destroyed by forest practices, especially road building and clear-cutting. The Nuu-Chah-Nulth members of the scientific panel took us on a tour of their homeland, explaining the significance of the different places, telling us stories that were set in this landscape and explaining their relationships to Nature and the sacredness and spirituality of their world.

The work of the Clayoquot scientific panel therefore reflected not only the local knowledge of the Nuu-Chah-Nulth participants but also recognized their deep connections to their territory. In addition, we followed as much as possible the Nuu-Chah-Nulth protocols and ways of working together, including listening respectfully to all points of view within the panel and making decisions consensually. Ultimately, we were able to produce a series of documents and recommendations to which all of us could agree and which were reasonably effective in directing less harmful and more sustainable forest use. An important lesson I took from this work was that our perspectives and attitudes—our ways of relating to the world—profoundly affect our actions and our treatment of the environment.

The idea for this book, then, is to demonstrate—and to try to better understand, myself—alternative ways of viewing the world and how these different perspectives might change the way society in general looks at the Earth. Consider, for example, the number of meanings and interpretations of our own English term "Nature." In his book *Home Place:*

Essays on Ecology, Stan Rowe discusses this very problem, presenting all the various perspectives that we in western society have about Nature, including the widespread belief that humans need to control and dominate Nature. Essays written by Sir Francis Bacon and later Enlightenment philosophers recommended that we "vex," or disturb, Nature to exploit her to the fullest. We have expanded the original concept of Nature to include "human nature," and yet seem to debate endlessly the dichotomy between "nature" and "culture," the notion that humans are not a part of Nature. Our very language is contradictory, reflecting our ambivalence about our relationship with our environment.

In developing the concept for the book I have struggled with many issues, the most difficult being the need to avoid appropriating or assuming the knowledge of others without properly recognizing and acknowledging the original sources or holders of that knowledge. Although I have had wonderful opportunities to learn about traditional ecological knowledge, I was not born into a traditional-knowledge environment.

The complex and sometimes overwhelming concerns around land and resource use for me are overlain with emotion and anguish in witnessing environmental destruction, which I have not been able to express or even explain. I have found, in working with and learning from people who are close to the the earth and close to their home places, a mirroring of my own distress. The knowledge that others are like-minded in their concerns about the land and the future of the earth has been empowering for me. I understand that there are many lessons to be learned, not just from the academic world of the sciences, social sciences and humanities, but from land-based societies and the wise people they have fostered. Writing this book is a form of medicine or therapy for me, to help me understand my own universe and to envision the changes that can be made to help the land to heal. More than this, though, I feel that the approaches to the environment I am documenting here are critically important and need to be more widely known and understood.

I have learned much from the wise teachers and elders of First Nations communities who have shared their knowledge and perspectives with me. As a non-indigenous academic, I have consulted at length with my aboriginal colleagues, teachers and friends to help guide me in the appropriate approaches and cultural protocols. The stories in this book that have been shared with me are published with the permission of those who told them. I sincerely appreciate their patience, support and confidence in me, and I hope that I have done justice to their wisdom. These advisers include (listed alphabetically): Art Adolph (Stl'atl'imx-Xaxl'ep), Dr. Richard Atleo (Chief *Umeek;* Nuu-Chah-Nulth–Ahousaht) and Dr. Marlene Atleo (*ʔeh ʔeh naa tuu kwiss*); Belinda Claxton *(Selliliye)* and Earl Claxton Sr. (ᴠᴇʟᴋᴀ́ᴛꜰᴇ; both Straits Salish–Tsawout); Pakki Chipps (Straits Salish and Ditidaht–Becher Bay); Chief Adam Dick (*Kwaxsistala;* Kwakwa̱ka'wakw–Qualicum-Dd^zawada7enux^w); Verna Miller (Nla-ka'pmx); Laurie Montour (Mohawk-Kahnawàke); Kim Recalma-Clutesi (*Ogwilogwa;* Kwakwa̱ka'wakw–Qualicum-Kwagiulth); Dr. Enrique Salmón (Rarámuri); Dr. Daisy Sewid-Smith (*Mayanilth;* Kwakwa̱ka'wakw-Mamaliliqela [Village Island], Campbell River); Dr. Mary Thomas (Secwepemc-Neskonlith); Pauline Waterfall (*Hilistis,* Heiltsuk–Bella Bella); Bill White (*Xelimuxw, Kasalid,* Coast Salish–Snuneymuxw-Cowichan, Victoria), and Barbara Wilson (*Ḵii7lljuus;* Haida-Skidegate).

Many, many others have contributed to the knowledge and teachings shared here and in making this book a reality, and I am deeply grateful to all of them, including (listed alphabetically within their nations, moving geographically from Vancouver Island to the North Coast, then inland): *Straits Salish:* Elsie Claxton, David Elliott Sr., John Elliott *(ꜱᴛᴏʟᴄᴇᴌ),* Ivan Morris, Christopher Paul, his son Philip Paul and their family (especially Chris Paul and Kevin Paul), Ernie Rice, Greg Sam, Dr. Samuel Sam, Theresa Sam, Tom Sampson, Edward Thomas (all Saanich); Bonnie Albany, Cheryl Bryce, Joan Morris, Robert Sam (all Lekwungen, or Songhees); *Halkomelem:* Bob Akerman, Arvid Charlie *(Lescheem),* Gordon DeFrane, Abel Joe, Abner Thorne, Theresa Thorne, Ellen White; *Ditidaht:* Chief Charlie Jones *(Queesto),* Ida Jones, John Thomas; *Nuu-Chah-Nulth:* Dawn Amos, Rocky Amos, Katherine Fraser, Chief Earl Maquinna George, Josephine George, Roy Haiyupis, Lena Jumbo, Alice Paul, Arlene Paul, Lawrence Paul, Stanley Sam; *Kwakwa̱ka'wakw:* Agnes Alfred, Agnes Cranmer, David Dawson, Flora Dawson, Christine Joseph *(Wata),* John and Mary Macko, Johnny Moon, Daisy Roberts; *Nuxalk (Bella Coola):* Willie Hans, Dave Moody, Dr. Margaret Siwallace, Felicity

Walkus; *Heiltsuk:* Cyril Carpenter and Jennifer Carpenter, Jessie Housty, Mary Hunt, Elroy White, Evelyn Windsor; *Haisla:* Ken Hall, Shirley Hall, Cecil Paul, Bea Wilson, Chris Wilson; *Gitga'at (Tsimshian):* Helen Clifton and Chief Johnny Clifton, Archie Dundas, Elizabeth Dundas, Belle Eaton, Ernie Hill Jr., Colleen and Gideon Robinson, Tina Robinson, Mildred Wilson; *Nisga'a:* Bert McKay, Deanna Nyce, Harry Nyce Sr., Harry Nyce Jr.; *Haida:* Diane Brown *(Gwaaganad),* Nika Collison, Florence Davidson and her family, Gwaai Edenshaw, Jaalen Edenshaw, Captain Gold and Mrs. Captain Gold (Bernice), Guujaaw, Golie Hans, Kathleen Hans, Roy Jones Sr., Emma and Willie Matthews (Chief *Weah*), Mabel Williams, Percy Williams, Emma and Sol Wilson, Ernie Wilson (Chief *Niiswes*), Ron Wilson *(Giitsxaa),* George Young, Ada Yovanovich; *Stl'atl'imx:* Ernie Adolph, Maggie Adolph, Marilyn Adolph, Herman Alec, Janice Billy, Nora Billy, Valerie Diablo, Tuffy Doss, Bill Edwards, Colleen Jacob, Roger John, Neawana John, Martina LaRochelle, Margaret Lester, Sam Mitchell, Edith O'Donaghey, Alec and Nellie Peters, Desmond Peters Sr., Baptiste Ritchie, Lucy Saul, Charlie Mack Seymour, *Nlaka'pmx:* Bernadette Antoine, Hilda Austin, Chief Leslie Edmonds, Mandy Jimmie, Mabel Joe, Julia Kilroy, Madeline Lanaro, Louie Philips, Arthur Urquhart, Annie York; *Secwepemc:* Dr. Aimee August, Irene Billy (originally Stl'atl'imx), Darrell Eustache, Ron Ignace and Dr. Marianne Ignace, Ida Matthew, Nellie Taylor, Louis Thomas; *Okanagan:* Jeanette Armstrong, Richard Armstrong, Willie and Lillie Armstrong, Martin Louie, Selina Timoyakin; *Sinixt (Lakes):* Nancy Wynecoop; *Spokane:* Nancy Flett; *Ktunaxa:* Catherine Grevelle, Troy Hunter, Pete McCoy, Frank and Mary Whitehead, Leo Williams; *Tsilhqut'in:* Minnie Charleyboy, Ubill Hunlin, Helena Myers, Linda Smith, Gilbert Solomon, Mabel Solomon, Maryann Solomon, Eileen William, Chief Roger William; *Ulkatcho (Dakelh):* Andy Cahoose, Annie Cahoose, Wilfred Cassam, Maddie Jack, Eliza Leon, Mack Squinas; *Tahltan:* Julia and Charley Callbreath, Garry Merkel, Curtis Rattray, Judith Thompson *(Edosdi);* *Gwich'in:* Alestine Andre, Chief Bill Erasmus, Ruth Welsh; *Mohawk:* Cecilia Mitchell; *Tohono O'odham:* Danny Lopez.

Many other friends and colleagues have provided advice or influenced the development of this book in various ways. I am so grateful to them all: Adrienne Aikins, Dr. Janis Alcorn, Dr. Eugene Anderson, Dr. Kat Anderson, Dr. Margaret Anderson, Doug Andrew, Dorothy Argent, Marguerite Babcock, Dr. Bill Balée, Bob Bandringa, Dr. Kelly Bannister, Dr. Brenda Beckwith, Dr. Marcus A.M. Bell, Dr. Fikret Berkes (especially for his helpful review of the final chapter), Sage Birchwater, Randy Bouchard, Dr. Robert Boyd, Dr. Chris Brayshaw, Dr. Cecil Brown, Dr. Conrad Brunk, Dan Cardinall, Dr. Catherine Carlson, Gianna Celli, Dr. Adolf Ceska, Fiona Hamersley Chambers, Kimberlee Chambers, Karen Chester, Dr. Mike Church, Wendy Cocksedge, Dr. Brian Compton, John Corsiglia, Dr. Harold Coward, Dr. Paul Cox, Juliet Craig, Stuart Crawford, Tara Cullis, Dr. Iain Davidson-Hunt, Dr. Douglas Deur, Adrienne Dewdney, Dr. Peter Dunwiddie, Dr. Don Eastman, Grant Thomas Edwards, Dr. William Elmendorf, Dr. Dick Ford, Dr. Jesse Ford, Dr. Kay Fowler, Ann Garibaldi, Dr. William Gibson, Tom Golumbia, Melissa Hadley, Dr. Gordon Hartman, Dr. Brian Hayden, Dr. Richard Hebda, Dr. Eric Higgs, Dr. Eugene Hunn, Dr. G. Brent Ingram, Dr. Timothy Johns, Dr. Leslie Main Johnson, Jim Jones, Larry Jorgenson, Dr. Elaine Joyal, Michèle Kay, Michael Keefer, Dr. Dorothy Kennedy, Freeman "Skipper" King, Dr. Harriet V. Kuhnlein, Dr. Andrea Laforet, Trevor Lantz, Dr. Dana Lepofsky, Kate Leslie, Bernadette Letchford (formerly Louisier), Dr. Robert Levine, Dr. Henry Lewis, Dawn Loewen, Dr. John Lutz, Karen McAllister, Nathalie Macfarlane, Dr. Quentin Mackie, Dennis Martinez, Jennifer Morrison, Dr. Gary Paul Nabhan, Dr. George Nicholas, Dr. Rosemary Ommer, Dr. Sandra Peacock, Dr. Devon Peña, Dr. Sinclair Philip, Dr. E.C. (Chris) Pielou, Dr. Darrell Posey, Hugh and Marilyn Price, Curtis Rattray, Dr. Amadeo Rea, Dr. Tom Reimchen, Dr. Leslie Saxon, Denis St. Claire, Dr. Gloria Snively, Dr. Michelle Stevens, Dr. Richard Stoffle, Dr. Wayne Suttles, Dr. David Suzuki, Dr. Duncan Taylor, Dr. Iain Taylor, Dr. Roy Taylor, Dr. Laurence C. Thompson and M. Terry Thompson, Dr. Jan Timbrook, Dr. Neil Towers, Dr. Ron Trosper, Robert Tyhurst, Dr. Jan Van Eijk, Dr. John Volpe, Dr. Paul West, Dr. Wendy Wickwire and Louise Wilson.

Of course, my family—Kate, Molly, Sarah, Damon, Shea, Janey, Isobel, Jan, Dave, Johnny, Linn, Kathleen and Wayne—has been an important part of my experiences and quests for knowledge. Words are inadequate to express my gratitude to my husband, Robert D. Turner, my companion through so much of this learning journey, for hundreds of hours of support, editing, advice and photography.

This research was funded in part through grants from the Social Sciences and Humanities Research Council of Canada (most notably general research grant number 410-2000-1166), and through a Major Collaborative Research Initiative grant, "Coasts Under Stress" (Dr. Rosemary Ommer, principal investigator). Much of the writing for this book was done through a faculty fellowship at the Centre for Studies in Religion and Society, University of Victoria (fall 2002) and through the Rockefeller Foundation's Bellagio Scholars in Residence Program (May 2003). Finally, I deeply appreciate the support and advice of Scott McIntyre and Saeko Usukawa and their confidence and energy in making this book a reality. I am especially grateful to Lucy Kenward, a perceptive and patient editor who is now a friend, and to Wendy Fitzgibbons, Naomi Pauls, Jessica Sullivan and the staff at Douglas & McIntyre and the University of Washington Press who have helped with this book.

PROLOGUE:

The LAND *and*

the PEOPLES

ANY OF THE STORIES and ideas in
this book were generated from the
landscapes and cultures of British
Columbia, Canada's westernmost province. Diversity comes immediately to mind when I think about this immense region of northwestern
North America and its varied geography, biology, cultures and languages. The coastline is rugged and indented, dotted with islands and cut
with deep channels and inlets. Since the time of the last glaciation around
10,000 years ago, the coastal land mass has risen and fallen so that parts
of the coastline have been both much higher and much lower than at
present. The mountainous landscapes have been scoured by sweeping
ice floes, the layers of rock carved through by torrential rivers and the
valleys filled by massive lakes, successively dammed and drained as
the ice melted and the stores of rock, gravel and sand it had trapped were
released and deposited.

As the landscape has changed, so has the plant and animal life it supports. Habitats we now find in the North and near the tops of mountains
once occurred in the southern and lowland regions, sustaining species,

now limited, that were once more common and widespread. Naturalists such as my friend Richard Hebda, a paleoecologist who studies the pollen deposited and preserved in wetlands by successive populations of different kinds of trees and other plants, can read the story of environmental change like a book. For example, on southern Vancouver Island between about 7,000 and 9,000 years ago the pollen of oaks and grassland species was even more predominant than today, indicating that the climate there was drier and warmer at that time. Western red-cedar *(Thuja plicata)*, the tree known as the cornerstone of Northwest Coast aboriginal culture, has been common in the coastal forests only within the last 4,000 years or so. In the interior similar changes took place, with first cooler, then warmer and then again cooler conditions prevailing since the time of the last glaciation. Some species, such as Rocky Mountain juniper *(Juniperus scopulorum)* and lodgepole pine *(Pinus contorta* var. *latifolia)*, have remained constant elements of the interior forests, whereas others have appeared only recently. Animals, too, have fluctuated in species and abundance, depending on the availability of their food sources and habitats. Salmon *(Oncorhynchus* spp.), however, have been part of the region's aquatic life for at least 15,000 years, as revealed by a series of amazing 15,000-to-18,000-year-old salmon fossils from Kamloops Lake near Savona.

Today the ecological regions of British Columbia are highly diverse, shaped by the localized and complex forces of geology, geography and climate to produce countless variations on the landscape. The result is an enormous range of forestlands and other types of habitats, from the dry, treeless grasslands and sagebrush steppes of the southern interior valleys to the magnificent forests of the west coast with their stands of giant western red-cedar, western hemlock *(Tsuga heterophylla)*, Sitka spruce *(Picea sitchensis)*, amabilis fir *(Abies amabilis)* and Douglas-fir *(Pseudotsuga menziesii)*.

At higher elevations on the coast, these forests give way to more cold-tolerant montane trees such as yellow-cedar *(Chamaecyparis nootkatensis)* and mountain hemlock *(Tsuga mertensiana)*. On the drier southeastern coast of Vancouver Island Douglas-fir predominates, together with grand fir *(Abies grandis)*, arbutus *(Arbutus menziesii)* and, in the very driest sites, garry oak *(Quercus garryana)*. The woodlands there are interspersed with meadows of camas (*Camassia* spp.) and other spring-blooming wild-flowers mixed with grasses and shrubby vegetation. Douglas-fir extends across the province and northwards as far as the Kitlope Valley on the coast, as well as inland to the Nass Valley.

In the hotter, drier forested regions of the interior, above the grass-lands and steppes of the valley bottoms and below the Douglas-fir zone, are open stands of ponderosa pine *(Pinus ponderosa)* with its clusters of long, decorative needles and pinkish pastel-coloured bark and tall bushes of Saskatoon berry or service berry *(Amelanchier alnifolia)*, mock orange *(Philadelphus lewisii)* and other shrubs. Rocky Mountain juniper is fre-quently found in these dry woodlands.

The coastal forest theme is replayed in the interior wet belt of the Kootenays and extends north into the Cariboo range, where abundant rainfall and snowfall again support the growth of large trees in dense forests: western hemlock and western red-cedar, as well as white pine *(Pinus monticola)*, lodgepole pine, western larch *(Larix occidentalis)* and Engelmann spruce *(Picea engelmannii)*. The spruce ranges into the high-elevation forests, with subalpine fir *(Abies lasiocarpa)*, spire-shaped in form, mixing with wildflower meadows that in turn blend upwards into the treeless alpine zone.

Deciduous trees—maples (*Acer* spp.), alders (*Alnus* spp.), cottonwood *(Populus balsamifera)*, trembling aspen *(Populus tremuloides)*, birches (*Betula* spp.) and willows (*Salix* spp.)—are also important players in the botanical landscape. They tend to grow in moister areas, along creeks, lakes and valley bottoms, but they are very versatile in their requirements.

The northern interior forests are less diverse and slower growing since they endure colder, longer winters, but they have their own beauty and bounty. An aerial view of the northern forestlands shows a mosaic of shades of green—from the dark foliage of the lodgepole pine and white and black spruce *(Picea glauca, P. mariana)* to the bright stands of aspens and birches—interspersed with dense thickets of willows and open muskeg dotted with and dissected by myriad lakes, ponds and rivers.

Through at least the past 11,000 years, and some say much longer, the land has supported communities of people who have relied on the plants and animals of their home regions for their survival. These people have, since time immemorial for them, adapted their lifestyles to the changing climates and the fluctuations in abundance of fish, wildlife and plants. If there is one overriding theme extending over time and space for human survival in this vast region, it is change—and adaptation to change. Being keen and vigilant observers, scientists in the broadest sense of the word, indigenous peoples have not only used the resources around them but maintained and enhanced them in various ways. They have developed ingenious and innovative methods for harvesting and processing their fish, shellfish, meat, berries and root vegetables for transportation and storage and have learned ways to optimize the nutritional and other benefits of these resources. At the same time they have found diverse means, through developing cultural institutions and protocols, to control their impacts on other species and to accommodate the changes that have occurred over millennia.

This is not to say that they have not made mistakes or that all of their choices and methods have been the best ones. There have been instances, probably many, when people took too much of a resource or neglected to put aside enough stored foods to carry them through the winter. There have been elites who have benefited unfairly from the labour of others, who have taken too much for themselves and not shared equitably. There has been warfare and slavery and plenty of conflict. The oral traditions of virtually every group of peoples tell about these occasions and warn of their consequences. These are a major part of the teachings and lessons that have guided and informed people's lives and from them, even in a contemporary context, all of us can benefit.

The First Peoples who have occupied the land are, like their environments, diverse both linguistically and culturally. In British Columbia alone they have spoken over thirty different languages, each with a range of dialects or variants. Today in many areas far fewer people are still fluent in their traditional languages, but programs are underway in many places, in schools and cultural centres, to revive these languages and teach them to the children and youth who will maintain them even as the elder speakers pass on. For example, my friends Ron and Marianne Ignace are dedicated to making sure the Secwepemc (Shuswap) language and cultural knowledge live on. They make a point of speaking Secwepemc-tsin to their four young children, and they and many others are working tirelessly to maintain this and other precious languages that embody so much knowledge and history.

Some of these languages are closely related. For example, Secwepemctsin, spoken since childhood by Ron Ignace and Dr. Mary Thomas, belongs to the Salishan family of languages. It is related to ten other languages spoken by people whose territory is within British Columbia, including SENĆOTEN (Saanich), Halkomelem, Sechelt, Squamish, Comox, Nlaka'pmx (Thompson), Stl'atl'imx (Lillooet), Okanagan, Sinixt (Lakes) and Nuxalk (Bella Coola), as well as several others in Washington, Idaho and Montana, including Flathead and Snchitsu'umshtsn (Coeur d'Alene). The languages of the Nuu-Chah-Nulth, Ditidaht, Kwakwaka'wakw (literally, "Kwak'wala-speaking people," also known as Kwagiulth or Kwakiutl), Heiltsuk (Bella Bella), Oweekeno and Haisla are all related to each other, being in the Wakashan language family. Two other major language families are Athapaskan (Tsilhqut'in, Dakelh or Carrier, Kaska, Sekani, Slave, Tahltan, Tsetsaut, Babine-Witsuwit'en) and Tsimshian (Coast Tsimshian, Southern Tsimshian or Kitasoo, Gitxsan, Nisga'a). Tlingit is distantly related to the Athapaskan group. There are also Cree and Saulteaux (Ojibwe) peoples in northeastern British Columbia. Two languages spoken in British Columbia and neighbouring areas—Haida in the northwest and Ktunaxa, or Kootenay (Kutenai), in the southeast—are linguistically isolated from all other languages, that is, they have no other known related languages.

Figure 1 shows the territories of the major language groups referred to in this book. Different names have been used historically and in the literature to refer to these various groups. I have attempted to use the names for peoples and their languages that they themselves prefer; sometimes these are different from those that have been most commonly known or used outside the communities, but I hope they will gain wider usage.

Indigenous peoples within the major areas of the province share cultural similarities in their traditional economies, social organization and lifestyles that are independent from the language relationships. Coastal peoples in British Columbia, for example, share a common, marine-oriented lifestyle and, together with other indigenous peoples

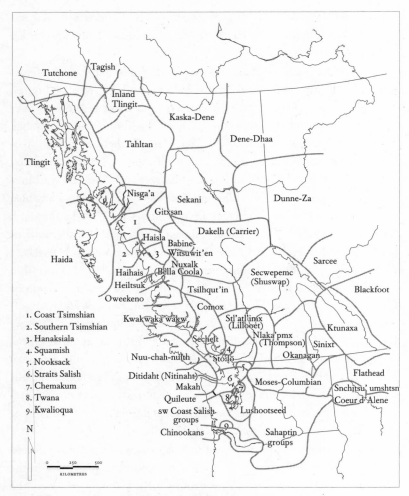

Figure 1. Map showing the territories of First Peoples of British Columbia and neighbouring areas (revised from Turner and Loewen 1998).

from northern California to southwestern Alaska, are considered to belong to the Northwest Coast Culture Area. These people, at least within the past 3,000 years or so, travelled mostly by dugout canoes made from western red-cedar and lived in large, multi-family houses constructed of red-cedar posts, beams and planks. Their major food, harvested from different sites within the traditional territory of each group, has consisted of the different species of Pacific salmon and other fish, marine mammals, shellfish, berries and various greens and root vegetables. Their art, narratives and complex ceremonies, especially for some Northwest Coast peoples such as the Haida and Kwakwa̱ka'wakw, are well known and widely profiled by anthropologists and others.

The First Peoples of the southern interior of British Columbia, from the northern Secwepemc territory around Williams Lake southward, are part of a broader cultural division known as the Plateau Culture Area. These peoples traditionally lived in semi-subterranean pit houses during the winter, and then, from spring through fall, they travelled through their territory, harvesting and processing fish, game and vegetable foods as these became available at different locations. Salmon migrating each year up the major river systems were a staple for them, as these fish were for the coastal peoples, and harvesting berries and root vegetables was also a major part of their seasonal round.

The northern interior peoples share cultural traits with other northerly groups and are part of the Subarctic Culture Area. They tended to live in smaller family-based groups that travelled widely over the landscape, relying heavily on caribou, deer and other game as well as on fish, berries and, to some extent, roots and greens.

All of these peoples, no matter where they lived or with which culture area they had affinities, depended completely on their environments and their communities for survival. All of them relied heavily on plants for food, materials and medicines and in their language, narratives and ceremonies. And all of them had deep and enduring ties with their homelands and territories that extended back for hundreds and sometimes thousands of years.

Since the Europeans arrived, however—first with the fur trade, then through the era of settlement and colonialism and, finally, with the development of an intensive, increasingly globalized economy with all the conveniences and trappings of the contemporary world—the cultures and lifestyles of First Peoples have changed dramatically. There is no question that many of the changes have been beneficial, but there have been costs, both social and environmental. The balance and harmony with the natural world that the people have striven to achieve has been elusive.

Chief Adam Dick
(Kwaxsistala; Kwakwa̱ka̱'wakw—Qualicum–Dᴣawadaꜰenuxw)

2

Wealth and VALUE
in a CHANGING *World*

LONG AGO, the ancestors of the present-day Nlaka'pmx (Thompson) Interior Salish formulated a concept that came from the depths of their being, from their deeply held belief in the integrity of their world and from their insightful understanding of the fragile and reciprocal relationship humans have with their environments. That is the concept of Earth's Blanket.

Earth's Blanket

Our knowledge of Earth's Blanket comes from the handwritten ethnobotanical notes of James Teit, a dedicated ethnographer who lived and worked with the Nlaka'pmx and other aboriginal peoples of the southern Interior of British Columbia in the late 1800s and early 1900s. Born in the Shetland Islands of Scotland in 1864, Teit emigrated to North America at the age of nineteen, moving to the small town of Spences Bridge along the Thompson River the following year. In 1892 he married Lucy Antko, a Nlaka'pmx woman. Although she died of pneumonia on 2 March 1899, seven years after their marriage, Lucy and her family probably taught Teit much about the language and traditional ways of the Nlaka'pmx. He obviously had an abiding interest in plants and natural history, as well as in language, and he put these skills to use helping legendary anthropologist Franz Boas to record and document what Boas viewed as the rapidly vanishing cultural and linguistic knowledge of the interior First Peoples.

So it was that, around the turn of the century, Teit was working on a manuscript, one of many he produced, in which he was meticulously listing and itemizing all the Nlaka'pmx names and uses of plants. There, about a third of the way down a page, within a sheaf of such pages in his notebook, are two major notations, beautifully scripted like all of his notes and letters. The first is: *".spákEm [sp'áq'm] flowers in general. Flowers are the valuables of the earth or mtns and if they are plucked ruthlessly the earth sorrows or cries."* Then, after an inscription in Nlaka'pmx, comes the entry: *"siekEm [s-yíqm] grass in general. Flowers, plants & grass especially the latter are the covering or blanket of the earth. If too much plucked or ruthlessly destroyed [the] earth [is] sorry and weeps. It rains or is angry and makes rain, fog & bad weather."*

These two entries represent a cultural belief, a sanction against destroying culturally and ecologically important species and habitats. The "valuables of the earth" and "Earth's Blanket" are powerful metaphors. They signify an attitude towards Earth and the plants growing upon it that would have guided the Nlaka'pmx people's behaviour, that would have reminded them of the importance of vegetation and constrained any harmful actions against it. Indeed, these words convey a positive, direct and reciprocal relationship between these people and their environment, in which the consequences of wrongful action are seen to be immediate and direct.

Many other environmentally based sanctions and taboos are embedded in the cultural traditions of the Nlaka'pmx and other First Nations, as in the cultures of long-resident peoples the world over. Stories and ceremonies that invoke Earth, the needs of Earth and the potential reaction of Earth to people's mistreatment demonstrate a long and multi-stranded tradition of viewing Earth and its landscapes as a living being, a vast, nurturing entity on which humans depend absolutely for their survival and well-being. In essence, the Earth's Blanket concept is similar to the Gaia hypothesis proposed by British scientist James Lovelock in his 1979 book *Gaia: A New Look at Life on Earth*. The basis of Lovelock's theory is that Earth is a self-regulating organism that adjusts to changes in order to maintain suitable conditions for life. Although he contends that life on Earth will continue no matter what humans do to it, he suggests that some life forms, including humans, may not survive the adjustments the planet is forced to make to accommodate the imposed changes.

Respectful Use and a Clash of Values

Neither the Earth's Blanket concept nor the Gaia hypothesis says that people should not *use* the grasses, the flowers or the other resources they need for survival. Rather, this world view implies the need for careful and thoughtful attention to such use. At the time that Teit was writing, the Nlaka'pmx, whose territory straddles the Coast and Cascade mountain ranges and extends along the Fraser, Thompson and Nicola River drainages, recognized and used more than 300 different species of plants and dozens of species of animals, birds and fish from a wide range of habitats. They and their neighbours, the Stl'atl'imx, Secwepemc, Okanagan, Stó:lō and other peoples of northwestern North America, tended the landscape and the plants too, burning over areas of brush to enhance the productivity of edible roots and berries, in some cases cutting trees for construction as needed, and harvesting an assortment of natural materials, foods and medicines. They travelled widely over their lands in a patterned seasonal round, harvesting quantities of these foods and materials, processing them for storage and winter use. But always they would have had a close familiarity with their valleys, forests, meadows and mountaintops and the resources they provided.

By the twentieth century the prevailing attitude towards the land had changed fundamentally and the Nlaka'pmx and other First Peoples were caught up in a clash of conflicting values. Consider, for example, the introductory statement from *Forests of British Columbia*, the 1918 report to the Canadian Commission of Conservation written by H.N. Whitford and R.D. Craig:

All the efforts of the Dominion must be devoted to production and economy. The vast resources of Canada, to which the term 'illimitable' has been so frequently applied, because of lack of knowledge, must be turned to some useful purpose. *Untilled fields, buried minerals or standing forests are of no value except for the wealth which, through industry, can be produced therefrom.* (Emphasis added.)

Later in their book, Whitford and Craig described the grasslands of Nlaka'pmx territory, referring to the very grasses described as Earth's Blanket by James Teit's careful hand. These men acknowledged the already evident problems of resource overuse at a time just a decade or two after Teit inscribed his notes. As representatives of the Dominion, however, Whitford and Craig saw a different future for this landscape:

The most characteristic plant of the natural grass lands in the southern part of the Interior system [of British Columbia] is the bunch grass (*Agropyron spicatum* [now *Pseudoroegneria spicata*]). Over some areas it has been practically exterminated by over-grazing. . . . Where irrigation is possible, the grass lands of the valleys are the best agricultural regions of the province. The crops raised are mostly fruit, vegetables and forage, with some grain.

Their view, an essentially utilitarian image of the land in terms of maximizing its usefulness to humans, was typical of the time. The "savage wilderness" was to be transformed into "civilization" and production in the likeness of European countryside and industry-based urbanization. Railways and highways, farms and hayfields, orchards, mines, canneries: these represented the "right" way to use the land. British geography professor David Demerritt summed up this view of "carving civilization out of savage wilderness" in a 1996 article on agricultural expansion in British Columbia: "Wilderness was wilderness—the opposite of the productive landscape of fences, fields, and small farms idealized by agrarianism. Mountains, forests, aridity—these were mere challenges to the hardy pioneer and his frugal wife. Agrarianism maintained that this wilderness would eventually yield and that social progress could be measured by the advance of agricultural settlement."

As the land was cleared and planted, even the Nlaka'pmx and other First Peoples were recruited in the drive to expand production from the land. Pioneer settler Jessie Ann Smith of Spences Bridge, whose family had come to Canada on the same ship as James Teit, observed extensive wooden flumes being built along the steep sidehills of the Thompson River valley to irrigate the benchlands for orchard and hay production. Around 1884, she noted that Nlaka'pmx men were employed in this project and was surprised that even the women had been enlisted:

> I was amazed to see the Indian women working too. With tump-line straps across their foreheads, the Indian women carried the flume boards on their backs up the side of the mountain to the men. They also carried up water from the Thompson River to cool the tools that the men were handling, for the heat was so intense.

What did these Nlaka'pmx workers think when they saw their lands being converted to European-style production in this way? How did they reconcile their participation with their traditional Earth's Blanket perspective? They were practical and adaptive people, but it must have caused them anguish and confusion. Secwepemc elder Mary Thomas well recalls that her own parents succumbed to the European way in the early 1900s at Salmon Arm along Shuswap Lake:

> But my father and mother, I guess they were willing learners; they were really busy clearing land, which was not traditional with us, cutting down trees—you can imagine what they had to go through, because of their connection to Mother Nature. I often heard my mother talk about this, that it wasn't their way of life, but they had no choice, they had to accept the way they were taught. How to survive was to chop down all these trees and cultivate it [the land] into a European way of living. I guess that's where we began to lose a lot of the traditional foods. And it was hard work going out and getting that stuff, and I guess it's equally as hard to put in a garden and keep it weeded and everything, but the sad part is losing the traditional values.

The traditional values Mary Thomas refers to are ones that her mother and grandmothers held, which she learned from them and has retained and strengthened. The values include the ways in which children are cared for, birchbark is harvested for baskets, berries are gathered, salmon is honoured and herbal medicines are prepared. Like other traditionally raised elders, however, she worries that these values of caring and respect for the land and all the life it supports are being subsumed by the dominant, materialist culture. On many occasions she has expressed this concern. Now in her late eighties, she has dedicated the last decades of her life to passing on her vast knowledge and sharing her wisdom with her own people and any others who are interested. She believes firmly that unless people become educated about these important cultural traditions and the values and philosophies on which they are based, the environment will continue to deteriorate, and the inevitable result will be a decline in the health and well-being of her people and all others on Earth.

Motivating many of the imprints we make on the land and resources is a quest for personal wealth and material goods. We accumulate wealth, at least in part, to get us through anticipated hard times. At the same time, however, by taking too much from the lands that support us we bring on hard times—for ourselves and for future generations.

Defining Wealth

Elders from many nations around British Columbia and beyond see value in the land and in their cultural traditions. No amount of gold or currency can make up for the loss of their traditional lifeways or of their ability to care for and benefit from their own homelands.

I believe that wealth—real wealth—is found among people who have a sound sense of their place in the world, who link their actions and thoughts with those of others and who are strong, vigorous and co-operative actors in their communities and ecosystems. Rich are those people who balance the benefits they receive in life with the responsibilities they assume for themselves, their families and communities and their environment. Wealth dwells in people who know about, appreciate and respect the other life forms around them and who understand the importance of habitats for people and all living things. These teachings are deeply ingrained in many traditional societies and would benefit contemporary societies in general.

"We were a wealthy people," explained *Kwaxsistala* (Adam Dick), one of the hereditary chiefs of the Dᶻawada7enuxʷ of Kingcome Inlet, when we were talking about the old ways of the Kwakwaka'wakw of coastal British Columbia. He was not talking about financial wealth; he was referring to the value of a viable and productive home place. The world of Adam's youth was full of vigour and beauty. The water was clear and sparkling, the air fresh and untainted and the forests teeming with birds and wildlife. He was familiar with the wolves, bears, beavers, mink and all the other animals of the forest and sea that inspired the magnificent and evocative representational art that is the hallmark of Northwest Coast indigenous peoples. (*Kwaxsistala*'s own daughter, Francis Dick, is a renowned artist who uses such natural imagery.)

As our discussion continued, *Kwaxsistala*'s eyes were raised in concentrated memory as he started to list all the different foods he and his family used to enjoy at their prime—the salmon, herring, eulachon (*Thaleichtys pacificus*, a small, oily smelt valued for the grease rendered from it), seals, deer, geese, salmonberries, crabapples, rice-root, clover roots and eelgrass and the dozens of other berries, root vegetables and greens. The memory of these valued foods made him smile and exclaim, "Oh, I can taste those berries now!"

Part of people's wealth in *Kwaxsistala*'s world, too, was sharing the bounty of Nature with the plants and animals that live in our habitats. These beings are so integral to the concept of riches in the society in which *Kwaxsistala* was raised that, without their presence and their participation, no matter how comfortable and well-fed the people were they would consider themselves impoverished. For example, the salmon were vital for people's existence not just because they were a major food source but because they were seen as essential cohabitants of the Kwakwaka'wakw world. Likewise, the western red-cedar tree *(Thuja plicata, wilkʷ)*, infinitely useful for its fibrous bark, clear and durable wood, aromatic boughs and tough, cordlike roots and prized for all these attributes, was honoured and revered for the quality of its magnificent tree-spirit, not just for the service it rendered humans. And so it was with all the plants of the forest and the fish of the river and sea. Their very presence, like the grass and flowers that comprised Earth's Blanket for the Nlaka'pmx, was part of *Kwaxsistala*'s feeling of comfort and security, part of his wealth.

At some point in our history, mainstream society has lost its reverence for the natural world; we have become more acquisitive and self-serving in our attitudes. For most of us in the urbanized, globalized society of today, being rich is readily equated with the amount of money we earn or manage to generate and with the extravagances we can afford—luxurious accommodations, expensive foods and exotic getaways to Paris or New York or the Bahamas. Even those of us who cannot achieve these particular goals often aspire to them, savour the idea of them and consider ourselves more successful the more we approach them. Many people use financial wealth to bolster their self-image. We say to ourselves: "I made it. I can do what I wish. I am the master of my own destiny!"

In the western world we generally do not have to occupy ourselves with actually gathering or harvesting our food, and so we do not often think about where our food comes from or how much it has cost in time, money or energy to produce. We quite happily drink wine from France or savour caviar from the Caspian Sea, pineapples flown in fresh from Hawaii, tiger prawns from the brackish aquacultural ponds of Thailand and beef from the stockyards of the Great Plains of North America or from the denuded tropical highlands of Guatemala and Honduras. This is the privilege of monetary wealth—never having to think about the environmental and social cost of the food we consume or the materials and tools we use.

However, more possessions, accumulations of material wealth beyond our basic needs of food and shelter, do not actually make us any happier. On the contrary, studies have shown that if we move up the economic ladder without the comforts of close family and social bonds, without a strong sense of identity, without intellectual challenge and stimulation or without strong ties with the natural world and a realization of our place within it, we become more stressed, more depressed and more discontented. Ironically, we often try to counter these feelings of dissatisfaction by acquiring more and more financial wealth and its trappings. To under-

stand real wealth, we must become familiar with the origins of our resources, with the processes involved in their production and with the
impacts we might be having as consumers.

Kwaxsistala has seen first-hand the damage from the pulp-mill and domestic sewage outlets near Campbell River, close to his home and in the
heart of the traditional fishing and seafood-gathering grounds of the
Kwakwa̲ka'wakw. Chemical and biological effluents have contaminated
clam beds and caused a decline in both the quantity and quality of salmon,
crab, octopus, red and green sea urchins (*Strongylocentrus* spp.), butter
clams *(Saxidomus giganteus),* cockles *(Clinocardium nuttallii),* edible laver
seaweed *(Porphyra abbottiae)* and eelgrass *(Zostera marina, ts'ats'-ayem)*
beds over the past several decades. People no longer feel safe harvesting
and eating their local seafood. The food-based riches of *Kwaxsistala*'s youth
have diminished and in some cases disappeared altogether. Where they
used to harvest the healthful laver seaweed, which he calls *łeq'estén,*
around the northeast coast of Vancouver Island, now he and his family
have to purchase this delicacy, when they can get it, from friends and relatives far up the coast.

Kwaxsistala lamented, "We were the richest people in the world. I'm
not talking about money, but everything that we had before. We'd just go
down to the beach and get a bucketful of clams, just enough for dinner,
like that. And we can't do this any more. We haven't got it any more.
Now we're really poor." In expressing these concerns, *Kwaxsistala* worries
not only about the health of his family and his community but about the
well-being of all the marine creatures, birds and trees of the local environment that are subjected to pollution and habitat loss.

Being an active and direct player in the ecosystem, at once an observer
and a participant, a learner and a teacher, a contributor and a user, can
make us sensitive to Earth's needs and dynamics, to the damage we are
doing to the planet and its life. When we slow down long enough to experience Nature, to remember what it is that gives us pleasure, we realize its
wealth.

I get a feeling of complete bliss from a long day of berry-picking,
searching the mountainsides and creek margins for the ultimate berry-
laden bush. There, amidst the tranquil sound of running water and the

spicy scent of evergreens, I surround the clustered berries with my fingers and feel the generous release when they part from the stems. I feel as if I am helping them to fulfill their ultimate evolutionary destiny, to multiply and disseminate themselves over the earth. As well as taking some for my own use, I leave behind plenty for the bears, the birds, the insects; to me, *that* is enriching.

The Wealth of a Place

The Earth's Blanket metaphor compels people to consider that which is valuable to *Earth*, and to link Earth's wealth and important possessions— the flowers, the grass and other vegetation—to human action. These are environmental treasures, and if humans do not pay attention to what is important to Earth the consequences to us will be serious. Focussing on the area where the phrase originated and the fate of the landscape there provides a context for a shift in our perceptions. To fully appreciate this phrase and its complexities of nuance and meaning, we should never lose sight of the fact that it comes from the Nlaka'pmx language and that it originated in the late 1800s from the Interior Plateau of British Columbia.

The area surrounding Spences Bridge has always been a geographical and ecological mosaic. There are trees and woodlands—mostly ponderosa pine, Douglas-fir and some Rocky Mountain juniper and cottonwood—on the moister slopes and funnelling into the steep-sided gulleys running down to the Thompson River and its tributary creeks. Farther up in the mountains are plenty of forestlands, with Douglas-fir, lodgepole pine, Engelmann spruce, subalpine fir, western red-cedar, aspen and birch. Downriver towards Lytton, where the Thompson and Fraser Rivers meet, and beyond in the lower reaches of the Fraser Canyon around Spuzzum, the forests form a dense, multicoloured and multitextured tapestry over the steep terrain. But around Spences Bridge and Ashcroft there are few trees; instead, vast swaths of mixed sagebrush and grassland steppe extend their soft pastel hues over the river benches and back up into the valleys and rolling tablelands beyond.

Some people would call this a desert landscape, but in its original state it was productive and biologically diverse. Bluebunch wheat grass, or bunch grass (*syiqm 7uy*—the "real/original grass or hay" of the

Bitterroot (Lewisia rediviva), *called sp'itlm or lhqwepn in Nlaka'pmx.*

PHOTO BY ROBERT D. TURNER

Nlaka'pmx) was the dominant grassland species, but in the swales or moist depressions large clumps of giant wild rye *(Elymus cinereus, pesenúlhten)* formed extensive patches.

Other than the bunch grass itself, one of the key species for the Nlaka'pmx was bitterroot *(Lewisia rediviva)*, called *sp'itl'm* or *lhqwepn.* Known by some as "desert rose," bitterroot is a low-growing, taprooted perennial bearing small, fleshy leaves in dense rosettes in early spring and soon after, in the month of May, producing large, exquisite, bright-pink flowers. The entire plants mature and dry out quickly, so that by mid-summer there is little evidence of their presence amongst the sagebrush and bunch grass. Nevertheless, they were there in the southern interior drylands in enormous numbers, and they were a staple food for the

Nlaka'pmx, Secwepemc, Okanagan, Sinixt, Flathead, Ktunaxa and other Interior Plateau peoples who had access to them. The roots were dug in their preflowering state, deftly peeled, then dried for later use and for trade. The Nlaka'pmx women around Spences Bridge and Ashcroft treasured these plants, harvesting them selectively and replanting parts of the root to ensure that they would replenish themselves and maintain their populations. They also transplanted bitterroot from one area to another and may have extended the plant's original range considerably.

In 1915 botanist John Davidson, fondly remembered as "Botany John," travelled through the lower Thompson River region accompanied by James Teit, and in mid-May he recorded his observations of bitterroot and its use by the Nlaka'pmx, from the open, undulating country of the Rattlesnake Hills near Spences Bridge. He described vast expanses of bitterroot, covering several square miles, and noted the bitterroot plants were "present in millions." At one point, he counted twenty-two plants in a square foot of ground and reported that commonly there was an average of a dozen plants per square foot. Davidson and Teit met several parties of local aboriginal women who, Davidson observed, travelled many miles by horseback to reach the bitterroot grounds. They collected the roots "by the aid of wooden or iron root-diggers." The quantities of these roots routinely harvested at that time, less than a hundred years ago, are significant:

> From an examination of several Indian camping-places it was seen that the women evidently collect a supply of roots and return to camp to strip them. One can picture half a dozen Indian women, squatted before the camp-fire at the close of a day's digging, busy peeling the roots preparatory to packing them. The small heaps of skins left at most of the camps indicated that each party returned with many hundreds— perhaps thousands—of roots.

"Botany John" had an opportunity to try these nutritious roots, which the camp cook "prepared . . . in the true Indian fashion for my benefit," and Davidson noted that they formed a pinkish starchy jelly that tasted slightly bitter, "like quinine."

Bitterroots, peeled and soaking in water before being dried.

Few of the European newcomers to the interior sagebrush country would have appreciated the importance of bitterroot to the Nlaka'pmx lifeways or have seen the plants for more than the appeal of a fleeting bright-coloured flower in an otherwise drab landscape. So it was with virtually all the diverse plants treasured by the Nlaka'pmx and other indigenous peoples. Bitterroot was so much valued that dried, peeled bitterroots were part of the complex trading arrangements between the Lower Nlaka'pmx, or Utámqt, around Spuzzum, and the Upper Nlaka'pmx of the drier regions from Boston Bar and Lytton to Spences Bridge. Nlaka'pmx elder Annie York, co-author of our book *Thompson Ethnobotany*, stressed, "That's expensive stuff, that [bitterroot]. . . . We don't have that bitterroot here [in Spuzzum] ... that's all up there [upriver]—comes from there and they trade. They trade with their vegetables here ... we have the fish here and then we trade with the bitterroot." On another occasion, Annie explained why people dried bitterroot by stringing it on Indian-hemp thread: "The reason why they used the string is to know how much they trade. And then, when that's dry [the bitterroots], the smallest little pieces that are broken, they take that and take Saskatoons. They pour the dried *speqpáq* [Saskatoon variety] and they mix it in there and then they put it in this bag, after they've dried it nice ... and they hang it up. ..."

OTHER CULTURALLY IMPORTANT species of the interior Nlaka'pmx region included mariposa or desert lily *(Calochortus macrocarpus, mek7-ú7sa7)*, whose bulbs were eaten raw; desert parsley *(Lomatium macrocarpum, qw'eqw'íle)*, whose celery-flavoured young taproots were dug and eaten, and balsamroot or spring sunflower *(Balsamorhiẓa sagittata, soxwm̓)*, a brilliant yellow-flowered, arrow-leaved plant whose large, fibrous taproots were carefully pit-cooked for many hours, usually twenty-four or more, after which they became sweet-tasting and more edible than the raw roots. With extensive slow steam-cooking, the main storage carbohydrate in balsamroot, a complex sugar called inulin, transforms into shorter-moleculed, sweeter and more digestible fructans and fructose. Balsamroot also yielded edible spring greens in the form of newly sprouting leaves and peeled bud stems, and edible seeds, which were ground to a meal and mixed with deer fat or put into soup as a nutritious thickener.

Prickly pear cactus *(Opuntia fragilis, O. polyacantha, skaẓkaẓ́)* was a life-giving food for the Nlaka'pmx. Not only were the succulent stem pads eaten routinely as a cooked green vegetable (after the spines were singed off in the fire, of course), but at certain times, especially in early spring when food was scarce, cactus became a critical part of the diet. For example, Annie York was told by her great-aunt about a famine that occurred before Annie's time, in the late 1800s. The fish did not come up the river, and deer were not to be found. People had to rely completely on their vegetable foods—the young peeled shoots of cow parsnip *(Heracleum lanatum, hékwu7)*; glacier lily bulbs *(Erythronium grandiflorum,*

Balsamroot or spring sunflower (Balsamorhiza sagittata).

PHOTO BY ROBERT D. TURNER

sk'émets); spring beauty corms *(Claytonia lanceolata, tetúwṅ)* from higher up in the mountains; bracken fern rhizomes *(Pteridium aquilinum, sá7eq)*, and cactus stems. Annie recalled:

> The *skaⱬkaⱬ* [prickly pear] they always eat it all right enough, but they *had* to eat it [during the famine]. My grand aunt told me, "We eat that three times a day!" she says. There was no fish, nothing. And that [cactus] was all the children, even to the babies, had to eat . . . after they steam it. That was in springtime. . . .

These examples are but a few of the plant and animal resources that the Nlaka'pmx people of the region used to sustain themselves. They did so with great care and with respect and appreciation. They sought to maintain and enhance the species they used, so that there would always be enough for themselves and those who were to come.

Early European travellers through the Nlaka'pmx region perceived the dry plains as generally stark and barren, although some of them remarked on the extensive summertime prairies with the grasses as high as their horses' bellies, as far as the eye could see. The sagebrush and other dryland shrubs, the cactus and the myriad other flowering plants, bryophytes and lichens that littered the ground they saw as useless at best, or as noxious pests to be eliminated. For example, pioneer gentlewoman Susan Allison noted from her travels in Nlaka'pmx territory around the 1860s: "Mountains covered with tall grass which could be converted into wheat fields or ranges for large herds of cattle." Jessie Ann Smith recorded in her journal, on seeing the countryside near Spences Bridge in 1884, that this dry region with scant rainfall and little vegetation save sagebrush and cactus could support excellent crops of many varieties if water could be brought to the land. Ironically, since Mrs. Smith wrote this observation the land has become even more desert-like through overgrazing, soil compaction and other processes leading to desertification.

The settlers were focussed on their own vision of what this landscape should and could be. They knew best the possibilities of the plow—that sharp-footed instrument of conversion—that churned and turned the soil and removed the entire constellation of life forms existing in a place to substitute another, seen as more desirable.

As a result, today, less than eighty years after John Davidson reported seeing bitterroot by the millions near Spences Bridge, it is hard to find more than a few bitterroot plants scattered sparsely here and there. Contemporary Nlaka'pmx elders all agree that the bitterroot has declined drastically in size and number. Saraphine Kirkpatrick, interviewed by University of British Columbia graduate student Bob Bandringa, echoed Davidson's early observations: "It was not very much long ago and you walk all over and you got to watch where you step 'cause you might step on it [bitterroot]." Now, as of the 1990s, she said, you can scarcely find them. The prime bitterroot digging grounds, known as *Schuchem-elch* ("Root-digging house") by the Nlaka'pmx and called "100-mile flats" by Davidson in 1916, are now privately owned by a ranch company. The main digging area is a winter holding pen for cattle. The grazing, trampling and seeding with pasture species has utterly destroyed the bitterroot that used to grow there, and it is further threatened by the Wastech Services Ltd. garbage dump, a wood-chip mill, irrigated hayfields and the expansion of tarpaulined ginseng monoculture. Chief Leslie Edmonds explained to Bob Bandringa, "*LhQuoopen* [*lhqwepn*, bitterroot] is harmed by cattle if they hang out in one area. Years ago the old time ranchers used to move their cattle around every day so that they didn't overgraze. Now people in 4x4s do it but in a much more casual way; the cattle stay in one area and they trample the ground until it is packed rock hard."

RAINS, WHEN THEY COME—and there are some horrific downpours—do not seep slowly into the ground but run off the compacted earth in torrents, gouging channels as they go, eroding the landscape rather than nurturing it. Grassland ecologists have estimated that it can take from twenty to forty years of full rest for overgrazed ranges in the southern Interior of British Columbia to recover their former productivity. Meanwhile, people who wish to harvest bitterroot today resort to small, localized harvesting areas. For the Nlaka'pmx, bitterroot is rare and endangered.

Aggressive introduced weeds have also virtually taken over many of the interior rangelands. Of these, knapweed (*Centaurea* spp.), Russian thistle *(Salsola kali)*, hound's tongue *(Cynoglossum officinale)*, mullein *(Verbascum thapsus)*, dalmatian toadflax *(Linaria dalmatica)* and crested wheat grass *(Agropyron cristatum)*—an intentionally planted range grass from Eurasia—are but a few. Unfortunately, many people passing through these landscapes and seeing only green hillsides, and even attractive purple and yellow flowers, do not recognize that these weedy invaders characterize a degraded environment. They do not realize just how much the original ecosystems have been transformed. Added to the erosion, soil compaction and general deterioration of the physical landscape, these species have been biological agents of ecological change, and they symbolize what environmental historian Alfred Crosby has termed "ecological imperialism." Crosby has documented the general displacement of native species in regions of the world settled by Europeans, by the plants and animals the newcomers brought along with them; not only the indigenous peoples but their original flora and fauna have been colonized.

The Perils of "Progress"

Was it these changes that the Earth's Blanket metaphor was warning against? By the time the Nlaka'pmx person spoke of this image to James Teit, the Nlaka'pmx must have experienced plenty of impacts to their landscape from the European newcomers. During the gold rush days of the late 1850s and early 1860s, the Cariboo Wagon Road was blasted up the Fraser Canyon. The Native peoples may well have worried about the landslides and other destruction Nature often wreaks as a result of the earth being opened and scarred by a large disturbance, just like a wound that once inflicted becomes more vulnerable to infection.

The Nlaka'pmx had witnessed landslides in their canyon-laced and mountainous terrain since the time of the mythical Transformers, a group of supernatural beings who travelled through the country using their magic to perform wonderful feats and to change the land, people and animals to their present forms: "putting things right." For example, to destroy a powerful cannibal they encountered just below the present site of Spences Bridge, the Transformers, called *Qwa'qtqwaL* (*qʷíqʷʌ́qʷəɬt*), kicked down a mountain on him and initiated a landslide, known as the Drynoch Slide, which has continued to move into the river since that time. Coyote, a major culture hero and Transformer, also was known to cause landslides by kicking down earth from the side of a mountain. Teit recorded these episodes in his book *Mythology of the Thompson Indians,* published in 1912. Through such stories, the impacts of catastrophic events that had visited the landscapes of the past would have been carried forward within the group's collective historical memory as manifestations of Earth's anger and sadness.

Cutting through the slopes and hillsides along the Thompson River to build the Canadian Pacific Railway in the early 1880s must have left a wake of landslides even greater than the effects of Coyote or other Transformers. The Nlaka'pmx themselves were hired to work on the railway, alongside labourers from China, Hawaii and Europe, and they would have watched the construction and dynamiting muddy the otherwise clear waters of the river and impede the runs of precious salmon—springs, sockeye and other fish—making their way up to their spawning grounds far beyond.

Not much later than when James Teit recorded his notation about Earth's Blanket, disaster struck in Nlaka'pmx territory. The Native peoples must have felt that the earth was angry about all of the building. In 1913, construction of the Canadian Northern Railway caused a slide of rock and debris above Spuzzum that blocked the Fraser River, preventing the sockeye from making their way upriver. In February 1914, another slide at Hells Gate compounded the damage.

As recounted by Andrea Laforet and Annie York in their book on the history of Spuzzum, the immense barricade of rubble and rocks sliding into the river filled the already restricted channel. Enormous numbers of fish—the heavy "fourth year" cohort of sockeye—congregated below the blockage. The Nlaka'pmx men, who understood the peril to not only themselves but also to all the nations upriver in both the Fraser and Thompson drainages if the salmon were prevented from continuing their journey, built a long, rickety wooden flume around the worst stretch of whitewater. Then they carefully dip-netted the salmon from below and carried them in buckets and baskets to the flumeway so they could proceed upriver.

In November 2000, journalist Stephen Hume reflected on this heroic episode, citing the famous Adams River near Shuswap Lake to which, especially every fourth year, people flock from far and wide to experience the spectacular effect of thousands of spawning sockeye colouring the river bottom red from bank to bank: "There'd be no Adams River sockeye run to enthrall tourists and school kids every fall if those long-dead aboriginal men hadn't set up their frantic bucket brigade to save the Fraser River's salmon 86 years ago."

Despite the heroic efforts of these aboriginal men, the Department of Fisheries banned fishing, first partially and then completely, on the Fraser River above Mission bridge. Not until 1922 was some permit-based fishing allowed again, and not until the 1940s was a fishway constructed at Hells Gate to alleviate some of the damage. Federal fishing permits and closures remain in effect, though many First Nations follow their own fishing guidelines, developed by their elders and based on traditional knowledge of the river and the fish.

The Cost of Wealth

This story of clashing values is repeated across different groups, from the nineteenth century until the present day. For example, the Haida, Gitga'at (Tsimshian) and other coastal First Nations have not been permitted to gather abalone *(Haliotis kamtschatkana)*, a prized traditional food for them, because stocks of this precious shellfish have plummeted. Why? Abalone stocks have been poorly managed and overexploited by commercial harvesters. Contemporary aboriginal leaders regard this situation as completely unfair, just as in 1914 James Paul Xixne7 of Spuzzum, quoted by Laforet and York, felt the injustice of the drastic cutback in salmon catch imposed upon him and his family because of the damage from railway construction.

Testifying before the Government of Canada's Royal Commission on Indian Affairs in November 1914 after a frustrating and worrisome season, Xixne7 asked, "Whose fault was it that I hadn't sufficient food to eat this year? Who was the cause of our poverty—it was not my fault that to-day we are poor—I was stopped from providing myself with food—No one should be stopped with providing themselves with food—when they came to stop me [from fishing] they told me if I did not obey I would be put in gaol."

Many indigenous people resisted the new laws and the changes to their lifeways that were relentlessly transforming their world. Smohalla, an indigenous leader and prophet of Priest Rapids, Washington, rejected the Euro-American world view and the transition to European-style agriculture, saying: "You ask me to plow the ground! Shall I take a knife and tear my mother's bosom? You ask me to dig for stone. Shall I dig under her skin for her bones? Then when I die I cannot enter her body to be born again. You ask me to cut grass and make hay and sell it. And be rich like white men. But how dare I cut off my mother's hair?" Smohalla's words portended the future for the First Peoples of the Interior Plateau, at once setting the stage for the inevitable changes they would endure and signifying the deep cultural implications for the people and their homelands.

Earth's Blanket is a cautionary lesson that human actions can have repercussions—some of them potentially severe and harmful—not just to an individual, but to all humanity and to the environment as a whole. It signifies a world view in which the individual, the family and especially the leaders of a community take responsibility and set an example to maintain the carefully constructed rules and norms of the society in order to avoid dire consequences. Children learned from an early age not to pluck too much or ruthlessly destroy the valuables of the earth. They learned responsible, caring behaviour both through stories, metaphors and focussed instruction at opportune moments and through observation, emulation and experience.

Metaphors such as Earth's Blanket are just one element in a complex array of beliefs that determine the influences humans have on their lands and on other life forms. Although these notions change—shaped by the physical, biological and ecological processes that interact with the ethnosphere (the total of human cultural attributes, including our languages, creations, institutions and social relationships)—metaphors and similar expressions remain a kind of shorthand to remind people about ideas. Many are language- and culture-dependent, but the effective ones transcend linguistic, cultural and temporal boundaries because they are drawn from universal experiences and lessons of the past. Consider the English expressions "Don't put all your eggs in one basket," "Make hay while the sun shines," "Do unto others as you would have them do unto you" and "As ye sow, so shall ye reap." As dated as the words may sound, the ideas of conservation and reciprocity they embody have been perpetuated, discussed, elaborated upon and perfected over thousands and thousands of years.

These days, metaphors that maintain and enhance Earth's vital ecosystems seem to predominate in traditional cultures of northwestern North America, though they are echoed and reinforced in hundreds of languages and cultures the world over. However, elders and even younger people are concerned that the rich environmental knowledge of previous generations that underlies and sustains these teachings is disappearing, or more rightly, is not being learned by today's children and youth. This book is one step towards recovering and preserving the stories and lessons for today and future generations and, with them, a world view that honours and respects Earth and the real wealth it brings us.

Elsie Claxton, W̱SÁNEĆ
(Saanich) elder and plant specialist, who passed away in 2000.
She is holding Oregon grape (Berberis nervosa).

2

Land-based STORIES

of PEOPLES

and HOME *Places*

WHEN I WAS A CHILD of ten or so, I heard for the first time a story about a place I knew. It had an outcome that I could see for myself, and I was enthralled. It was a story about the Saanich (W̱SÁNEĆ) people who lived at the estuary of the Goldstream River and about the inlet known as Saanich Inlet, and it was told to me by Freeman King, a beloved local naturalist we all called "Skipper." He had been told the tale a long time previously by one of his W̱SÁNEĆ friends.

The story, as I recall it, was about a time, eons ago, when the indigenous people who lived at the Goldstream estuary had easy access to all the salmon they ever wanted because an enormous whale, residing at the mouth of Saanich Inlet, blocked the fish from leaving, just like a giant fish trap. The people, having all the food they wanted, became lazy. With time on their hands, they started to fight among themselves. Then, Skipper recounted, the Creator sent his little watchman bird, Chickadee, to tell the people not to fight but to be kind and generous to one another. The people improved their behaviour for a while, but then they began to argue and fight again. The Creator sent Raven, his big black watchman, to warn the people that they should mend their ways. They did for a short time, but, alas, they reverted to their arguments and squabbles. Then one day, without further warning, the sky became black even though it was the middle of the day. A gigantic bird—Thunderbird—flew overhead. "The beat of his wings was like thunder, the gleam of his eyes was like lightning and the lake on his back spilled over and it rained in torrents." (I can still hear Skipper saying these words to a circle of entranced children, myself among them.) The people were so frightened that they hid their eyes, but Thunderbird flew right past their village. He headed directly to the mouth of Saanich Inlet, and with his enormous talons he picked up the whale by its back and flew with it to Mount Newton (ÁUWELNEW). He deposited the whale there on the side of the mountain, turning it into stone.

After telling the story, Skipper took a group of us to John Dean Park to look at the rock that was once a whale, so we could see for ourselves the basis for the story. The rock *was* shaped like a huge whale, and it had been set down on the side of the mountain so lightly that a child could crawl into a large cavern underneath it from several different points around the edges. I went there many years later with Christopher Paul, my friend and ethnobotany teacher from Tsartlip (W̱JOȽEȽP), and we talked about this story of which he had heard, though he did not know it in detail. The story ends with a lesson: Without the whale to keep the salmon in the inlet, the fish swam away into the wider ocean, only to come back at a certain time of the year. Since that time, people have always had to work hard to get the salmon they need to survive and they had no time for strife.

This story was undoubtedly westernized and modified from the original W̱SÁNEĆ version, but for me its charm and fascination—and the reason I have remembered it for many decades—is that it is a situated tale. It is set in a landscape familiar to me, it relates to a large whale-shaped rock I have seen with my own eyes, and it features people who, though they are not my own ancestors, are ancestors of my friends. This tale is real to me, more real than the Europe-based stories of my childhood.

In urbanized, globalized societies, our stories—the stories we read or tell to our children—if they relate to lands and habitats at all, are usually more generic. The places they refer to are vaguely distant and impersonal. They seldom feature locations we know intimately, where our own footsteps tread or where we can cast our eyes. Most of the stories I grew

up listening to or reading as a young child were about locations in Eng-
land—*Peter Rabbit* or *Winnie-the-Pooh,* for example—or in the vast expanses of pre-industrial eastern Europe, as in the Grimms' fairy tales and
Peter and the Wolf. They, too, had their important lessons, but they taught
me nothing about the places where I lived or about the plants, animals and
habitats I might encounter. In fact, most of the fairy tales taught me that
the woods and forests are scary and unfriendly places for people to be,
that they are full of fierce, wild animals and dangerous witches.

Many years later my W̱SÁNEĆ teachers, Elsie Claxton of Tsawout and
Violet Williams of Pauquachin, told me other stories set in and around
ȽÁUWELṈEW̱. This mountain is sacred to their people, and they explained
the sadness they felt when developers subdivided, cleared and covered a
huge part of the mountain with large, expensive houses, without any consultation with the W̱SÁNEĆ. They pointed out that Dunsmuir Lodge, a
large three-storey building on the north side of the mountain, now owned
by the University of Victoria—where I work—and used for conferences,
workshops and special courses, was also built on traditional W̱SÁNEĆ
lands. On one occasion the late Philip Paul, Christopher Paul's son and a
well-known leader and former chief of the Tsartlip Band, gave a welcoming address at a university symposium at Dunsmuir Lodge. He started by
telling the story of the mountain and describing the bonds his people have
with it. It is difficult for those of us from western, urbanized society to
really understand the concept of a mountain being sacred or to feel what
that means. For the W̱SÁNEĆ people who hold strong traditional beliefs,
Philip Paul said it evokes a reverence, a special emotional sense of awe
and wonder similar to that a cathedral such as St. Paul's, Westminster
Abbey or Canterbury inspires in Christian worshippers, and an equivalent respect and wish to protect it from harm. To see their sacred place
ravaged by bulldozers and cut through by roads brings the same heartfelt
sadness that one can imagine in seeing a cathedral, mosque or synagogue
being desecrated or destroyed.

Although these stories come from aboriginal tradition, I remember
them because they are about places and animals that I know and care
about. Another favourite story that Skipper used to tell us was about how
Raven captured sunlight for the people. The sun was stored in a box at the
back of a deep cave whose entrance was guarded by Seagull. Seagull

was blind. Raven scattered sea urchin spines around the mouth of the cave, then called Seagull to come out. Seagull trod on the spines and cried to Raven to help him pull them out. Instead of extracting them, Raven drove them more deeply into Seagull's foot, saying he couldn't see well enough to pull out the spines. Seagull told Raven to open the box a bit, letting out a little of the sunlight. Raven said he needed more light, and Seagull, in great pain, agreed that he should open the box wider. Finally, Raven opened the box all the way, grabbed the sun and flew with it high up into the sky, thus bringing Light to the world. Ever since that time, poor Seagull has been crying piteously because of the sea urchin spines in his foot.

Even now, every time I hear the seagulls crying along the shore I think of Skipper telling us this story. Only recently, I found a recorded version of the tale, a Snuneymexw (Nanaimo) story transcribed into German by Franz Boas and recently translated into English as "The Origin of Daylight" in a volume edited by Randy Bouchard and Dorothy Kennedy (2002).

Stories like this, complex and deeply symbolic, are told and retold all over the world about local places, plants and animals. Tom Sampson, another Saanich leader and cultural specialist, explained this relationship between people and their homelands in relation to the oral traditions of the W̱SÁNEĆ: For the First Nations people of Saanich Inlet, he said, intersection between culture and landscape is reflected best in the concept of *tcelengan,* which in the SENĆOTEN language means "teachings of the places where you come from." People identify themselves with culturally significant places that offer spiritual teachings, often imparted through stories, to guide members of the community in their relationships with one another and with the resources on which they depend.

One of the special places in the Saanich landscape is *Yaas,* the highest part of the Malahat Ridge, on the western side of Saanich Inlet. The elders refer to *Yaas* as the "teachings" of their community and they acknowledge this place as integral to their identity as a people. As this high ridge and its total environment—the plants, the animals, the streams and pools and the spirits—provide for the physical and spiritual well-being of the W̱SÁNEĆ, the people consider it to be sacred in its entirety. Relationships such as this one between the W̱SÁNEĆ and the Malahat mountain are powerful and ancient; in fact, *Yaas* is the home of Thunderbird, the giant bird that removed the whale from Saanich Inlet. This place also figures prominently in the origin of the w̲sáneć.

Origin Stories of Place: Beyond the Depths of Time

Outsiders may never fully understand traditional narratives, because the meanings are embedded in prior cultural knowledge and words that only a speaker of the language can completely appreciate. Nevertheless, stories can have some wider interpretation and understanding in other cultures, and perhaps this is why some themes transcend cultural and linguistic boundaries. The Nlaka'pmx narrative "Old One and the Earth, Sun, and People," recorded and translated by James Teit in the early 1900s in his book *Mythology of the Thompson Indians,* is a creation story that speaks to people of one place but also has significance for a wider audience. In this case, Teit recorded several similar but distinct accounts from a number of Nlaka'pmx storytellers, and even with this version he noted variations in particular points or details.

I have never heard this story told by a Nlaka'pmx storyteller, and I can only imagine what intense meaning it would convey when told in its original language by an expert orator: It would be easy to imagine the characters in the story as family members, with their own personalities and struggles. The significance of the story and the tensions within it as it unfolded must have been spellbinding. Even in the English version provided by Teit it is a powerful, compelling commentary, embodying humour and drama and imparting lessons about human nature, loyalty, technology, ecology and a people's place in the world.

Old-One of the Nlaka'pmx

The story begins with a broad and ancient setting:

A long time ago, before the world was formed, there lived a number of people together. They were the Stars, Moon, Sun and Earth. The latter was a woman, and her husband was the Sun.

The Earth-woman and her husband are personified in ways that all of us can relate to. In the story, the woman always found fault with her husband. She was disagreeable with him, saying that he was "nasty, ugly and too hot." The Sun, for his part, was annoyed with her complaints, and he abandoned her. His relatives, the Moon and Stars, also left, moving away to where the Sun had taken up residence. At this desertion, the Earth-woman "became very sorrowful, and wept much." At this point Old-One, the Creator, appeared, and he transformed the Sun, Moon and Stars into their present forms, which he placed up in the sky "so that they should look on the Earth-woman, and she could look at them." Old-One said, "Henceforth you shall not desert people, nor hide yourselves, but shall remain where you can always be seen at night or by day. Henceforth you will look down on the Earth."

Old-One then transformed the woman into Earth as we know her to-day. He changed her hair into the vegetation—the trees and grass. Her flesh became the clay and her bones the rocks. Her blood was transformed into the springs of water. He said to Earth-woman, "Henceforth you will be the Earth, and people will live on you and trample on your belly. You will be as their mother, for from you bodies will spring and to you they will go back. People will live as in your bosom and sleep on your lap. They will derive nourishment from you, for you are fat; and they will utilize all parts of your body. You will no more weep when you see your children."

After he had created Earth, she gave birth to humans, who were said to be very similar in form to those of today but were completely ignorant, having "no appetites, desires, knowledge, or thoughts." Old-One travelled over the world and among the people. He gave them the appetites and desires that humans have today. He also created the birds and fish, gave them their names and their different "positions and functions."

He taught the people how to make use of all the things he provided for them. The Creator told them, "Where you see fish jump, there you will find water to drink. It will quench your thirst and keep you alive." He instructed the women in making birchbark baskets and mats and lodges of tule (*Schoenoplectus acutus,* round-stem bulrush) and cattail *(Typha latifolia)*. He also showed them how to dig roots and gather berries for food and how to dry and store them for the winter. The men he taught how to make fire and how to catch fish and hunt for game with snares, traps and spears. He showed them the different kinds of stone for making arrowheads, knives and spear points. And he told them how to harvest the tough fibres of the *spats'en* (*Apocynum cannabinum,* Indian-hemp) plant and how to clean and twist them to make thread and rope for snares and fishnets. All the other skills and information the people needed to survive, he instructed them on: how to make deadfalls for marten, how to snare grouse, how to fix feathers on arrows so that they might go straight, how to cook and eat salmon and other food, and how to make pipes from pipe-stone and how to smoke tobacco. He also taught them how to have sexual intercourse and how to give birth to children.

The story concludes:

> When he had finished teaching them, he bade them good-by, saying, "I now leave you; but if you forget any of the arts I have taught you, or if you are in distress and require my aid, I will come again to you. The Sun is as your father, and the Earth as your mother. When you die, you will return to your mother's body. You will be covered with her flesh as a blanket, under which your bones will rest in peace.

I can only imagine that for the Nlaka'pmx this story would help people to situate themselves and their lives comfortably and appropriately within a geographical, cultural and historical context. It would, in short, bring meaning, purpose and continuity to their lives. As well, and perhaps most importantly, it would surely foster an attitude of caring and appreciation towards the earth itself, its landforms, its waters and its plants and animals.

ANOTHER OF MY FAVOURITE ecological stories from our region, situated at least in part right off the coast of where the city of Victoria is located today, is the Saanich story "Origin of Salmon," recorded from an unidentified W̱SÁNEĆ storyteller by ethnographer Diamond Jenness and found with other narratives in his unpublished notes from around 1930. These remarkable fish, the salmon, undergo a life cycle that connects them to their freshwater, estuarine and marine habitats. Five species of Pacific salmon—coho (*Oncorhynchus kisutch*), chinook (*O. tshawytscha,* also known as spring), chum (*O. keta,* also known as dog), pink (*O. gorbuscha*) and sockeye (*O. nerka*)—as well as steelhead (*O. mykiss*), a sea-going trout often classified with salmon, occur in North America. As juveniles they leave the lakes, streams and rivers of the northwestern North American watersheds and migrate to feeding grounds in the north Pacific Ocean and as far away as the Bering Sea. After periods ranging from a few months to three or four years, depending on the species, the adult salmon re-enter rivers and creeks and travel sometimes hundreds of kilometres to spawn and complete their life cycle. Not only humans but bears, eagles and many other types of wildlife rely on the salmon for sustenance. These fish are indeed cultural and ecological keystone species.

Origin of Salmon

This story begins at a time when there were people on the earth, but they had no salmon to eat; the salmon were in their own land, far away. The W̱SÁNEĆ (Saanich) were facing starvation because the seals, elk and other game they relied upon had disappeared.

There were two brave young men who said to each other, "Let us go and see if we can find any salmon." Setting forth in their canoe, they headed out to sea in no particular direction. For three and a half months they journeyed, until finally they came to a strange country. When they landed, a man came out of a house and spoke to them as if he expected them, saying, "You have arrived." The youths had no idea where they were, but they answered, "We have arrived." They stayed with their host, who fed them and looked after them. He told the youths to look around, and they noticed that smoke rose from the aromatic seeds of qexmín (*Lomatium nudicaule*, Indian celery, also known as Indian consumption plant), which everyone was burning in their houses. It turned out that these were all Salmon People—steelhead, chinook, sockeye and the other kinds of salmon—and the smoke from the qexmín was their food.

After about a month, their kind host said to the youths, "You must go home tomorrow. Everything is arranged for you. The salmon that you were looking for will muster at your home and start off on their journey. You must follow them." So the next day the youths left, following the salmon. They travelled with the fish, day and night, for three and a half months. Following the instructions of their host, they burned qexmín seeds every night, "that the salmon might feed on its smoke and sustain themselves." After a long time they reached Discovery Island (TĆÁS), off the coast of Oak Bay in Victoria. Here they burned qexmín all along the beach,

Seeds of qex̱mín, *Indian celery* (Lomatium nudicaule), *an important ceremonial and medicinal plant of the* W̱SÁNEĆ *(Saanich) and other peoples of southwestern British Columbia and Washington.* PHOTO BY ROBERT D. TURNER

as they had been instructed. They had been told, "Burn qex̱mín along the beach when you reach land, to feed the salmon that travel with you. Then, if you treat the salmon well, you will always have them in abundance."

From the area around Discovery Island the salmon went on to other places, including around Nanaimo on the east coast of Vancouver Island, and up the Fraser River. In the story it was explained that, because the journey from the land of the Salmon People had taken them three and a half months, the salmon are absent from the coast for that period of time each year. In the story, too, the coho said to the other salmon, "You can go ahead of us, for we have not yet got what we wanted from the lakes," and that is why the coho are generally the last of the salmon to appear.

As well as providing the W̱SÁNEĆ people with salmon, the "leaders of the salmon," who had the forms of a man and a woman, taught them how to construct the reef nets to catch the salmon and all the proper ways or protocols to ensure that the salmon would always return. They told the young men how their people should dress when they caught the salmon and that they should start to use their nets in July, when the berries were ripe.

"So today," Jenness recorded in his manuscript, "when the Indians dry their salmon they always burn some qexmín on the fire (or on top of the stove), and they put a little in the fish when they cook it. Also, when they cut up the salmon, before inserting the knife they pray to the salmon, that they may always be plentiful."

In this story, the mystery of the origin of salmon and their long absences, the close and reciprocal interactions between humans and salmon on the Northwest Coast, the "gift" of the salmon to the people for their use and benefit and numerous details of geography, salmon ecology and their seasonal availability, fishing technology, and ceremonial and food roles of plants are all represented. Gratitude for the salmon—indeed, blessing them—and responsibility for the salmon are elegantly conveyed.

FROM ORAL TRADITIONS such as this one we can also learn about species that can no longer be found in an area. Most people never think twice about the origins of the name Elk Lake, one of the lakes on the Saanich Peninsula that is bordered by the Patricia Bay Highway along one side. This story, however, notes that people were eating elk before they had salmon, an indication that these large, stately ungulates lived on the Saanich Peninsula in the past, although they have not been seen around Elk Lake for many decades.

Origin stories can provide many other important linkages between a group's history and its contemporary practices. The seeds called qexmín are revered as a medicinal and ceremonial species not only by the W̱SÁNEĆ but by other Coast Salish peoples, as well as the Kwakwa̱ka'wakw and Nuu-Chah-Nulth, right up to the present. Saanich elder and language specialist Earl Claxton Sr. explained to me that the root of this name, qex-, refers to the plant's ability to protect someone against a curse or evil thoughts. Kim Recalma-Clutesi, a cultural specialist of Kwakwa̱ka'wakw Nation whose home is at Qualicum, confirmed that her people still burn the seeds as an incense at funerals, to honour and respect the deceased person. Singers chew the seeds to ease their throats and to give them a good, clear voice. In the past, these seeds have also been chewed as a medicine for tuberculosis, hence the earlier name "Indian consumption plant."

Another W̱SÁNEĆ story that situates people in their home environment was recorded in part by Diamond Jenness but also shared with me, in more detail, by Philip Paul. Philip's version features Ḵ'EḴ'IEȽĆ' *(qweqwey-íĺhch)* *(Arbutus menẓiesii,* arbutus or Pacific madrone), an often gnarly broad-leafed evergreen tree with bright, thin, striking, reddish-brown bark that peels and sheds every year. Arbutus is a special tree for those of us living on southern Vancouver Island and elsewhere within its range, but it has particular significance for the W̱SÁNEĆ because of the assistance it provided to their ancestors during the Great Flood.

How the Arbutus Saved the W̱SÁNEĆ

In this story, once, long ago, it rained and rained until the water of the sea began to rise. The people started to twist the tough, flexible branches of western red-cedar *(Thuja plicata)* into a thick, very long rope that they could use to secure their canoes in the rising flood. They attached their largest canoes to the top of ȽÁU,WELṈEW̱ (Mount Newton) on the Saanich Peninsula, fastening them to the trunk of a tough, deeply rooted arbutus tree. The waters rose to the top of the mountain before they started to recede and many people were drowned. Those who anchored their canoes to the arbutus tree, Philip Paul said, were the ones who were saved.

At the time that Diamond Jenness recorded this story, around 1930, it was reported that in certain places you could sometimes hear the drowned people and they were still talking about the rising waters. Philip Paul added that the W̱SÁNEĆ people do not usually burn arbutus as firewood. Although not everyone today realizes the reason for this, those who know the story of the arbutus tree recognize that it is preserved out of respect for its life-saving gift to the ancestors.

STORIES ABOUT the Great Flood are told in many different traditions around the world, including, of course, the flood endured by Noah and his family in the Old Testament of the Bible. Among the First Nations in northwestern North America, each cultural group and territory has its own story about a special local mountain that served as a refuge from the rising waters during the flood. As Saanich elder Edward Thomas explained:

> The Malahat mountain is one of the mountains that didn't go down in the flood. Mount Newton [ȽÁU,WELṈEW̱] didn't go down. There are

names for mountains up and down the coast—that's where the Indian people went, that's why there are people up and down the coast. When the flood went down, the Creator left bushes, all medicines.

In all of the traditions many people were lost in the flood, but some were saved, often with supernatural assistance. First Nations populations believe the survivors became their ancestors. It could be that the floods of legend are metaphorical, but science shows that they may well be linked to actual natural catastrophes. The floor of Saanich Inlet, for example, shows that a massive torrent swept across the Strait of Georgia to southern Vancouver Island at the end of the last ice age, possibly when a melting ice dam released water from Lake Kamloops in the Interior. Sediment core samples taken from the bottom of the inlet in 1996 by the international Ocean Drilling Program vessel JOIDES *Resolution* record this event.

THE SACRED CEDAR TREE

My friend Dr. Daisy Sewid-Smith *(Mayanilth)* explained that her family's ancestor, *c̓ǝqamǝy̓*, survived the Great Flood not on the top of a mountain but within a colossal hollow western red-cedar. Daisy comes from a family of storytellers. Her grandmother, Agnes Alfred, used to take her and her aunt (who was just a little older than Daisy) home to her house on weekends when they were little girls. Long into the night, as they lay snuggled in her bed, Agnes Alfred would recount the history, stories, customs and traditions of their people. Daisy has herself become an expert and teacher in Kwakwa̲ka̲'wakw culture and in the Kwak'wala language because of the training she received from Agnes Alfred, her other grandmother, Daisy Roberts, her father, James Sewid, and the other elders of her childhood and youth. In 1998, she received an honorary degree from the University of Victoria in recognition of her knowledge and of her work over many decades in teaching others about her language and culture. She recorded the story of *c̓ǝqamǝy̓*, which she had been told on many occasions by Agnes Alfred, in a book chapter we worked on together.

Origin of the Cedar Bark Ceremony of the Kwakwa̲ka̲'wakw

C̓ǝqamǝy̓ was my ancestor. At the beginning I said I'm m̓am̓aliliqǝla, but actually I'm m̓am̓aliliqǝla-q̌ʷiq̌ʷasut̓inux̌ʷ. Every tribe has its origin, what people call their sacred origin, and they talk about how they originated, and how their ancestors came down. And that's exactly what they call it, *gelgalis*—how they originated, and how they survived after the flood. Every tribe has its own flood stories. And my ancestor *čaqaməý* was told that this flood was coming, and he was told how to prepare for it. And he was told to go to look for a large cedar tree, and to hollow it out. And when I talk about a cedar tree, today, people cannot even visualize what the great trees were like. When I talk about a cedar tree, they think about a little cedar tree that you see [today] in comparison to the trees we had before. But the cedar trees were enormous. They were like big huge buildings, if you hollowed them out, they were so enormous. I'm talking about first-growth forest cedar trees.

And so *čaqaməý* was told to go and look for one of these [giant cedar trees] and hollow it out. And then he was told to put [spruce] pitch on all the different holes in the trees, so that the water wouldn't come in. And he was told that out of his whole tribe only himself, his wife, his daughter and his four sons were to enter this cedar tree. And it was to be sealed with pitch when he went inside the hollow tree, and he was not to open it until he was again told when [to do so], even though people would be begging to go into the tree. And so that's what he did. He prepared the tree and he put all the food and all the things he would need in the tree, and then he sealed himself and his family in this tree.

And then bumblebees were ordered to guard the tree, and to sting anyone who tried to swim toward the tree and get into it. . . . While he was inside the cedar tree, *čaqaməý* was told to weave the first cedar headdress, the first cedar neck ring, wrist rings and ankle rings. And he was told to put the faces of men all around his cedar head ring and his cedar neck ring, and this was to signify two things . . . that he was saved, from out of all his tribe, and also that from that day on, he was to honour and respect the cedar that saved his life, and that he was going to be the first one ever to perform what we now call the cedarbark ceremony. And, he was told how it was going to be performed.

When he entered the cedar tree, his name was *hawilkʷala*, which means "cedar tree," but when he came out, he was told, "you will no longer be *hawilkʷala;* your name will be *čaqaməý*, which means that you will be the first person ever to perform the cedarbark ceremony. And, from there, it'll spread among your nation." And so, when he came out [when the flood waters receded], this is what happened. Through him, the cedarbark ceremony spread among all the Kʷakʷak'wakʷ [Kwakwaka'wakw] people.

Daisy explained that the name ćəqaməy̓ has the same root as ćeqa. She said, "We call the red cedarbark ceremony ćeqa. If we refer to someone as being ćeqa, it means a person who is doing whatever chore they're doing very slowly and very pompously—regally, yes, very regally. And you could call a person ćeqa, like if you're in a hurry to go somewhere and you're taking your sweet time, they will say that you're ćeqa, meaning that you're taking it slow and regally, not in a hurry for anything. So that word is used every day in that term."

Ever since the time of ćəqaməy̓ and the Great Flood, people have honoured the cedar tree in a special ceremony during the Kwakwaka'wakw Potlatch (see chapter 4). For Daisy it is especially hard to see the giant cedars, so significant spiritually and materially to her people, felled without proper respect or without recognizing their sacredness or their deep historical relationships with human societies. She worries about what will happen to her people when all the magnificent old cedar trees and their associated ancient forests are gone.

Origin Stories of Plants: The Spirit Within

Humanness, the spirit, the soul of all Nature, predominates in the stories of indigenous peoples everywhere. Trees, in particular, are imbued with personality, sacredness and power. In Diamond Jenness's w̱SÁNEĆ notes is part of a longer account of x̱ÁLS, the Creator and Transformer, and his activities, set in the ancient times when trees and animals were people. This story illustrates both how trees are personified and how they came to have the features for which they are known today.

The Saanich Story of How Douglas-Fir Got Pitch

Pitch was a man who used to go fishing before the sun rose and retire to the shade before it became strong. One day he was late and had just reached the beach when he melted. Other people rushed to share him.

Fir arrived first and secured most of the pitch, which he poured over his head and body. Balsam [grand fir] obtained only a little and by the time Arbutus arrived there was none left. Arbutus said, "I shall have to peel my skin every year and have a good wash to keep me clean." But just then *XÁLS* appeared and said, "You shall all be trees, and Fir shall be your boss." So now the arbutus sheds its bark every year, and fir has more pitch than any other tree.

I HAVE HEARD many versions of this story from different parts of the Northwest Coast. All have similar themes, and all reflect the general transformation from the original world to the conditions and elements of the earth as we know it today. In all of these transformations, such as the creation of Earth by Old-One, earlier beings have made sacrifices to produce a world full of gifts to benefit humans. For example, in all of the different variants of the story Pitch was originally a human being—a man who, in some versions, enjoyed halibut fishing and had a loving wife who looked after him and took care of his needs, reminding him not to stay out in the sun. Inevitably, Pitchman forgot this restriction and was transformed by the sun into a gummy, aromatic substance, taken up in different amounts by various kinds of trees. Today, pitch is supremely useful to people: it is gathered and applied as a glue, as waterproofing or as a healing salve. This story helps teach children which trees have the best-quality pitch. Aside from Douglas-fir *(Pseudotsuga menziesii)*, Sitka spruce *(Picea sitchensis)* and grand fir *(Abies grandis)* are two other trees known for the quantity and quality of their pitch.

The Haida, Tsimshian, Kwakwaka'wakw and other coastal peoples—as well as First Peoples right across the continent—still value tree pitch for its medicinal properties. Many people recount stories of its effectiveness in helping draw out slivers and in curing infections from cuts, burns or scrapes. Gitga'at elder Tina Robinson recently showed me a huge Sitka spruce tree behind the cabins at Kiel on Princess Royal Island on the North Coast of British Columbia. The Gitga'at, a Coast Tsimshian people, have gone to Kiel every year for generations to harvest edible seaweed and to fish for halibut and spring salmon in the month of May, and this ancient spruce tree has probably been used for a hundred years or more as a source of pitch for medicine.

Tree pitch is a complex blend of resins and aromatic oils, and it is known to have antibiotic properties. Every once in a while, a person wishing to obtain the medicine would make a cut or two on the trunk with an axe, through the bark and down to the wood. Over several days or weeks, pitch would seep out of the cut and accumulate and harden on the surface, where it could easily be scraped off when needed; Tina Robinson demonstrated how you can use a giant California mussel shell to harvest the pitch from the tree trunk. You heat the pitch until it is soft and runny, strain it through cheesecloth, then mix it with Vaseline or, formerly, deer or other animal fat to produce a creamy healing salve for cuts, scrapes, burns, slivers and infections. To this day, pitch trees have special significance for healers.

The giant spruce tree itself is a centrepiece for the Gitga'at community, especially for the children who come to learn and play at the seaweed camp. The tree's mighty branches support a rope swing on which the children fling themselves from the high landing point and out around the trunk, spiralling and twirling in excited chaos. Playing around its massive trunk, they are all the while unknowingly learning about the toughness of wind-strengthened wood, about the laws of physics and the laws of Nature, about sharing and participating, about the gifts of trees and the joy that life can bring.

For the adults, this and similar trees in communities up and down the coast are like living pharmacies, continuous sources of healing medicine for those who know how to gather and prepare it. Pitch is a good example of a traditional medicine that may have wider applications, but anyone wishing to use it for healing should not forget the sacrifice of Pitchman, or that it is a gift from the trees, to be used with care and appreciation.

Countless other stories link people to their home places, give meaning and life to the resources they use, and teach them everyday lessons about the foods that are good to eat and where they grow.

Another story that goes back to that magical time when trees were people is the Hesquiaht (Nuu-Chah-Nulth) story about the origin of yellow-cedar trees *(Chamaecyparis nootkatensis)*, told by Alice Paul and many others before her.

The Yellow-Cedar Sisters

Three young women were down on the beach drying salmon. Raven came along and wanted their salmon, so he kept asking them if they were afraid to be there by themselves—if they were afraid of bears or wolves or other such animals. They kept saying "No" to everything he asked them about until he said, "Owls! Aren't you afraid of owls?" At this they said, "Oh, don't even talk about owls to us; we are afraid of owls!" [They said this because owls are associated with death and ghosts or spirits.]

Raven went away but hid in the bushes nearby and began to imitate owl sounds. The women were so frightened they ran away into the woods. They kept running until they came partway up the side of a hill. They were so tired, they decided to stop and rest. They said to themselves, "We'd better stand here now on the side of the mountain; they will call us *ṣalhmapt.*" And they turned into yellow-cedar trees. Raven snuck out and ate all their dried salmon. This is why yellow-cedars are always found on the mountainsides and why they are such nice-looking trees, with smooth trunks and few branches, because they used to be attractive young women with long, shining hair.

Basket weavers today harvest yellow-cedar bark, which peels off the tree in long strips. The smooth, lustrous inner bark separates easily from the brittle outer bark when it is harvested at the right season. The inner bark is split, dried and pounded until soft, then used to weave hats, baskets, blankets and clothing.

Another story about the infamous Raven, who is at once a glutton, a helper for the people and a Transformer, is about the gift of soapberries, also known as soopollalie or buffalo berries *(Shepherdia canadensis)*. These small, soft, somewhat bitter fruits are highly valued by First Peoples throughout British Columbia; in fact, the berries are named in every language and known to almost everyone, even children. The all-around-favourite food made from this fruit is a light frothy whip, of the consistency of beaten egg whites, made by thoroughly whisking the berries with water until they form a stiff, whipped-cream-like mixture. Sometimes called "Indian ice cream," this special confection (nowadays sweetened with sugar, honey or even bananas) is served especially at family gatherings and feasts. The bottled, dried or frozen berries are also considered to have medicinal value and are a precious gift or trade item. Common throughout the interior forests, soapberries are more sporadic towards the coast; hence, knowing where they occur is of considerable interest to coastal people.

From the Nuxalk, or Bella Coola people, comes the following story, recorded by ethnographer Thomas McIlwraith. It relates how *nuxwski*—soapberries—came to grow at the head of the Bella Coola Valley, a long, narrow, glacier-scoured valley on the central coast of British Columbia. Like the Hesquiaht story of the Yellow-Cedar Sisters, this narrative teaches an ecological lesson, namely where a certain culturally important plant can be found. The story provides information that the soapberry is common on the inland mountain slopes and that it is spotted here and there towards Bella Coola. It also gives people the message of the soapberry's value and quality.

How Raven Brought Soapberries to the Bella Coola Valley

Long, long ago, *słexłekwaiłx*, a mountain in the Carrier country above Burnt [B]Ridge, was a chief possessing human characteristics. Buffalo berries flourished on his slopes, and he wanted to keep them as food for his guests. On one occasion he invited all of the animals and birds, including Raven, to a feast and a dance. The chief's house was the interior of the mountain, and when all had assembled he carefully closed every opening so that none of the berries could escape. Raven was determined to obtain some of this food for the people of Bella Coola and accordingly used his power to force one of the guests to go outside. As soon as a door was opened to let the guest out, Raven seized some of the whip and flew away, scattering drops of it in his flight. Berries grew wherever the drops fell, and since that time everybody has been able to make this luxury. *Słexłekwaiłx* was very angry but could do nothing.

Such stories are brought to life in peoples' day-to-day activities. For countless generations, Nuxalk children have been hearing this and similar accounts of their lands and resources and, being taken out on the land to harvest the fruits of Raven's labours, begin to grasp the real meaning of

Soapberry, or soopollalie (Shepherdia canadensis), *a bitter fruit that is whipped with water into a frothy confection, is widely enjoyed by many indigenous people in northwestern North America.* PHOTO BY ROBERT D. TURNER

the soapberries, or of the other foods and materials that are so important to their lives.

One day in July in the early 1970s I went with Nuxalk elder Margaret Siwallace and her family especially to pick *nuxwski*. We went to Stuie, at the head of the Bella Coola Valley. I had just read the story of how the berries came to be there and it gave me special pleasure to see them, bright red and translucent, crowded around the dark-green leaves near the ends of the coppery twigs. Closing my eyes, and hearing Raven's raucous calls far overhead, and in the background fresh water tumbling over the rocks on its way to join the Atnarko River and then the Bella Coola River, I could almost see the drops of pinkish-coloured whip falling from the sky each time Raven opened his beak.

Reading the story was only the beginning of the lessons of the soapberry. I had always thought that berry-picking was fairly straightforward—until I tried to pick *nuxwski*. These berries are not like any other;

they are small, soft and juicy, and drop easily from the bushes when ripe. Trying to pick them with my fingers, one at a time, was tedious and ineffective and I learned that the hard way. I returned with a modest cupful of berries. Margaret, who had collected a litre or more over the same time, laughed at my inexperience and demonstrated the "right" method. She placed a large bucket under a berry-laden branch, held the branch firmly, then whacked it lightly with a small stick; all the berries dropped into her bucket, and she moved on to the next branch. It didn't take long to fill her bucket this way. (The other important detail I learned was that one must never let any oil or grease come in contact with the berries, or they will not whip.)

Another valued berry—the prize of all berries in the eyes of many— is the black mountain huckleberry *(Vaccinium membranaceum)*. The name for this sweet, delicious, juicy berry in Nuxalk and several other languages simply means "berry." An origin story is associated with this berry, too, this time from the Sinixt (Lakes) tradition, from the Arrow Lakes region of the Columbia River in the Kootenay district of British Columbia. The story was told to anthropologist William Elmendorf in 1935–36 by Sinixt elder Nancy Wynecoop.

The Origin of Black Huckleberries

In this story, Eagle was a very beautiful young woman who lived at Kettle Falls. She had many suitors, and the old grandmothers, who were her teachers, decided to hold a big running competition, with the winner of the race to become her husband. The course for the race was extremely challenging and led over rough rocky ground and steep precipices along the Columbia River. Mountain Goat sent his sons to compete in the race. The eldest son was one of those courting Eagle, but she and all the other people there despised him because of his ugliness—his bony legs, big horns and thick body. Old Mountain Goat sent a gift of huckleberries with his sons, but because the goats were so unpopular, their contribution was set aside from the other gifts. The eldest mountain goat brother sat down despondently. His younger brothers, however, planted one of the huckleberry bushes they had brought from home in front of him. The eldest brother ate all the berries from the bush, and felt much better, regaining his self-respect because of his brothers' kindness.

Nobody thought the mountain goat brothers could win the race, but they were allowed to enter the competition. When the race began, the people laughed at them with their awkward gait. When they came to the cliff, however, the goat brothers raced right across the face of it, a feat that none of the other animals could achieve, and because of this they easily won the race. Eagle's grandmothers had almost been ready to throw the goats' gift of huckleberries into the river, but the women were astonished to see the goats racing across the face of the rock. The agile mountain goats won the esteem of the grandmothers and the others. The grandmothers then brought the choice gift basket of huckleberries over to Eagle for her to taste and name—she named the fruit "sweet berry." The story goes that from the bush the goats had planted now come all the huckleberries in Sinixt territory.

After the race, meanwhile, the mountain goats set out for home, but Eagle, forgetting her earlier disdain for them, followed. Although they had seemed very shabby when they first arrived at Kettle Falls, she noticed that as they travelled towards home, their coats became as white as snow. She admired how they nibbled only the dewy tips of fresh grass. Paying special attention to old Mountain Goat, she accompanied the goats about the mountains. Eventually, the goat adopted Eagle, then she married his eldest son and stayed in the mountains, where she still builds her nest to this day.

This story weaves together primary ecological and cultural teachings, among the most important being the high regard people hold for black mountain huckleberries. Okanagan elder Selina Timoyakin told me that all the plants and animals, and even the different kinds of rocks, formed discrete communities, each with its own leader or chief. For the berries, Black Huckleberry is the chief. Annie York said that among her people, the Nlaka'pmx, black huckleberries were so highly valued that if anyone gave you a gift of them you would certainly be obligated to give a gift of food or some other valuable in exchange. My Secwepemc friend Mary Thomas said that her grandmother would bring huckleberries as a gift to friends or neighbours, even if she knew they already had some; you could *never* have too many huckleberries! For Margaret Siwallace in Nuxalk territory, black huckleberries, like soapberries, were worth a full day's trip into the mountains just to get a taste. If they were plentiful—enough to freeze or, formerly, to dry in cakes—everyone would go up to get them, and groups of families would meet and enjoy each other's company while they picked.

THE BLACK TREE LICHEN

Another food, little used today but nonetheless culturally and nutritionally significant in the past to the Okanagan, Secwepemc and other Interior Plateau peoples, is the black tree lichen, or "black moss" *(Bryoria fremontii)*. It hangs in long, hairlike wisps from the branches of coniferous trees such as Douglas-fir, ponderosa pine and western larch.

A delightful story, part of a much longer narrative, is told by Okanagan-Colville storyteller Mourning Dove, among others, and published in her 1933 book of Okanagan stories.

How Coyote . . . Happened to Make the Black Moss Food

Coyote, travelling with his son, *Top'-kan,* tried to capture some white swans resting in a large lake. The swans were tricking Coyote by pretending to be dead, but two young swans allowed Coyote to catch them. He tied his little son to the seemingly dead swans while he climbed up a pine tree to get the pitchy top for fire-kindling. Just as Coyote reached the top of the tree, the swans came to life and started to fly away with his son. Coyote tried to jump, but his long braided hair was caught up on a branch of the tree. He swung there, helpless and unable to free himself. The swans flew away with his son. Coyote had to cut himself down with his flint knife, and he fell to the ground, leaving his hair caught in the branches. He then looked up at his hair and said, "You shall not be wasted, my valuable hair. After this, you shall be gathered by the people. The old women will make you into food." With this, Coyote transformed the lichen, called *sqwilíp,* into its present form, and it has been used as food ever since.

Black lichen is not a food that is easily prepared. Formerly, it was harvested by extending long poles among the tree branches, twisting them around the hanging lichen and pulling it off. People were careful to taste the lichen before gathering it in any quantity because it varies significantly in taste. Apparently genetics and ecological differences have a bearing on the concentration of bitter-tasting lichen compounds the different populations contain. Secwepemc elder Mary Thomas explained that people would look for the darker-coloured ones; the greenish ones, she said, are more bitter. Sometimes enormous bales of the lichen were bound up and rolled down the hillside to people's camps below. Although the lichen can be eaten raw, it is best after proper processing and cooking. It is soaked for a long time in running water, then kneaded with the hands "like bread dough," according to Mary, one of the last elders who knows how to cook it properly. After it is thoroughly washed and cleaned, it is cooked for a long time in an underground pit.

Mary learned about pit-cooking this lichen from her mother, Christine Allen, and the story Mary tells about this experience only adds to the legend of the black tree lichen. Her mother was a teacher of few words. Under her mother's instruction, Mary dug a large pit and lit a fire in it to make the sides "like a ceramic pot." She heated hot rocks by placing them on top of two beams positioned over the pit. When the beams had burned through, the rocks, now presumed to be thoroughly heated, fell down into the pit. The unburned wood was removed, the hot rocks spread out and covered with a dense matting of bunch grass and wild rose and Saskatoon twigs, and the black lichen was placed within a woven cattail tray and put into the pit. The lichen was covered with more twigs and grass. Mary would have placed a pole in the centre of the pit before she started to fill it, and after the pit was full she pulled the post out and added water to create steam. At this point she covered the entire pit with dirt, until no steam escaped, and left it to cook.

The next morning, when the lichen was supposed to be cooked, Mary returned and carefully uncovered the tray. She was appalled to see not a nice homogeneous layer of cooked lichen that resembled a cake of rich black licorice but, instead, dry lumps that looked, in Mary's words, "like something that the Coyote had left behind after he had eaten a gopher!"

"Mom!" she said. "What did I do wrong?" She remembered that her mother had grunted slightly at one stage of the preparations the day before but Mary hadn't thought too much about it. It came back to her as her mother said reproachfully, "Since when did Indians use *two-by-fours?*"

Mary had decided to apply the material she had at hand—firwood two-by-fours, instead of the green cottonwood logs that people traditionally used to heat the cooking rocks. Of course, two-by-fours burn too fast—much faster than green cottonwood logs—and by the time they had burned through, the rocks resting on them were not nearly hot enough.

Mary laughs and laughs when she tells this story today. "Well, I never made that mistake again, so I guess Mom was a good teacher," she says. Today, she herself is the teacher and she patiently instructs her own grandchildren—and hundreds of others—about the importance of traditional food and traditional values. She, like Daisy Sewid-Smith, received an honorary doctorate from the University of Victoria in recognition of her work.

Many more examples are to be found of transformations of plants and animals from their ancient, humanized forms to their present forms in First Peoples' origin stories. For example, more colourful and flamboyant plant than the black tree lichen, but also an important food in times of scarcity, is the yellow skunk cabbage *(Lysichiton americanum)*, also and perhaps more aptly named "swamp lantern."

THE LIFE-GIVING SKUNK CABBAGE

Although yellow skunk cabbage is valued for its large, waxy-looking leaves, which are used to wrap food and as a surface for drying berries, it was seldom actually eaten. Plants in the arum family (Araceae)—and skunk cabbage is no exception—have microscopic crystals of calcium oxalate embedded in the tissues of their leaves, stems, roots and flowers. This renders skunk cabbage unpleasant to eat, if not downright poisonous, unless it is carefully processed to reduce the crystals. Even when cooked, skunk cabbage roots (rhizomes) are said to be "hot" and "peppery." However, if they are dug in early spring, and well roasted or cooked for a long time, they can be consumed.

Long ago, skunk cabbage was a life-saving famine food for the Kathlamet (Chinook) at the mouth of the Columbia River, as recognized in several versions of a Kathlamet narrative called "Myth of the Salmon," which was recorded around the turn of the last century by ethnographer Franz Boas.

Skunk cabbage (Lysichiton americanum). PHOTO BY ROBERT D. TURNER

The Myth of the Salmon

The people of mythical times were dying of hunger. They had only sagittaria-roots [wapato: *Sagittaria* spp.] to eat. They had only small sagittaria-roots and skunk-cabbage and . . . rush roots [probably *Typha latifolia*] to eat. In the spring of the year the Salmon went up the river. They had first arrived with many companions. . . . Then the Skunk Cabbage said: "At last my brother's son has arrived. If it had not been for me, your people would have been dead long ago." Then the Salmon said, "Who is that who is talking there? Oh, that is the Skunk Cabbage who is talking. Let us go ashore." They gave him five elk skins and put war clubs under his blanket, one on each side. . . . Then they carried him inland and placed him among willows.

Although people often scorn skunk cabbage because of its pungent smell, this story demonstrates a gracious side to this truly spectacular golden-flowered plant of wet places. In the time of the people's need, Skunk Cabbage and the other lowly roots of the marshes saved them from starvation; even the Salmon People recognized and rewarded their generosity, which is still seen today in the club-shaped flower spike and brilliant yellow spathe. Our attitudes and prejudices are manifested in many ways. Sometimes we need to look at things—and at other people— with a different eye, and we may be surprised at what we discover.

NETS AND NETTLES

Another story of supernatural intervention in the workings of humans and other animals is the Nuxalk narrative, recorded by Thomas Mc-Ilwraith, about the origin of fishing nets for eulachon (also written as "oulachen" or "ooligan"), a small smelt whose oil is rendered as a valuable food and condiment:

> One of Raven's inventions was the making of nettle-fibre oulachen nets, an art which he taught spiders as well as men. In the beginning of time, Raven told two men to make a net according to a pattern which he showed them, and gave them some fibre. It was not sufficient, and when the workers asked for more, Raven told them to draw it from their own intestines. This they did, and ever since spiders have had the same ability.

In another Nuxalk story, Raven saw a nettle-fibre eulachon net being made in one of the distant villages that he visited during his travels and learned the details of its manufacture. In the same generous spirit he exhibited when he brought home the whipped soapberries, Raven taught the Bella Coola people how to make the nets once he returned home.

ONE FINAL STORY of invention and discovery illustrates the diversity of origin stories that recognize both the gifts and the sacrifices of those ancient beings—human, animal and plant—who came before to make the lives of the people today more comfortable and pleasant. This short story, from the Tlingit traditions of southeastern Alaska, explains how people came to learn the arts of basketry with Sitka spruce roots *(Picea sitchensis)* and other plant fibres, and why the Yakutat people are said to be the most experienced basket weavers among the Tlingit:

The Sky, the Earth and the People

Back in Raven's time, Sun's beautiful wife, who was human, fashioned the first basket from some roots up in Sky-land at a time when she was longing for the Earth-life for herself and her children. Sun, understanding her homesickness, increased the size of her basket until it was big enough for his wife and their eight children, then gently lowered them down to the Earth. The basket settled at a place near Yakutat on the Alsek River, and that is the reason that the first baskets in southeastern Alaska were made by Yakutat women.

These stories and hundreds of others like them—connecting us with the land and the other beings of Nature—teach us to live our lives with humility and respect. Wherever we live, we should learn about and honour these stories and the people who told and continue to tell them. It is important to remember, however, that many stories are personal property, in some ways similar to copyrighted books and movies. Just because they are orally reproduced does not make them free for others to use and tell without consent. Some of the stories—like the ones told by Skipper—have lost their original identity, but as much as it is possible to do so the origins should be acknowledged, and where ownership is attributable a person should seek and receive permission to retell the tales.

All of the resources that people use in stories such as these have been given to us as gifts, sometimes at great personal sacrifice and cost. We are taught to value what we have and to take responsibility for looking after these offerings. Perhaps one key to sustainable living is for all of us to become rooted to a place and, if we don't have them at first, to evolve our own stories about our relationships to our special places and to the trees and other life forms that live there. We need to commit ourselves to those environments and to their well-being in any way we can. Knowing and caring about places is probably the very best thing we can do for ourselves and for the earth.

LEFT TO RIGHT: *Kim Recalma-Clutesi*
(Ogwilogwa; Kwakwₐka'wakw—Qualicum–Kwagiulth;
elected chief, Qualicum) and Dr. Daisy Sewid-Smith (Mayanilth;
Kwakwₐka'wakw—Maṁaliliqəla).

3

A KINCENTRIC

Approach

to NATURE

"WE ARE ALL STAR-STUFF!" I can still hear that exclamation from the late Carl Sagan, famed astronomer and journalist. I was watching his television series *Cosmos,* and he was musing about humans' connections with the stars as he pondered the origins of the universe and our place in its vastness. I remember Dr. Nancy Maryboy, Diné (Navajo) educator and cultural specialist, stating in a lecture that the Diné word for "star" means, approximately, "my ancient ancestor from whom I come."

To me these two ideas, from two entirely different knowledge traditions, represent a profound convergence of thinking and understanding. Fundamentally, the basic building blocks of matter—atoms and molecules and the particles they comprise—and the energy that mobilizes them are the same everywhere, as far as we know, whether on Earth or on a distant star.

Not all peoples of the world assume, as is common in western societies, that humans are superior to other life forms. In fact, most aboriginal traditions from the Americas recognize a time when there was no distinction between humans, plants and animals. Trees and other plants, birds, fish, deer and all the other creatures of the forest and the sea were—and still are, to some—capable of taking on human form and performing human actions. Only in the modern era, it is said, are humans unable actually to view the humanness of other life forms in their day-to-day lives. The human attributes of the animals and plants are represented in the narratives focussing on the mythical times, including those I have already described, such as the Nuxalk stories of the origin of soapberries and eulachon nets, the Saanich story of the origin of salmon and the Kathlamet tale of how Skunk Cabbage fed the people in the very early days. Many of the actors in these stories, like Raven and Coyote, are represented as superior to humans, having magical, superhuman powers. They are the ones who used their magic to transform the beings and landmarks of ancient times to their present-day likenesses.

Another group of indigenous people, the Rarámuri, or Tarahumara, of northern Mexico, have a world view that is remarkably parallel to that of northwestern North American peoples.

Iwígara: A Rarámuri Concept of Relationships

Dr. Enrique Salmón, a good friend, ethnobotanist and member of the Rarámuri people, describes humans' relationships to the other entities in their universe as "kincentric." That is, they regard all of the earth's beings as relatives, different from humans in form but not in substance. Not only are animals and plants considered members of the same big family, they are the ones who assisted humans to enter the world, according to many cultural traditions. Salmón refers to the Laguna Pueblo people of New Mexico as an example. He suggests that the Laguna's long existence in the arid region of the Southwest could not have been possible without recognizing that humans were sisters and brothers to all the other dwellers there: the badger, antelope, clay, yucca and sun. It was not until they realized this, Salmón says, that the Laguna people could "emerge" from the dark place under the earth where they originally existed.

Salmón describes his own people's homeland, called *Gawi Wachi* ("the Place of Nurturing"), in the eastern Sierra Madres of Chihuahua, Mexico. A region highly diverse, biologically and geographically, *Gawi Wachi* has

Dr. Enrique Salmón, Rarámuri ethnobotanist and cultural specialist.

been carefully managed by the Rarámuri for more than 2,000 years, and Salmón estimates that even today 95 per cent of the population still practises some form of traditional ways, including speaking the Rarámuri language and participating in ceremonies. The Rarámuri hold a concept called *iwígara*, which embodies "kincentric ecology," even though this latter phrase itself would not be used by Rarámuri and other indigenous-language speakers. These languages have their own terms for expressing ideas and fundamental interrelationships that fit with their own world views. (It is almost always difficult to translate accurately the words of one language into another and retain their essence, let alone the subtle nuances of humour, irony and other important elements of conversation and story-telling. No English word corresponds even roughly to *iwígara*, for example. The best that can be done is for someone such as Enrique Salmón, who converses in both Rarámuri and English, to provide corresponding phrases and examples of how and under what circumstances the term can be applied. In this way outsiders may approach an understanding, but we must accept that we will never fully comprehend such a term.)

Salmón defines *iwígara* as "the total interconnectedness and the integration of all life in the Sierra Madres, physical and spiritual." On hearing this term, a Rarámuri person would understand it to mean life in all its forms and would recall the origins of Rarámuri life and of the relationships the people have to animals, plants, their home place and their guiding entities. *Iwígara* ties people to their songs and ceremonies, to their foods and to the land that nourishes them. Significantly, too, it makes reference to the Rarámuri concept of soul. Salmón writes, "It is understood that the soul, or *íwi*, sustains the body with the breath of life." For the Rarámuri, unlike for most members of western society, everything that breathes has a soul: plants, animals, humans, stones, the land—all these share the same breath, and all have souls.

There is so much more to *íwi* and its Rarámuri significance. When humans and animals die, their souls become butterflies that visit the living and also travel to the Milky Way, where past souls of the ancestors reside. A caterpillar that weaves its cocoons on the madrone (or arbutus) tree (the same kind of tree to which the Saanich anchored their canoes during the flood) is identified as *íwi* too, with the implication that *íwi*, and the caterpillar, represents the whole cycle of metamorphosis and renewal, from birth through death and rebirth. *Íwi* and *iwígara* epitomize the continuous cycle of life and the interconnections between the spiritual and physical elements of life. As Salmón summarizes, "We are all related to, and play a role in, the complexity of life."

Everything Is One

Far to the north and west of the Rarámuri homeland, on the west coast of Vancouver Island, the concept of *iwígara* is echoed in general terms in the Nuu-Chah-Nulth phrase *Hishuk ish ts'awalk*, "everything is one." Dr. Richard Atleo, educator and hereditary chief of Ahousaht, explained this concept further, noting that the Nuu-Chah-Nulth belief system from which their traditional values arise can be articulated as follows:

The Creator made all things one.
All things are related and interconnected.
All things are sacred.
All things are therefore to be respected.

Essentially, these philosophies from the Rarámuri and Nuu-Chah-Nulth confirm and reinforce the idea that humans do have a kinship with all the other elements of their world. Ceremonies, customs and stories recognize and validate this connection, as do the ways in which people relate to their lands and resources. This kinship supports and nurtures humans, but it brings with it obligations. The same responsibilities that most humans feel towards their own family members are, in the kincentric view of indigenous peoples, extended to all life. It is the duty of humans to acknowledge, and to look after, *all* of their relatives and to consider their health and well-being as inextricably bound to humans'. It is seen as a sacred trust to care for Earth and its inhabitants, as they care for us.

Iwígara ensures that the Rarámuri treat the plants and animals and the lands from which they derive their sustenance with special care and respect. Their entire agricultural system—from the way they grow and process their crops to the way they treat even the weeds in their fields—is influenced by recognizing kinship with these things. In the Rarámuri origin stories, people were actually part plant in a previous world. When the people came into the present world, many of the plant and animal beings emerged with them and took up their lives as people in a different form: peyote cactus *(Lophophora williamsii)*, datura or thornapple *(Datura meteloides)*, maize, coyotes, bears and deer. These living entities are all seen as cousins and siblings of humans.

The Nuu-Chah-Nulth treat salmon respectfully—carefully returning the bones to the river after the flesh is eaten—for the same reason that a canoe-maker approaches a tree he wants to use: they recognize the kinship, the humanness of these life forms. Nuu-Chah-Nulth elder Roy Haiyupis described what should be done when a tree is to be cut down: "Talk to it like a person. Explain to the tree the purpose, why you want to use it—for the people at home and so on. It may seem like you're praying to the tree, but you're praying to the Creator."

Datura or thornapple (Datura meteloides), *a plant-being of high importance in the American Southwest.* PHOTO BY ROBERT D. TURNER

Halkomelem cultural specialist Arvid Charlie spent a lot of time as a boy with his great-grandfather *Lescheem* (*Leschím,* Louis George), who was born in about 1871. *Lescheem* taught Arvid traditional lifeways as well as about respecting all of Nature, and this automatically instilled in Arvid a sense of conservation that is a major part of his teachings today. In 1999, Arvid recalled some of *Lescheem*'s wisdom when I asked him how he gained his knowledge and understanding of conservation:

> I never got told directly about some of these things [conservation], but one of the main things that Lescheem, Grandpa Lescheem [taught]: re-spect. And that goes for everything. One of the main things for a youth,

an Indian youth here, in Quamichan—[we] lived right by the river—
was the chum salmon. He always really stressed, you don't take any
more than you can use. [If] you get too much, you give it away. If you
have only one fish, you cut the best off and give it to who you're going
to give it to. And, keep the spirit part for yourself.

. . . And he always said, respect the fish, and your elders, your people, including the trees. Even the *sqweyalth* today, the wind. Everything. He included everything. Talk to it. Thank it. They all have their
own spirit. And even one person, you take one person, well he's got one
spirit. But every part of his body has its own spirit: the elbow, the feet,
each part of your foot. And everything's like that. If you treat everything right, how you treat things comes back many times. So, if you're
respectful to everything, they'll do the same. If you help everything,
they'll help you back.

Arvid Charlie's words summarize eloquently an attitude, a way of
life, that was, and still is for some, a part of living as an aboriginal person
in British Columbia and in many parts of North America. Another
Cowichan (Quw'uts'un) healer, Theresa Thorne, conveyed similar
thoughts in describing the healing properties of water and other elements
of the environment:

The water is strong, the water is alive. Talk to the water, always face
east when you go in. Everything around you is alive, the trees and
rocks. Always pray when you pick medicines. Always have a clear
mind when you pick medicines and talk to the plants.

My friend Kim Recalma-Clutesi, like Arvid Charlie, received teachings from traditionally trained people, and she explained a similar kind of
relationship instilled in her as a child and young woman by her
Kwakwaka'wakw and Nuu-Chah-Nulth relatives:

All of our rituals, taboos and ceremonies revolved around the careful
gathering of what the great Nature provided us, and we honoured each
life, whether it be plant, animal or marine, by using it and not wasting it, being careful not to overharvest . . . to carefully cultivate and

enhance the resources so they would be there for use by our grand-children. . . . We believe that all life, whether it be animal, plant or marine, is sacred and is as important as human life. We are but one small part of the big picture and our food-gathering practices and cere-monies remind us of that.

Animals and People: Shared Customs

A story told to me by Daisy Sewid-Smith, Chief Adam Dick and Kim Recalma-Clutesi illustrates the human attributes of other life forms in the Kwakwaka'wakw world view.

At one time, just before the coming of Captain George Vancouver to circumnavigate the island named after him, the salmon did not make their usual spawning run up the Nimpkish (*'Namgis*) River. The chiefs of all the communities along the river that relied on these salmon runs decided to bring the people down to the mouth of the river to live on shellfish and other seafood until the salmon returned. They built extra houses for these people, and Daisy Sewid-Smith said that at that village you can still see the human-built terraces where they placed the houses. At the time that the salmon did not come, however, the people understood that the chief of the under-ocean world, *Mayisilah* (described as the Kwakwaka'wakw counterpart of Neptune, the Roman god), was hosting a wedding for his daughter. The salmon did not come up the river that year because they were attending the wedding.

This representation of a society of under-ocean beings, with all of the cultural institutions of the people themselves—including salmon as wed-ding guests—reveals a very different attitude than most of us have to-wards the fish and other life of the sea.

Likewise, in the Interior Mary Thomas vividly remembers her elderly Secwepemc grandmother walking along the banks of the Salmon River near her home at Salmon Arm after the sockeye had spawned, gently pushing the dead salmon back into the river to float away in the current. Her grandmother did this with a combined sense of respect for the salmon and, she explained to Mary, for all the other life in the river that the dead salmon would nourish. Mary recalls that different people did this all along the river. The children, including Mary, were taught to return the dead fish to the river and to respect the dead and dying salmon. Under no circumstances were they allowed to play with the dead and dying salmon, poke them or make fun of them.

Mary remembered, "Our grandmother would tell us a little legend and at the end of the legend she would say, 'Now you see, if you don't do it this way, or if you do it that way. . . . ' They always used something in Mother Nature to teach us our lessons, our values." One of these stories related the life history of the sockeye salmon with the life changes, roles and responsibilities of young people.

The Story of the Sockeye

The story starts with the baby sockeye, just hatched from its egg: so delicate you could see almost through it. . . . The little fish would get together in schools, to protect each other, like in schools. Although the mother and father salmon were not there, Mother Nature is looking after them. . . . As the fish is going down along the lake, travelling to go down to the ocean, it's starting to grow, it's growing. That filmy part is disappearing and they're beginning to mature, and it's a normal thing, they will tell the young boy, the young girl. 'It's just like you. Your body will change. It's a normal thing, it's nothing to be ashamed of, it's part of life.' "

(Mary also recalls that this is how the Secwepemc taught children to understand and take pride in their own roles in society and family life. She explained that when the salmon were young, silvery and gorgeous-looking, out in the ocean, the salmon were prideful of their appearance and careful to maintain their beauty.)

As the fish started up the Fraser River on their long, arduous journey to their spawning grounds, Mary's grandmother told the children, they started to pair off and to care for each other more than for themselves. The males, once sleek and flashing with silver, began to develop ugly hooked noses and became bruised and battered on the rocks of the river. Still, they didn't care. Each one told his wife, "When you get tired, come over and hold onto my tail and you can rest." They cared more about their families, and the baby salmon they were going to bring into the world, than about themselves and their own beauty. Finally, when the salmon reached their spawning beds in the Salmon River, they carefully deposited their eggs and milt, fanning the beds with their tails and putting all their energy into ensuring the survival of the babies. They died giving life to the next generation, and they also gave life to humans and to all the other living things along the river.

From this story, Secwepemc children learned why the salmon are to be so respected and admired, and they understood why Mary's grandmother admonished them to care for the dying fish and not to make fun of them. Mary explained that sex was talked about to young people in a way that was sacred. Youths were taught to have pride in themselves and their bodies. And the girls were reminded that their bodies were the givers of life. They were told, "You have to be true to your husband, encourage him to be your protector, your provider." And the boys were taught, "When your mate is carrying your child, you forget about yourself. All you think of is that mate; you have to look after her, give her the utmost love and care. That way she will bear you strong, healthy children. People should live just like the salmon when they pair off to come up the river."

ANIMALS AS PEOPLE

The Sinixt story of the mountain goat brothers and their introduction of black mountain huckleberry is one of many indigenous narratives about these animals that show the animals' humanness. The close relationship between the Nlaka'pmx people and mountain goats *(Oreamnus americanus)*, for example, is reflected in "The Goat People," recorded, like many other Nlaka'pmx narratives, by James Teit.

In this story, the mating season for the Goat People is identified as the time when the dog salmon, also known as chum salmon, ascend the Fraser River on their spawning migration. Each day the mountain goats made a special delicacy for their guests: "a large basketful of soup of black and white moss."

The "black moss" referred to here is actually the black tree lichen *(Bryoria fremontii* and related species), the same one featured in the origin story in which Coyote transformed his hair braid into food for people; the "white moss" is old man's beard lichen *(Alectoria sarmentosa)*. Both lichens are recognized as a favourite food of mountain goats, whereas humans would usually eat only the black lichen.

This detail of the delicacy served is a good example of both differences and similarities between the foods of humans and the foods of animals. Black bears *(Ursus americanus)* and grizzlies *(U. arctos horribilis)*, for example, are known to relish yellow glacier lily *(Erythronium grandiflorum)* bulbs, called sk'émets in the Nlaka'pmx language and scwicw *(sxwixw)* in Secwepemc-tsin. The bears also enjoy other foods that humans like, such as huckleberries and blueberries (*Vaccinium* spp.). However, unlike humans, they eat grubs and such fruits as cascara berries *(Rhamnus purshiana)* and black twinberries *(Lonicera involucrata)* that humans do not usually consume; these were "the bear's own berries," as described by Mary Thomas and others.

One prepared Nlaka'pmx food that Black Bear and other animals of the stories from ancient times really enjoyed (and that reflects the love of roots and berries that bears demonstrate today) is nkéxw, a dish perhaps best referred to in English as "pudding." Its ingredients are typically Nlaka'pmx: salmon eggs, deer fat, black tree lichen, sk'émets, tiger lily bulbs *(Lilium columbianum)*, spring beauty corms *(Claytonia lanceolata)*, dried bitterroot and dried Saskatoon berries. Nlaka'pmx elders Annie York and Hilda Austin, both of whom really enjoyed their traditional food, liked to make this dish. Once, Hilda served it when my friend Harriet Kuhnlein and I visited her at her home near St. George's School in Lytton. What she made must have been the deluxe recipe, as it contained all the possible ingredients. It was both delicious and filling; one bowlful kept us going for the rest of the day. Bernadette Antoine of Coldwater, who also loved serving traditional food to her family, used to make the dish for her grandchildren and she noted: "The kids just go crazy over it. . . . When you don't make any of it for a long time, you can't seem to get any of it for yourself!" In the old times, the animal people, too, enjoyed nkéxw, and it is featured in the stories about them, such as in the following excerpt from a story about Skunk, recorded in Teit's *Mythology of the Thompson Indians:*

> Skunk pretended to be sorrowful, and wept. He said to his wife, "I am sorrowful. Cook much *nqáux* [nkéxw], roots and fish, that my guests may have plenty to eat." Then he asked all the people to come and see

him, and all his younger brothers the animals repaired to his house. Grisly [sic] Bear, Fisher, Marten, Wolf, Wolverine, all went. . . .

These and similar stories are set in the distant mythical times when not only could animals become people but so, too, could people sometimes become animals. Those fortunate enough to undergo such a transformation learned from the fauna some of the important lessons of human existence, since the animals then were able to understand people as well as or better than we do ourselves. Especially valuable teachings from the animal world included how people should relate to their animal kin and how to use them respectfully.

For example, in "The Hunter and the Goats," a Nlaka'pmx hunter—a reverent and competent young man—is taught by the goats themselves the right way to hunt. The story begins as a father and several of his sons set off to hunt mountain goats. One night when they are in camp, a goat comes into sight in the distance. The youngest son has been training himself in running and shooting, so his father bids him to run out and shoot the goat, which he does. He is successful in killing it, and, having received a good education, he prays and treats the goat's remains with care and respect as he skins and cuts up the meat. He carefully lays the pieces of meat on fir boughs that he has spread on the ground, then he ties everything together with his packing line, wrapping fir twigs around the bundle.

When he has finished his work and is ready to carry the meat back to the camp, he sees a woman approaching him. He does not recognize her, but he notes her good looks and white complexion. She turns out to be the goat that he has killed, and she invites him to come home with her. First he resists, saying, "No, I cannot go with any woman. I am training, and it would ruin me for hunting. I must keep myself pure." The woman praises him for his hunting skills and for showing care and respect for the goats when he handled the meat. She tells him that if he goes home with her, he will gain great knowledge and become an even better hunter.

Thus, the young hunter goes to live with the Goat People, and he learns all about the habits of goats. He himself becomes a goat and eventually ruts with all the female goats. For four days and nights he stays with the goats, then the goat-woman leads him back to the place where he left his bundle of meat. She hands back his weapons and instructs him: "You will now be a great hunter and will be able to follow the goats on the precipices where they walk. When you kill goats, treat their bodies respectfully, for they are people. Do not shoot female goats, for they were your wives and will bear you children. Do not kill kids, for they may be your offspring. Only shoot your brothers-in-law, the male goats."

This narrative illustrates how, embodied in a story of prowess and success, is the message that goats are actually relatives of humans and have families and societies of their own, and serious instructions are given about how to respect these animals, hunt sustainably and maintain the goat populations.

Respecting Our Relatives

In this kincentric world view, it is understood that all forms of life need to eat each other and they willingly give themselves to each other as food, if the proper protocols are followed. Most important among these rules of conduct are treating all life with respect and never wasting or wantonly using animals, plants, foods or medicines. Elders will explain that, just as one should not joke about other beings, so too children should never joke about, tease, play with or waste animals or plants, because these living beings have generously given themselves to humans for our benefit.

Secwepemc elder Ida Matthew recalled how her own mother taught her about the treatment of animals when she was a little girl: "It was pitiful enough that we had to kill them," she said. "[My mother] instilled in us that we were not to waste the food, that we had to kill the poor animal. With any kinds of animal that we would hunt and eat, you have to respect them."

The observations of ethnographers such as Charles Hill-Tout, who worked in the territories of several Salishan peoples in the latter part of the nineteenth century and early twentieth century, confirm this reverential and appreciative attitude:

Nothing that the Indian of this region [Lillooet; Stl'atl'imx] eats is regarded by him as mere food and nothing more. Not a single plant, animal or fish or other object upon which he feeds is looked upon in this light, or as something he has secured for himself by his own wit and skill. He regards it rather as something that has been voluntarily and compassionately placed in his hands by the goodwill and consent of the "spirit" of the object itself, or by the intercession and magic of his culture-heroes; to be retained and used by him only upon the fulfilment of certain conditions. These conditions include respect and reverent care in the killing or plucking of the animal or plant and proper treatment of the parts he has no use for, such as the bones, blood and offal; and the depositing of the same in some stream or lake, so that the object may by that means renew its life and physical form. . . .

Respect for all the life on Earth is stressed over and over by indigenous elders. In his book *The Tlingit Indians,* George Emmons explained the world view of the Alaskan Tlingit, noting that they never took life unnecessarily or needlessly because they believed in the existence of spirits in all of Nature.

Even inanimate objects possessed for him [a Tlingit person] something more than the mere material form. The shadow cast by the tree in the sunshine [was its spirit], and the winter wind, *hoon* [xú.n], was the breath of the ice spirit. Animal species formed families [clans] like those of men, and in the early days of the world, all living beings were much closer to one another. . . .

Helen Clifton, an elder of the Gitga'at Nation (Coast Tsimshian) from Hartley Bay, explained that all animals and plants, whether they are used for food or not, must be treated deferentially, with appreciation and reverence. She explained that you should never joke about them because this is disrespectful. She stressed, "They all have their societies and their families, and you have to respect them, whether it's a plant, a little mouse or a wolf—any living creature." You have to be careful, Helen cautioned, even about the words you use in the Sm'algyax language; you should never use terms that demean or show disdain to others, even in jest.

She shared these teachings with me after we saw wolves down at the beach at the Gitga'at spring harvesting camp at Kiel, when I was there in

May 2002 with Helen and her husband, Chief Johnny Clifton, and members of the Gitga'at community. The immediate concern of some people at the camp was for the children who might stray and be taken by the wolves (*Canis lupus columbianus* is the British Columbia wolf). The elders, however, refrained from shooting the animals and simply scared them away with a gunshot over their heads; the elders would not harm the wolves unless it was absolutely unavoidable.

The canines' behaviour on that occasion—coming right into the camp—was seen as unusual and aberrant. Usually, Helen told me, the wolves keep to their own societies, living their own lives. They do not bother humans or, at least, they only communicate with people from a distance. Human society and wolf society do not mix: Each respects the other and does not interfere, except in certain mediated ritual situations. People do not eat wolves, and these animals are not killed for sport. They are treated respectfully and left alone. They are considered to bring special power and can spiritually impart their hunting skills to humans, according to Tsimshian and other First Nations traditions.

Children of First Nations up and down the coast are taught about the special relationship humans have with wolves. When I recently attended a Nuu-Chah-Nulth celebration, Dr. Richard Atleo, Chief *Umeek*, explained to me that the singers of a traditional song of honour we were listening to were actually imitating wolves. The way they stood in a circle while they were singing and the way the chorus of singers echoed the single lead singer in the lines of the song recreated wolves' howling, when the pack follows the single leader who initiates and directs the group.

Violet Williams and Elsie Claxton told a version of a story about a young man from Pauquachin, a community within the Saanich Nation, who was adopted by wolves when he was seeking power. The animals had captured the young man, who had inadvertently seen them in their human forms, without their wolf skins. Some of the wolves wanted to kill him because he had caught sight of them as humans, but one female wolf said he should be spared, so they let him live. They began to train him, teaching him to run like a wolf and to hunt deer, and they finally accepted him as a wolf. The young man lived with the wolves for many years, becoming an exceptional hunter. When he finally returned to his human community, the young man's wolf family kept watch over him. Every morning they would leave a deer for him and his family at his door. And once, when he was digging clams at Deep Cove, the young man was surrounded by enemies from the north, who derided him because of his reputation as a wolf man. He howled like a wolf, and immediately his wolf protectors appeared. The enemies ran away and never bothered him again.

The Woman Who Befriended a Wolf

A different story about wolves comes from the Nuxalk tradition and starts with another lesson about the humanness of even the berries that people pick and eat. In the story, recorded by Thomas McIlwraith, a woman named *Ksninsnimdimut* was out picking wild blueberries *(Vaccinium ovalifolium, V. alaskaense)*. She was starting to climb a steep bank to a shelf where she noticed that the fruit was plentiful, when she heard one of the berries speaking to the others: "Let's hide," it said, "that foulmouthed woman is coming." The berry was speaking about the woman herself, calling her "foul-mouthed" because she had a habit of eating the berries as she picked instead of putting all of them into her basket. *Ksninsnimdimut* hurried up the bank so fast that many of the berries were unable to hide, and she saw them in their human forms: "a host of goggle-eyed little boys sitting on the berry shoots." After this lesson, she was more careful about respecting the berries' wishes: she never ate the fruit as she picked, but chewed on dried salmon instead. She became a very successful berry picker because, from then on, she was always able to see the berries in their hiding places.

Later, the story goes, *Ksninsnimdimut* encountered a wolf giving birth to its cubs: "In some way the delivery was being retarded so that the mother wolf was in agony; without hesitation *Ksninsnimdimut* went to her assistance, an evergreen bough in each hand. First she drew forth the four cubs, one after another, and finally the afterbirth. The grateful wolf gave her midwife the power of a shaman." On another occasion, the woman helped a wolf who was choking on a bone; she inserted her hand into the animal's throat and drew forth the cause of the blockage. From these experiences and the special powers she was given, *Ksninsnimdimut* became a famous shaman and healer among the Nuxalk.

More Stories of Learning from Animals

In another Nlaka'pmx story recorded by James Teit, "The Hunter and the Wolf," a wolf teaches a man how to prepare sagebrush buttercup *(Ranunculus glaberrimus)* as a poison for his arrowheads. With this knowledge the man became a great hunter, and the Nlaka'pmx acquired this skill. Nowadays buttercup is well known to contain an irritating compound, protoanemonin, in its leaves, stems and flowers, and children are told not to handle these flowers because they will cause sores on their hands. The wolf is thus given credit for first conveying this knowledge to the people.

The Blackfoot of the central plains just east of the Rocky Mountains in Alberta and Montana also had a special relationship with wolves. For them, *Makoiyi,* the wolves, were the first Earth Beings to take pity on people. The animals brought fresh meat to a starving family one winter, then they showed the young man of the family how to co-operate with others when he hunted buffalo and other animals. From wolves, people learned to live and travel in clans, like wolf packs, and to work together for the good of the group. In the Blackfoot language, the Milky Way is called *makoi-yohsokoyi,* the Wolf Trail, and these stars are a constant reminder for people of how they should live together.

RECOGNIZING SPECIAL TALENTS

The animals in traditional stories, like the mountain goats and the wolves, often bring their characteristic traits, habits and foods to their human form. Woodpecker in his human form is often a master carver and canoe builder. Mallard Duck Woman and Goose Woman like to eat Pacific silverweed *(Potentilla pacifica)* and wild clover *(Trifolium wormskjoldii)* roots along the tidal flats of the Pacific coast where these roots grow. Grizzly Bear tends to be cantankerous, and Chipmunk is quick and flighty. Raven and Crow are always trying to get other people's food. Owl and Eagle are excellent hunters. Deer is a swift runner. Snail moves very slowly. Mouse Woman, in Haida traditions, lives beneath a clump of sword fern *(Polystichum munitum)*.

Beaver lives in water and is generally knowledgeable about wood. In a Nlaka'pmx episode recorded by Charles Hill-Tout, Beaver was the one who taught the people how to make and keep fire. Beaver was travelling down the river with the people, and he "threw fire on all the trees they passed." Most of these trees were cottonwoods *(Populus balsamifera* ssp. *trichocarpa),* and, as the story explains, wood from the cottonwood was the best for making fire from that time onward. Today, those who know the art of firemaking affirm that few woods are better for starting a fire than the dead, dry wood of cottonwood, especially the roots.

In this story, Beaver continued to throw fire on the trees until he reached the coast and all his fire was used up. Then he assumed a human form and taught the people how to make fire with a drill, by working it between their hands and twirling it rapidly into a grooved wooden base or hearth. The other valuable device he taught them about was a "slow match," which is a means of keeping and carrying fire from one place to another: He obtained a quantity of inner bark from the western red-cedar *(Thuja plicata),* which can be easily shredded into fine strands when it is dried. He then formed the cedar bark into a long rope and covered it with the bark of another tree that was not as easily burned. When the end of the cedarbark rope is ignited, it continues to smoulder inside its covering for several days, until it is all burned. When people were travelling and likely to be away from camp for several days, they always carried one of these fire-ropes coiled around their shoulders. The story concludes, "After this great gift to them the Indians thought very highly of Beaver, and he was usually called by them 'our head brother' because of his wisdom and goodness."

A wonderful Saanich story, with a theme that echoes up and down the coast, tells about the "salmonberry bird," Swainson's thrush *(Catharus ustulatus)*. It is said that Swainson's Thrush's singing in the springtime makes the salmonberries *(Rubus spectabilis)* ripen. This small brown speckle-breasted bird blends into the dappled shade of the forest thickets, but its melodic song in rising notes reverberates throughout the forest, touching the soul of all who hear it. The Saanich name for Swainson's thrush is *xwexwálesh,* an onomatopaeic imitation of its song: "*xwexwelexwel-exwelexwesh!*" Elsie Claxton told me that if you translate the bird's full song, it sounds something like: "Come on, all you dark ones [*nenel'q'-xelíqw*]! Come on, all you light-coloured ones [*nenel'pq'íqw*]! Come on, all you red-coloured ones [*nenel'kwemíqw*]! Come on, all you golden ones [*nenel'pxwíqw*]! Ripen, ripen, ripen, ripen [*xwexwelexwelexwelexwesh*]!" The story that goes with this song was told to me by Elsie Claxton and Violet Williams.

Salmonberry Bird (Swainson's Thrush) and Raven

One time, Salmonberry Bird invited Raven to her house for a meal. She told her kids to take their baskets out to pick berries. She started to sing her song, and as she sang her children's baskets filled up. The children came home, and everyone had a wonderful meal of deliciously ripened salmonberries of all the different colours. Afterwards Raven said, "You come to my house tomorrow." So Salmonberry Bird came along the next day, and Raven gave baskets to his children and told them to go out to get the berries. Raven's children went out for their dad, and

Salmonberry (Rubus spectabilis), *golden colour form.* PHOTO BY ROBERT D. TURNER

Raven sang and sang in his croaky raven voice. They waited and waited, but the Raven children's baskets never got full, and finally Salmonberry Bird went home without any berries.

This is one example of many that are referred to in folklore studies as the "bungling host" stories. Raven and Coyote are prime bungling hosts, always trying to imitate the talents of the other animals and always getting in trouble for it in some way. These stories are fun, but they also teach the children important lessons. In a gentle way, they remind children both that the birds and animals have human traits and that everyone has their own talents in which they should take pride, but they should not be envious or try to imitate the talents of others.

Plants, Rocks and Mountains as People

For the Okanagan, and other peoples, every group of beings has its communities and its chiefs. Just as Black Huckleberry is the Chief of the Berries for the Okanagan, so do the trees, grasses, edible roots and things that crawl along the ground have leaders. There are societies of beings all around us. In this world view, even the rocks have a chief, Black Flint. Figure 2 shows how some of these relationships work for the Okanagan, with the Old Man, the Creator, as the one overseeing them all. The Sweathouse, for the Okanagan and others, is a mediating entity, and sweatbathing can transcend the space between the Old Man and the people.

Many stories illustrate the human qualities of plants, rocks and mountains. There is a common tradition, for example, that trees like alder *(Alnus rubra)* were once women. In one of the Nlaka'pmx "Transformer Tales" recorded by James Teit and published in his *Mythology of the Thompson Indians,* there is an episode in which the four brothers who are the Transformers go to Coyote's house and discover that Coyote has a make-believe wife consisting of a piece of firewood with a knothole in it. Unbeknownst to Coyote, who is away from his house, the Transformers burn this piece of wood to warm themselves. Coyote enters and, not noticing the Transformers' presence, carries on a conversation with his

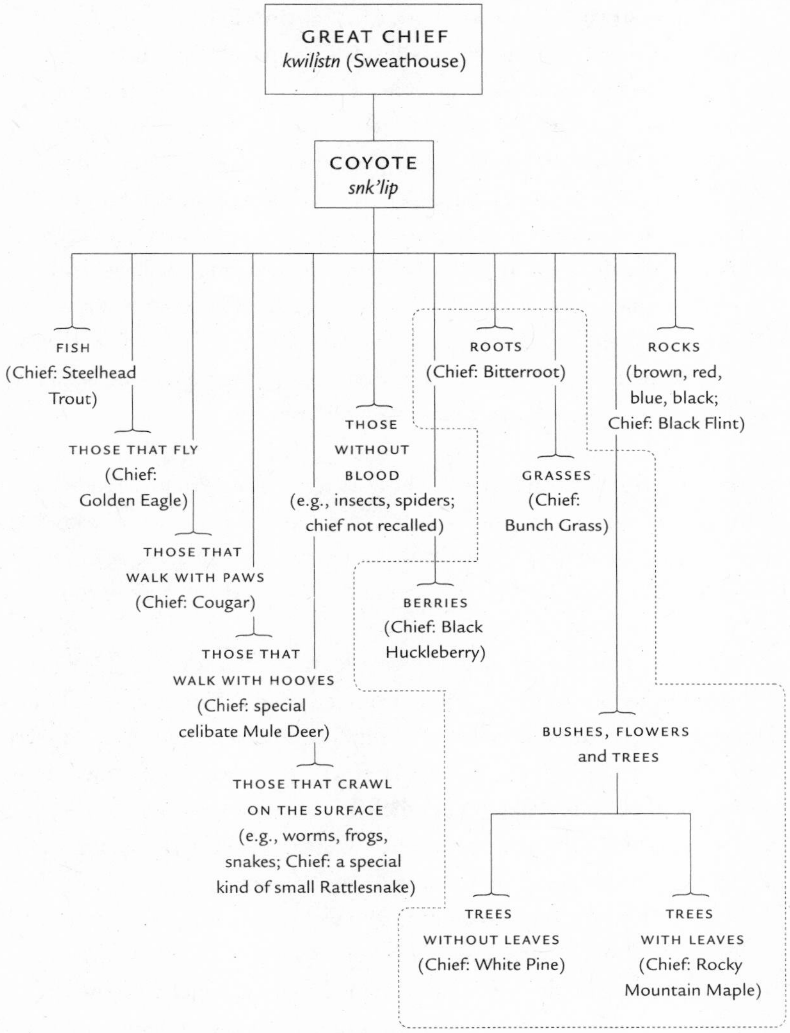

Figure 2. An Okanagan classification of living beings, shared by the late Selina Timoyakin of Penticton.

"wife," changing his voice to hers as he answers himself. Then he goes to find the piece of wood, which he had left under a heap of robes, but cannot find it:

He searched throughout the house, but, failing to find [his wife], he sat down and wept. The brothers could not restrain themselves any longer, and laughed from their hiding-places. They said, "We will give you better wives than the one you had." Borrowing an adze, they went to a bluff of trees nearby, and, cutting a short piece of alder (*kwiê'lp*) [*kʷy'éɬp*] and a longer piece of [trembling aspen] (*ōloltcê'tcêlp*) [*wəl'wəl'céɬp*] they fashioned them into the shape of women, and made them alive. . . . Before long the short woman, who was of alder, entered the house without speaking, and closely following her came the tall woman of [aspen], who said, "*alá*" as she reached the top of the ladder. The alder woman was of the Lower Fraser tribes, and the [aspen] woman of the Upper Thompson tribe, and they became Coyote's wives. . . .

In one Saanich tradition, a whole race of Tree Giants lived within Saanich territory long ago. Even today, people perceive trees as beings with special powers. As elder Ernie Rice explained, "You have to respect trees, speak to them so they will understand and they give you their strength."

Mountains, too, were formerly people in many traditions. In his two-volumed book on the Bella Coola, originally published in 1948, Thomas McIlwraith recorded a number of mountains in and around Nuxalk territory that used to have human forms before they were transformed. Even today, the mountains may reveal their human or supernatural traits and must be treated with special deference. Cultural traditions often prohibit people from pointing directly at certain mountains because it would show disrespect. In Saanich territory, for example, pointing at a mountain such as Malahat mountain near Victoria is said to cause thunder and lightning. Mountains are sometimes powerful humans like the chief who owned the soapberries in the Nuxalk story, who have their own personalities and their own powers. Some of them even have wives and children who also are mountains or hills and are often located close by.

Many other narratives tell of humans who were transformed into trees or rocks or other landmarks. For example, on Mount Tolmie (S̱NÁX̱E) (near the University of Victoria campus), Earl Claxton Sr. was told by his elders, two large rocks that are prominent in profile and easily visible from some locations represent a man and his wife; they were transformed into stone by xÁls, the Creator, according to a w̲sÁneć narrative, because the man had transgressed a cultural taboo and revealed a secret to his wife.

The Special Power of Medicine

Among the Kwakwa̱ka'wakw, everything that was used by people was honoured with special words acknowledging its healing or nurturing role and its power to help. The following passage was recorded by ethnographer Franz Boas in his 1930 book *The Religion of the Kwakiutl Indians*. The word for the address is translated from Kwak'wala by Boas as "prayer," but this translation is inaccurate according to Daisy Sewid-Smith. The original term connotes "words of praise and appreciation." The words are spoken by a medicine gatherer to an alder tree *(Alnus rubra)* along a riverbank. The man wishes to use the alder's bark to treat his wife, who is spitting blood [from tuberculosis]:

> I have come to ask you to take mercy, Supernatural-Power-of-the-River-Bank, that you may, please, make well with your healing power my poor wife who is spitting blood. Go on, please, pity me for I am troubled and, please, make her well, you, Healing-Woman, . . . and, please, stop up the source of blood, you Causing-to-Heal-Woman, and, please, heal up the cause of trouble of my poor wife, please, you, great Supernatural One. . . .

After this, the man would carefully remove four pieces of the bark from the standing tree, take them home and prepare and administer the healing solution with additional appeals and words of appreciation to the "Healing-Woman" alder.

Another example from the same volume is shown in the words of praise directed towards the salmonberry bush, whose bark is to be used for medicine. A man goes to the salmonberry plant and talks to it:

> Don't be startled, Supernatural One, by my coming and sitting down to make a request of you, Supernatural One. . . . This is the reason why

I come to you. . . . to pray you, please, to [let me] take some of your
blanket, Sore-Healer, that it may heal the burn of my child, that, please,
may heal up his burn, Supernatural One . . .

After he has carefully taken the bark that he needs, the man prepares
the medicine and talks to it [the medicine] once it is ready to administer:

O, Supernatural One, now I put you on to the sore [or burn] of my
child that you may lick off this great sickness, that you, please, make it
heal, you, Supernatural One, . . . Healing-Woman, you, Long-Life-
Maker, please, take pity on me that my mind may be at rest, you, Supernatural One.

Several healing practitioners from First Nations along the coast have
stressed that all medicine harvested must be used; if it is thrown away or
wasted, the person could suffer hardship in some way because of the disrespect shown. Careful harvesting and use of such medicines allowed them
to be used continually over many generations—in other words, sustainably. For example, in harvesting bark for medicine from a tree it is important to take a vertical strip of bark from the trunk, being careful not to cut
too far around its circumference. Also, many elders have told me that bark
harvested for medicine should be taken from the sunrise side of the tree, or
sometimes from the side of the tree facing the river. Trees usually grow
faster on the side that receives the most sun. Examine a cross-section of a
log or stump: you will see that the tree rings are wider (which means faster
growth) on the sunny side than on the shady (usually north) side. The
people who gather medicine know this, and they know that the bark on the
faster-growing side will heal faster over the wound. They say, too, that the
person for whom the medicine is prepared will likewise heal more quickly,
just as the tree heals itself. For example, Theresa Sam explained:

Each person has [their] own place to go for medicine. To our people,
everything is sacred. My granny thanked the tree before taking bark for
medicine. After two or three days, you go back and see if the tree is
healed and, if so, that means the person is healed.

Part of a Greater Whole

The recognition of humans' relationship to Nature and the respect given to life is seen over and over again in the different traditions of First Nations across North America and beyond. For example, the Blackfoot shared their perspective in an exhibit and the guidebook that accompanies it at the Glenbow Museum in Calgary. The name, *Ihtsi-pai-tapi-yopa*, is given in the Blackfoot language to "The Essence of All Life . . . Creator, the Source of All Life." In Blackfoot teachings, *Ihtsi-pai-tapi-yopa* made all living things, and all living things are equal. Humans have no right to rule over or exploit the rest of Nature. Plants, animals and even rocks are considered other living beings, different from humans but in no way inferior.

In the Blackfoot traditional world, each plant and animal has its unique abilities and gifts that it shares with humans. Plants can cure diseases and supply important nutrients in people's diet. The bison was a mainstay for the people, providing much of what they needed to survive. The birds, swift fliers, helped human warriors to be quick and stealthy. The Blackfoot Gallery Committee notes: "These animals visited us in human form and taught us how to call on them for their special gifts. This is how we became so closely connected to all the beings with whom we share the Earth."

Thus, everywhere are environmental features and entities imbued with humanness. The ultimate message is that we have relatives all around us: the rocks, the mountains, the trees, the edible roots, the animals and birds and the fish . . . all are our kin, all are related to us and to each other. People are only one form of a large and diverse family of beings and entities, including both physical and spiritual realms, which are not generally separated in First Nations perspectives. We are all part of creation and this connects us.

The relationships of kinship give rise to the special ceremonies and rituals to honour those entities that shaped and fostered the human condition and who, through their generosity, kindness and wisdom, continue to nurture humans, as long as humans in their turn respect, value and recognize their contributions and the wisdom they impart.

Dr. Mary Thomas (Secwepemc–Neskonlith).

PHOTO BY ROBERT D. TURNER

4

HONOURING *Nature* through CEREMONY and RITUAL

C HRISTINE ALLEN, a teacher of traditional Secwepemc ways, lived to a
golden age of more than one hundred
years. Throughout her lifetime, and even when she was in her nineties,
Christine enjoyed outings into the forests and hills around Salmon Arm.
She was especially delighted when her daughter, Mary Thomas, or other
family members gave her a handful of fresh-picked Saskatoon berries,
wild raspberries *(Rubus idaeus)*, blackcaps *(Rubus leucodermis)* or huckleberries. Much as she loved these treats, she never ate them without first
extending the handful of berries towards the sky and pronouncing with
feeling, "*Kwukstsámcw, Kwukstámcw, Kwukstsámcw!*" ("Thank you,
thank you, thank you!") to convey her gratitude to the Creator for this
wonderful gift of food and life. Then, and only then, did she pop them into
her mouth to savour and eat them. Her enjoyment of the berries included
this modest but significant ritual, which was for her as important a part of
their use as their actual consumption.

Christine's words of thanks before she ate her mouthful of wild berries
are typical of traditional practices all over North America. Ethnobotanist

Priscilla Kari reported similar practices for the English Bay and Port Graham Alutiiq of Alaska:

> People left the powerful medicinal plants a gift when they gathered them to thank them and to encourage their effectiveness. Medicinal plants that grow in the mountains were usually given something such as a thread or match or bit of tobacco. Highly valued medicinal plants of the lowlands were also treated this way. To an extent, this practice still continues.

When I was at the Gitga'at village of Hartley Bay recently, I went out with a couple of friends to harvest devil's club *(Oplopanax horridum)* for medicine for another friend. Before we set off, elder Helen Clifton gave us careful instructions that she, in turn, had been taught by her elders. She cautioned that people gathering medicine, especially an important plant like devil's club, should always approach this task with a serious focus. They should not laugh or joke, or think or talk about anything other than the medicine and how it is going to help someone. They should go to a remote place away from the village or other frequented area. The plant will reveal itself to the harvesters if they follow this practice. They should give the plant an offering of tobacco or even a copper penny, to signify giving something back to the earth in exchange for what they are taking. Then, they should take only four stems—no more—at any one time: never take more than you need. If a person follows this practice, Helen said, not only will he or she be successful in finding the medicine, but the person for whom the medicine is being collected will have a better chance of being helped.

Acknowledging and expressing appreciation and thanks reflects people's understandings of their relationships with all the elements of the environment and the Creator. Not just taking but recognizing, valuing, caring for and giving back are integral to people's lives in the traditional ways of belonging to the world. Mary Thomas recalled, "I went with my mother and my grandmother gathering medicines. My mother never took a piece of bark off a tree without acknowledging it. She always acknowledged—she said her prayer and a thanksgiving before she put a cut into a tree. And I've learned the value of that."

Interpreting Ceremonies and Rituals

Ceremonies and rituals, even small and very personal ones, are completely embedded within a cultural context. In this chapter are examples of some rites practised by indigenous peoples that reveal interconnections between humans and the environment. Most of these examples come from northwestern North America; however, there are common approaches and perspectives in other indigenous traditions, and I have drawn on some of these, as well, to illustrate similarities. As a non-indigenous person, I acknowledge that I will never be able to achieve a perfect understanding of these ceremonies and rituals because they are so much situated within particular world views and traditions.

In the history of the interface between Europeans and indigenous peoples many rites have been seriously misunderstood and misinterpreted by outsiders. Saanich elder Earl Claxton Sr. described how a Saanich hunter, even today, will specially address a deer he has just killed, thanking the Creator and the spirit of the deer for giving itself to him and explaining that he needs the deer to feed his family. He noted that the Christian missionaries who came to the coast never witnessed the hunters' respectful ceremony of thanks and praise, or the address to the cedar tree by the woman who wished to harvest its bark. They only noticed that indigenous people did not give thanks for their food at the time they sat down to eat it, and therefore portrayed them as heathen and irreligious. If they observed the First Salmon Ceremony or similar rites that showed gratitude for the food the people received, the missionaries did not see them as resembling their own Christian practice of prayer and they soon set about making people's religious practices conform with Christianity. Today, Earl explained, people will say grace just before a feast or other meal because the missionaries demanded it, but this was not a traditional practice.

Similarly, when famous North West Company explorer Simon Fraser passed through Nlaka'pmx territory in June 1808 on his arduous voyage down the Fraser River from near its source to the Strait of Georgia, he described in his journal some impressions of the people he encountered. The Nlaka'pmx in particular interested him, and his descriptions of the people living in a village near the present town of Lytton were positive.

He noted in his journal that some of these people appeared very old, and that they were clean-living and made use of wholesome food, some of which Fraser and his men had already shared. On 16 June 1808 he wrote, "The chief invited us to his quarters; his son, by his orders, served us upon a handsome mat, and regaled us with salmon and roots. . . ." Later, on June 19, they had a chance to witness further not only Nlaka'pmx kindness but also a welcoming and honouring ceremony of obvious great significance:

> After having remained some time in this village, the principal chief invited us over the river. We crossed, and He received us at the water side, where, assisted by several others, he took me by the arms and conducted me in a moment up the hill to the camp where his people were sitting in rows, to the number of twelve hundred; and I had to shake hands with all of them. Then the Great Chief made a long harangue, in course of which he pointed to the sun, to the four quarters of the world and then to us, and then he introduced his father, who was old and blind, and was carried by another man, who also made a harangue of some length. The old [blind] man was placed near us, and with some emotion often stretched out both his hands in order to feel ours.

This ceremony, in which the Sun and the four directions were acknowledged, is one of the first that European chroniclers described for indigenous peoples of western Canada. Fraser conceded that the people "appear to be good orators, for their manner of delivery is extremely handsome." However, he obviously did not hold the same values of honouring the environment or respecting visitors and elders that were integral to the Nlaka'pmx world view. Some of the Nlaka'pmx considered Fraser, who wore a shining emblem on his hat that resembled the symbol of the Sun, to be the son of the Sun and hence an important and honoured figure from the past, equivalent to the Transformers of mythical times.

The Nlaka'pmx deemed Fraser's visit so significant that people who had been camping at Botanie Valley northeast of Lytton and men from as far away as Spences Bridge hurried down to witness the event. The Spences Bridge chief ran all the way and arrived in time to meet the strangers and deliver a "great speech." Fraser took advantage of the awe the Nlaka'pmx had for him and the privileged position in which he was placed; he ordered his men to fire their guns for added effect, to reinforce their evident supernatural status.

James Teit recorded an account of the Nlaka'pmx meeting with Simon Fraser and his men from a woman named *Semalítsa* from Stein Creek. Her grandmother was a young girl, playing on the shore there when the strangers came through. Teit reported that some people saw Fraser's arrival as a portent of changes to come:

> Very many people thought they were beings spoken of in tales of the mythological period, who had taken a notion to travel again over the Earth. . . . They believed their appearance foreboded some great change or events of prime importance to the Indians, but in what way they did not know.

Perhaps, even then, the Nlaka'pmx feared irreparable damage to the earth. Fraser revealed little understanding or appreciation of the Nlaka'pmx world view or of their relationships to the natural world. If they had been able to convey to him the idea that the trees and vegetation constituted the Blanket of Earth, what would Fraser have thought about this? It is unlikely that he would have embraced such a concept.

Some of these misinterpretations have reflected differing perspectives of land use and environment and, as such, have had major implications for First Nations' land and resource rights. In the 1840s, James Douglas, chief factor of Fort Victoria and later governor of the Colony of Vancouver Island, attempted to purchase the traditional lands of the local Salish nations. However, he did not fully appreciate the complexities of the First Nations' occupancy of the land. He and other colonial officials considered the area to be only minimally used, since the indigenous people were not cultivating their lands in the European style. Although it was unacknowledged and unrecognized by Douglas or the churches, the people were fully using the entire range of lands and resources. They not only hunted and fished there but harvested root vegetables and berries, gathered their medicines and used everything from giant cedar trees for their canoes to willow bark and other fibrous materials from which to fashion their ingenious reef nets. Their entire existence was based upon fully using their lands.

Traditional Land Use and Ceremonies

First Nations spiritual life is completely tied to territory, to their home places. For example, the rituals of acknowledging and paying tribute to the First Salmon and the training that accompanies the quest for spirit powers leading to success in hunting, healing and social relations both require enactment on a land base. Those in training to strengthen their relationships with the land and its spiritual embrace need remote, private places for praying and bathing, places without the perceived profanity of development or human impact. The importance to the Saanich people of the Malahat mountain is a prime example, illustrated in the following quotation from a report on a potential housing development at Bamberton on Saanich Inlet:

> Today, as in the past, the Malahat mountain area is used by the First Nations people for ceremonies associated with the transition from childhood to adulthood for young men and women, as well as for ritual bathing associated with the longhouse traditions and the winter ceremonies, all of which form the foundation of the religious principles and practices of the Saanich Inlet peoples. Without revealing the specifics of these practices, and thereby diminishing their spiritual powers, suffice it to say the water on the Malahat—its creeks, streams, ponds and lakes—are central to these rituals, as are the plant and animal medicines associated with each. This is what the elders say.

Today, people of the Saanich, Lekwungen and many other First Nations are struggling to maintain these traditions on their drastically diminished lands. People still bathe in their sacred pools and retreat to remote forests and hills for their spiritual cleansing rituals. They still take their children and grandchildren to instruct them in these traditional ways of thought and practice, but without the land areas they once held exclusively it is more and more difficult to do this. Today, even remote areas are subjected to such intrusions as the droning of airplane engines or the roar of off-road vehicles. Many elders have expressed concerns over the destruction of their sacred places where their rituals and ceremonies are undertaken. Quoted in the same report on the Bamberton development, elder Ernie Rice explained:

> Areas of bathing and washing are very important and, provided they are not altered, will always have that power and will never go away. Once altered, it becomes a disaster for the First Nations people who use them.

In all, Ernie related, there were formerly six ceremonial bathing creeks on the Malahat, each one named in the SENĆOŦEN language and each with a specific use and medicines associated with it. Only one is intact today; the others have been lost to development and pollution. Purification through ritual bathing and scrubbing is a widespread spiritual practice for indigenous people and is considered necessary preparation for any important undertakings, from hunting and fishing to successfully harvesting cedar for canoes. Many profane influences can adversely affect people's relationship with the spirit world; cleansing removes any unclean elements that might interfere with a person's ability to communicate with spiritual helpers. People carry out such rituals alone and in isolation to ensure their success; today, however, they are in constant fear of being interrupted and intruded upon. For this reason, the First Nations in this region see protecting the Malahat and other sacred sites as one of the most urgent issues they face.

Many other elders expressed similar concerns that confirm the inextricable links between their lands and their sacred activities. Nuu-Chah-Nulth elder Roy Haiyupis, a participant on the Scientific Panel for Sustainable Forest Practices in Clayoquot Sound, was constantly reminding the scientists on the panel of the importance of the spiritual values of the Nuu-Chah-Nulth lands:

> Our ancestors still live with us in these forests where we encounter our spiritual values, our powerful healing medicines which were gifts of the Creator. The forests that are our very sustenance for everyday living are also being blessed by our ancestors. The natural setting needs to remain stable.

Many times during the scientific panel's deliberations, Roy Haiyupis talked about the concept of his people's connections to their lands and the importance of ceremony and ritual in Nuu-Chah-Nulth life that both took place on the land and celebrated people's oneness with their environment. On another occasion, he described how people's spiritual connections to the land were expressed according to the seasons:

> It is on the basis of Man's interconnectedness to nature that the opportunities for festivities in the winter months, to acknowledge their place in Creation, took place.... The underlying spiritual elements instituted into our cultural exercises allowed for the therapeutic measures contributing to the healing of those encountering distress and grief within the food-gathering season. The cultural customs also demonstrated the need to acknowledge the Creator for the many gifts received through the year.

THE CRUCIAL ROLE OF FEASTS AND POTLATCHING

The Nuu-Chah-Nulth and others held dances, ceremonies and celebrations, often collectively referred to as "Potlatches," during the sacred winter season, to recognize their connections to their lands and environments and to reaffirm the family and community ties that existed throughout the entire year. After the growing and harvesting season people congregated in their winter villages, where such formal observances were generally made. This was the time when the stories were told and performed in dance and ceremony to reinforce and re-emphasize cultural teachings. This was the time when feasts were held, and during the feasts the great orators would retell the histories of the people, to bring a common understanding of their rights and responsibilities.

Chief Earl Maquinna George, hereditary chief and HawiiH (hereditary leader, person of high status) of Ahousaht, recalled the feasts of his boyhood:

> There was an old man called *Tushka*. He had a cane, and after the dinner was . . . eaten, he got up and banged the cane on the floor, and he was the start of what was going on. He announced what the feast was

for, who it was for, and the reason why the feast went on. He started with the historical stories of where our people came from. And this was *Tushka*. He must have been one of the leading historians of our culture. He knew about the songs, and the dance that goes with each family. . . . The people were proud of the many things that were said through the long talks by *Tushka*.

Tushka . . . knew a lot about the Keltsomaht relationship, how we [Ahousaht] were linked to the tribe, mostly by being close relatives to the hereditary chiefs of Keltsomaht, hereditary chiefs of Manhousaht (neighbouring communities), and various HawiiH. . . . This is what *Tushka* used to talk about, how things came about, ownership of all the beaches and land, resources. Not just covering forestry. There's a lot to do with fishing grounds, halibut banks, codfish banks, salmon banks. There were several other people that spoke, and it would become a long, drawn-out day, going into the evening or the night, when these expert people talked for hours at a time. A lot of people did listen to them, the ones that learned very well. They are the ones that know the history today, that *Tushka* brought out.

Earl Maquinna George recalled that *Tushka* would talk for hours at a time, and "nobody moved, nobody made noise, but they listened to what *Tushka* said. . . . " *Tushka* talked about the abundance of salmon and how it was used for the feasting throughout the winter months. It was the chiefs, like Earl Maquinna himself, who had the responsibility to care for all the rivers and streams of their territory, as named by *Tushka*, and to ensure that enough salmon were caught and put away for the feasts in the winter. The children, too, were made to sit and listen to *Tushka*, but afterwards, when they got home, they were able to ask questions and learn about their family history and its relationships to their territories. Gradually, through this process, they gained knowledge and understanding of their own place in society and in their environment.

Earl Claxton Sr. and John Elliott of the Saanich Nation also talked about winter as "a time to reaffirm family ties and history and hold other gatherings as well." These important winter ceremonies, they said, included */stanek/* (memorial Potlatches), namings, weddings and blessing ceremonies. "Potlatching," they stressed, "enabled the more fortunate to share and distribute goods with those less fortunate than themselves."

THE MEANING OF POTLATCH

The Potlatch—or at least what is now called "Potlatch"—is perhaps one of the best known but most misunderstood ceremonial complexes in all of northwestern North America. Much has been written on the Potlatch and its interpretations by anthropologists and others. To the government and church officials the Potlatch ceremonies, especially as they were practised by the Kwakwaka'wakw, Nuu-Chah-Nulth and neighbouring peoples, were so alien to any of their own practices and experiences that the Potlatch was seen as destructive, degrading and "evil"—a term applied to it by William May Halliday, the Indian agent for Alert Bay whose chief aim was to completely eliminate it. The Canadian government banned potlatching in 1884, threatening severe punishment to anyone who hosted or attended one, including confiscation of all Potlatch goods and imprisonment. All across North America, indigenous peoples were coerced and forced to abandon their sacred ceremonies that reinforced their ties to each other and to their lands, and to replace these with Christian rituals, as a way of "civilizing" them and curbing their "savage" ways. It wasn't until 1952 that the ban was lifted, following an appeal by the Native Brotherhood of British Columbia.

The term "Potlatch" is derived from the Nuu-Chah-Nulth verb *pachitle*, meaning "to give," and the noun *pachuck*, which means "article to be given," according to my friend Dr. Richard Atleo, Chief *Umeek*. The Potlatch and the ceremonies it embodied had numerous functions, many of which are still important. In general, it integrated social, economic, political and spiritual aspects of life. More specifically, *Umeek* explained, it redistributed food and other resources within and among communities. It promoted people's well-being by sharing extra provisions without violating the principles of balanced stewardship of lands and resources, and it was undertaken in such a way as to render respect and honour to chiefs, nobility, people, plants, animals, spirit powers and, through all these, to the Creator.

George Clutesi, a Nuu-Chah-Nulth of the Tseshaht Nation, attended a Potlatch, or *tluqwanah,* in the 1950s. In his book *Potlatch* he provides a translation of part of the opening oration, given by the official speaker:

Hear again the stories that are old;
Traditions that our ancestors told.
The laws they made are still with us
They are here and have not changed.
Our lands, our streams, our seas remain
To provide for wants, that are yours and mine.

See again my dance of joy and gladness.
Cast your woes to the winds from the north.
Stand with me and share my happiness;
Take my hand, with me stand forth.

Do the dance your forebears and also mine
Did leave for us to perform as one.

Thanks, many thanks, are due you for your own.
The presence of your House here in mine
Reassures that friend is nigh.
Arise, renew the friendship of all time
Show the goodwill to all mankind
Share with me the abundance of our seas.

This speech exemplifies the meaning and importance of the Potlatch as a ceremony that celebrates community, culture, history and environment and the interrelationships among them all. The Potlatch emphasizes ancient stories, teachings, laws, names, lineages, songs and dances, which in turn validate people's occupancy of their territories and their responsibility for the integrity of their lands, waters and resources.

One of the most remarkable Potlatch-related documents is an unsigned letter apparently written from Alert Bay, one of the centres famous for potlatching, by a group of chiefs of the 'Namgis (Nimpkish)

Nation and addressed to the deputy superintendent general of the Indian Affairs Department in Ottawa. It is dated 6 April 1919.

Sir,—

We have been informed by our Indian Agent that the government is re-considering the Indian Act, particularly that part known as Section 149 which deals with our old custom of giving away. The Indian Act makes this an offense punishable by imprisonment and we pray you to recon-sider this matter. We have been appointed and committed by our peo-ple and we think that if you understood our customs from the beginning that you would amend the law to allow us to go on in our old way. In order to let you know how it was carried on and why it was done we are sending you this letter.

We all know that things are changing. In the old days the only things that counted were such things as food: dried fish, roots, berries and things of that nature. A chief in those days would get possession of all these things and would pass them on to those who had not got any and in many instances would call another tribe and help them out too. We wish to continue this custom. In the old days when feasts were given, those who remained at home were remembered and those who attended would carry stuff home for their wives and children. This is all about our feasts, and we want to have the same thing today.

In the old days we got fire from the west coast of the Island, we trained a man known as a deer to go to the west coast for this fire, we split up some pitch wood and gave it to him, so that when this man was set on fire he could carry it back to us, that's why we like big fires at our feasts.

In the old days Indians specialized in some particular branch of work, some were trained to make canoes, some to hunt, some to catch fish, some to dry fish, some to get material to make our clothes, then we divided this up amongst the others. This was the beginning of our feasts of giving away.

At one time there were no rivers for the fish to come in, and there was a man known by the name of "Omath" (the Raven). He was the man who knew the place to get water and he borrowed a sea lion's

[Eumetopias Jubatus] bladder, then he walked around where he thought would be a good place for the rivers to run and when he found a suitable place he would break the bladder and let some of the water run, this made all the rivers, he did this so that the salmon would go up for the people to use, so that they could get it to dry and have a feast when they went home to their own places, that's why we want to keep up these feasts.

Men came into the world first as animals and birds and were turned into men, and the things that those men did are what we are still doing today; in the old days these animals and birds had dances like the cedar bark dance, and they acted a part so that all those who were looking on would understand what they were doing. Omath had a dance called "Towheet." He was dressed in limbs and cedar brush and we still want to keep up this dance; these things happened, so we have been told by our forefathers, before the flood, and after the flood these animals and birds were changed into men.

A man by the name of Kawawnalalase was asked by the Lord what he wanted to do. Did he want to be a big tree? He said "no." Did he want to be a rock? He said "no." Did he want to be a mountain? He said "no," a piece of him might break off, fall down and hurt somebody; then after thinking a long time he said he would like to be a river so that he might be useful to people in after days, so he was changed into the Nimpkish River. That's why we call it Gwalana and claim it as ours.

After this a man by the name of Numokwistolis was the first man that lived on the hill called Xwulque, then there was another man named Kwunoosala, he was a thunderbird, he took off his feathers and let them blow up into the air again and left him as a man. There was another man named Kwakwus, he was from a fish. Omath was the chief over all these.

And he gathered up all these feathers and tied them into bunches and gave them to his people; after that he got skins such as Marten, Mink, Coon and Beaver, and sewed them up to make blankets. He invited all his people and gave these things to the people that he invited and he distributed these cedar boards, paddles, Indian wedges and mats, after the fur was given away. He also found out that yellow cedar bark was good to make clothes, so he had his people get the yellow cedar bark and beat it with a club to make it soft and made dresses of it, that's why we use the cedar bark today, when we are giving away.

After this a ship came in with some white men on. We didn't know what the white men were, so we called them "Poopaleepzie." They bought our furs and gave us in exchange blankets and tobacco and many other things, and the chiefs gave them away to the rest of the tribe, and this is the habit that we've kept up ever since.

We now come to the part that affects us most in this custom, not only us, but all the other tribes. In those days people that had sons to marry or maybe wanted a wife himself would hear of another man's daughter, and would want to marry her particularly if she was of a chief's family. When the young people are married, the father of the woman would give to his daughter's husband canoes, food, a name and other different things which have a part in our dances and a *copper*. This is what a man gets when he is married to a woman and that is what has been passed on until today. The bridegroom would give a feast with what he got and would invite everybody from his own tribe or other tribes to partake of what had been given to him, and we wish to continue this custom as it helps our old people and young people as well. Each one gets his share and can use it for his own purposes either to get clothing or other things. The coppers that we got in those days were different from those we got from the white men. These coppers were as they were found, only beaten out with a hammer, and we have a lot of money invested in them.

The copper is the main holder of our customs because the value of them is rising and as they are passed on to others they increase in value. The copper forms the chief strength of a man who intends to give a feast and he sells the copper and what he gets for it he uses to make a feast. All the other things that we have would be quite useless to us if the copper is thrown out of our custom; it is used in marriages in order to get the thing to give the feast. If a father would die and leave the copper to his son, no other man could get the copper except the son who would hold it until he thought it time to sell, then he'll figure out what it will bring. When he is finished figuring, he will call all the people together and will dance for them and give what it is worth and afterwards whatever is given away if any of the other chiefs return it to him, and it will be of use to him for many years. These coppers are sold for a large sum of money, and no one will force a person who sells it to give it all away, so that he always has considerable left for his own use. When a man buys a copper he pays a deposit on it and the next man may buy it from him and pay a deposit on an increased valuation and so on, it may be through the hands of four or five and still payment not be completed. If our custom is done away with these coppers will be useless, and will entail a big loss, as all those who have an interest in them will lose all they have put in. Each tribe has its own coppers and each copper has its own value. . . .

In this single letter, the chiefs connect the potlatching tradition to their world view, their origin stories, their ties to the land and their responsibilities to provision their people. They also stress that the Potlatch is an intricate system of investment and exchange, with coppers being the main currency.

The letter, remarkable in its calm, reasonable tone, ends as follows:

We do not want to fight the government, nor do we expect the government to repay us the price of our coppers, but we do ask to be let alone and left free to follow our own old ways, and these coppers represent the chief things in our customs. The way things are now, we try not to disobey the government in any of the criminal laws and we hope the government will allow us to continue our old customs so far as they do not come in conflict with the criminal law. In the old days and in all villages our forefathers followed this custom and we cannot see any bad results from it. If it suits us and does not interfere with or hurt anyone else, why should we be stopped?

The original law banning the Potlatch was passed in 1884, but because the law was appealed and ruled unconstitutional it was revised in 1906 and amended again in 1927. Obviously the Nimpkish chiefs' appeal was unheeded, because this amended law was passed several years after their letter was written.

The Kwakwa̱ka'wakw Investment System

Banning the Potlatch thus affected an entire complex system of resource sharing and exchange, as did the fur trade and the new economic system it brought.

Daisy Sewid-Smith further elaborated on the complex Kwakwa̱ka'wakw investment system called *p'ə́lxalasgəm,* after *p'ə́lxala* "fog," because they originally traded white mountain goat furs. She explained: "It was our cash. We would use it to buy things from other tribal groups or within our own nation. . . . And eventually, Hudson's Bay [Company] changed the mountain-goat fur into Hudson's Bay blankets. . . . They would give a certain amount of Hudson's Bay blankets to our people for one of the mountain-goat furs. And they could use Hudson's Bay blankets to purchase things at the [Hudson's Bay] store."

Hudson's Bay Company found it advantageous to trade blankets for the mountain goat furs because they could sell the furs in China for a tremendous profit. When Hudson's Bay brought in their blankets "to take the fur off our hands," Daisy said, the people named the blankets by the same term in Kwak'wala, "because it was equivalent to the mountain goat fur as trade." Daisy said that a canoe, for example, might be worth 1,000 mountain goat furs; later, that would be 1,000 Hudson's Bay blankets. The observers of the Kwakwa̱ka'wakw Potlatches often remarked with surprise about the piles and piles of Hudson's Bay blankets that were given away. To outsiders, the blankets were a waste; to the Kwakwa̱ka'wakw, they represented money and sound investment. They were used to pay the witnesses of the important business transactions of the clans, including transference of property rights and inherited rights and responsibilities for management of lands and resources. These rights cannot be separated from land and resource stewardship and are tied into sustainable occupation of territories.

When Daisy Sewid-Smith's family hosted a Potlatch, they would re-enact the story of their ancestor *c̓ə́qaməy̓* and perform the cedarbark ceremony taught to him when he was sheltered with his family within the trunk of the giant cedar tree during the Great Flood. *C̓ə́qaməy̓* was the original source of the cedarbark ceremony that spread among all the

Kwakwa̱ka'wakw people and their relatives, as far north as Bella Bella and Kitamaat. The Sacred Cedar Bark Ceremony and the formal recognition of a family's or clan's rights to use and maintain resource-harvesting areas were interrupted and eroded when the Potlatch was banned. Only in recent years have people been able to pick up and reweave some of the threads of these practices, thanks to the knowledge and cultural memory of such people as *Kwaxsistala* (Chief Adam Dick), who as a child and young adult received formal instruction in Potlatch protocols and the meanings behind them. To this day, *Kwaxsistala* is called on to help plan, interpret and officiate at Potlatches, and he has brought back some of the sacredness and deeper meanings behind the enactment of the Cedar Bark Ceremony and other rites that link people to their lands.

Connecting with the Spirit World

In indigenous societies, individuals participated, in the course of their lifetime, in a number of important ceremonies and rituals relating to their relationship with the environment. The transition to adulthood, for both boys and girls, was a time to practise self-discipline and learn about the new roles and responsibilities that they would be taking on. At puberty they were often isolated from the family and the community, making it a time for learning and reflection and for ceremonial cleansing. Frequently they fasted and observed dietary restrictions, and they made time to connect with the spiritual world and to learn skills and patterns of thought for their lifetime ahead as an adult, husband or wife, parent, and community leader or participant.

A Halkomelem girl at the time of puberty, for example, underwent at least four days of seclusion and dietary restriction, as described by ethnographer Charles Hill-Tout:

> For the first two days she must abstain from food of any kind; after this she might eat a little dried salmon, but no fresh meat or roots. After the fourth day the girl's face was painted, and she was permitted to walk abroad for a little distance in charge of some women. On her return, four *olia* [ceremonial officials] would meet her and dance round her,

each holding a salmon of a different species in his hand. When this ceremony was over, she was taken to a lake and made to undergo a ceremonial washing and cleansing. She was never allowed to enter a stream frequented by salmon, or they would shun the stream thereafter. Throughout the four days of her seclusion she was kept busy in making yarn, as among the Squamish. When her menses are upon her a woman must never eat . . . fresh foods.

Training for boys at puberty often meant travelling for a considerable distance—to lakes, deep forests or mountaintops (such as the Malahat range for the Saanich people—where they might encounter a spiritual helper or supernatural guide. No matter what his chosen role, whether carpenter and canoe-maker, or doctor, hunter or fisher, a young man's work could be made easier and more successful by this discipline and training.

Young men seeking spiritual strength and power would bathe and pray at many different sites, especially at little lakes, creeks or pools. After exercising strenuously, fasting, bathing and scrubbing himself with western hemlock *(Tsuga heterophylla)* boughs or the even tougher boughs of Pacific yew *(Taxus brevifolia)* or western red-cedar, a youth might fall asleep and dream about the supernatural power he would receive. Alternatively, the power might come to him in the form of an animal, bird or other being. For example, Haida Eagle Chief *Weah* Willie Matthews explained to me once why his lineage holds a number of names, passed from generation to generation, relating to a supernatural wood-being, or "fairy," called *skil* in Haida. Willie Matthews' own name, *skilda k̲'ahljuu*, means "waiting for a *skil*." These names go back to one of his ancestors who, travelling far away from his village, came across a gigantic devil's club *(Oplopanax horridum)*, which was like a tree, with leaves more than a metre across. The ancestor scraped off the bark and chewed the inner bark of this giant *ts'iihlanjaaw* plant, then fell into a kind of trance. At this time a wood-being came to him and endowed him with exceptional spiritual powers. To this day, descendants of this man have inherited names that commemorate this special encounter.

This training of young men, which involves bathing, fasting and prayer, is called *Uusimich* in Nuu-Chah-Nulth. Young men who wish to follow the traditional lifestyle of their ancestors still practise it today. They might go to a remote island, to a prayer pool with a waterfall in a remote valley, or up to a mountaintop to practise their spiritual observance.

Richard Atleo told the members of the Clayoquot scientific panel:

> Sacred areas are pivotal to Nuu-Chah-Nulth culture. They are important to the well-being, survival and sustenance of the Nuu-Chah-Nulth in the same way that any logging company may consider forests to be [essential to the company's survival].

For the Ahousaht and others of the Clayoquot Sound area, the Clayoquot River valley is a highly spiritual site where people have gone to train for thousands of years. For this reason, Roy Haiyupis was adamant that this valley should never be logged. He wrote:

> The power of the spiritual history of the people who lived there . . . still has to be there. The specific sites for those spiritual searches and vision quests, to me, seem apparent. . . . Nature suggests to us with all its might that this is the central cathedral for meditation and cleansing in readiness for major hunts and excursions. This is where the greatest bear and whale hunters entered into harmony with the Creator and Nature. This is even the valley where those seeking and given healing powers found their alliance with the spiritual for good and destructive powers . . . Plants and medicines used primarily for the *7uusimich* were obtained in the [Clayoquot] valley.
>
> Today, Clayoquot Valley is encountering a very serious threat from the outside world in the logging industry. . . . Even allowing for a passage through the valley [a road] would certainly destroy something of the spiritual treasure and quality that is there.

The increasing scarcity of and encroachment on remote, pristine lands has caused tremendous conflict between First Nations people—whose religious practices and spiritual beliefs still connect them to special places in the landscape—and outsiders, including logging companies, who see these places only as resource banks or recreational grounds. Mountains are particularly important places for maintaining spiritual and medicinal well-being. Mary Thomas explained:

> The old [Secwepemc] people would say medicines that grow up in the high mountains they believe have more strength than the ones that you pick down below. Because here you're closer to the mountain, which they appreciated, and the clear air, with all the water fresh from the mountain snow—it made the growing of the plants more powerful.

Saanich elder Edward Thomas explained why mountains are particularly important:

> Church steeples reach up high to the Lord. It's the same with the mountains. When you want to be closer to the Creator, go up there. Mountains have always been sacred and that's where the medicines are—rocks, leaves, everything from the mountains are medicine.

Tom Sampson, also Saanich, described the Malahat mountain, called *Yaas,* as "who we are . . . This is our *tcelengan,* our 'teaching,' this mountain." It is *Yaas,* and all it contains—plants, animals, streams, pools and spirits—provides for the physical and spiritual well-being of the people. Hunters, berry pickers, medicine gatherers and spirit questers all ventured, and still venture, onto its rocky slopes and into its dense forests, always with a deep sense of respect. This mountain embodies an ancient and powerful relationship: it is, in Saanich traditions, the home of Thunderbird, and a landscape that is used and respected. *Yaas* is a sacred landscape.

Honouring the Season's First Foods

Food harvesting, not surprisingly, has primary significance in traditional peoples' lives, and the First Foods Ceremony is an important ritual that links people to their lands. Many variations on this ceremony exist, including the types of foods honoured from one locality to another. Most often celebrated was the First Salmon Ceremony. In their book on the Saanich reef-net fishery, Earl Claxton and John Elliott describe the salmon ceremony for their people:

> Amongst the Saanich Inlet peoples, a sacred ceremony is associated with the arrival of the salmon: The medicine man, *snamen,* would paddle to the farthest point east and call on our ancient relative (the salmon) to come and feed the Saanich people. He prayed, sang and mentioned all the family reef net locations that the salmon would pass. . . .

Salmon are a primary food for people almost everywhere in British Columbia. Of the five different species of Pacific salmon, the sockeye is one of the most generally valued, but all of them have their special qualities and uses. Charles Hill-Tout described the Chehalis sockeye salmon ceremony:

Spring salmon, also known as chinook (Oncorhynchus tshawytscha), one of the five species of Pacific salmon.

When the sockeye salmon run commenced, the first one caught was always brought to the chief, who called all the people together for prayers and dancing. Only the chief himself prayed, and my informants could not tell me the tenor of these prayers, as they were never uttered aloud, they said. During the prayers everybody must shut his eyes. . . . The salmon was afterwards cooked, and a small piece of it given to each person present. This ceremony was only observed in the case of the sockeye salmon, which the Chehalis regarded as the prince of salmon. It is worthy of remark that the Squamish people held the spring salmon as the first of salmon.

Many other First Foods ceremonies took place, but even in regions where no formal ceremonies were observed in acquiring or harvesting the first foods of the season, individuals were taught to honour and consciously acknowledge the animals and plants that provided them with sustenance, as well as with their materials and medicines. Ernie Hill Jr., who is the head Eagle hereditary chief of the Gitga'at (Tsimshian) at Hartley Bay, told me that when someone from another clan—Raven or Blackfish— brings him his very first salmonberry of the season, he is obligated to acknowledge this symbolically with a small gift of some kind. He usually brings a small item—a baseball cap or a small toy—from Prince Rupert to pay the person, usually one of the schoolchildren, since Ernie is the principal at the Hartley Bay School. Even this small tradition marks the seasons and signifies respect for the bounty of Nature and for each other.

Charles Hill-Tout also described a Chehalis ceremony to celebrate the first harvest of the shoots *(satske)* and berries of thimbleberry *(Rubus parviflorus)* in the spring. This plant, like salmonberry *(Rubus spectabilis)*, has delectable sucker shoots that were, and sometimes still are, snapped off, peeled and eaten in quantity by First Peoples up and down the coast. He wrote:

Another of these ceremonies was kept in connection with *satske* . . . the young succulent suckers of [thimbleberry] which the Indians of this region eat in large quantities, both cooked and raw. When cooked, I am told they eat like asparagus. The time for gathering these was left to the judgment and determination of the chief. When ready to gather, he would direct his wife or daughter to pick a bunch and bring them to him; and then, the people all being assembled, a ceremony similar to that connected with the salmon ceremony would take place. After the ceremony anyone might pick as much as he liked. A similar ceremony took place later in the summer, when the berries of this plant were ripe.

Few people eat these wild vegetables any more, but many elders remember their use. Earl Maquinna George recalled the thimbleberry shoots, called *chashxiwa7* in the Nuu-Chah-Nulth language, as being bright green, juicy and "very tasty." He said that the women of Ahousaht used to go by canoe to the offshore islands beyond their home island of Flores, a distance of about ten kilometres, and gather canoeloads of the shoots in June and early July. As the paddlers approached the shore on their return, they called out to all of the other women to come down to the beach to get the shoots. All of the women feasted on them together. Earl said the kids used to ask to eat some of the thimbleberry shoots, and the women would give them a little bit, but mostly it was "a woman's plant." The children used to bring a little sugar in which to dip the ends of the shoots before they ate them. The women ate the shoots with "cheese" made from dogfish (dog, or chum, salmon) roe, which was dried and smoked in the smokehouse.

Similarly, the Ahousaht people picked salmonberry shoots, called *ma7yi*. Earl Maquinna George said that people used them as a travelling food. The young people would pick them by the armload when they first came out and then share them with the whole village. Halibut fishers used to take the shoots with them to the fishing grounds and trade them for other food there. People really looked forward to this time in the spring when they could harvest these fresh delicacies.

Things have changed now, though, Earl said; they don't gather food like that any more. Today, people eat rhubarb, lettuce, cabbage, carrots and potatoes; very few people go to the bush. Nevertheless, Earl and his wife, Josephine, do go and have a feed of these wild foods when they can. They go to the islands in the early part of June, at the first laying of the seagull eggs, before the eggs become too mature. They have a feed on the eggs, and they harvest *ma7yi* and *q'ilhtsup*, the shoots of cow parsnip, which is also sometimes known as "wild celery."

Charles Hill-Tout found First Foods ceremonies in general hard to understand and pondered their purpose and meaning. Despite the derogatory tone of his words, he did in fact draw the link between these rituals and people's quite different relationship with the natural world than anything he was used to:

> I have been led to the opinion . . . that they [First Foods ceremonies] were always propitiatory in intent. They were intended to placate the spirits of the fish, or the plant or the fruit . . . for if these ceremonies were not properly and reverently carried out there was danger of giving offence to the spirits of the objects and being deprived of them. . . . It must be remembered that, in the mind of the savage, the salmon or the deer or the berry or the root was not merely a fish or an animal or a fruit, in our sense of these things, but something more. . . . Animals

Peeled young stalks of cow parsnip (Heracleum lanatum), also sometimes called "wild celery." Knowing how and when to harvest and prepare it is essential because this plant contains phototoxins that are activated in the presence of sunlight (ultraviolet light) and that can cause skin irritation, blistering and discoloration. Only the young shoots are eaten, and they are always peeled. Identification is important, too, because other somewhat similar plants in the celery family are extremely poisonous. PHOTO BY ROBERT D. TURNER were not regarded as lower in the scale of life than himself, but rather the opposite, being more wonderful and "mysterious" in their ways and able to do many things that he could not.

Hill-Tout reported on a similar First Foods feast for the Nlaka'pmx (Thompson):

> No one under penalty of a severe punishment could take a fish, pick a berry or dig a root until after the Feasts of First Fruits had been held. These feasts were conducted as follows: When the salmon, for instance, begin to run, the word is brought to the divisional chiefs that the fish are coming up river. Messengers are then sent to the neighbouring villages, calling a meeting of the people on a certain day, at which all must attend at the appointed place. When the day has arrived and the people have assembled, the head chief, attended by the other lesser ones and the elders, opens the ceremony at daybreak by a long prayer. When the prayer is being said everybody must stand with eyes reverently closed. . . . Exactly to whom these prayers were addressed my informant could not tell me. All I could gather was that the "old Indians" believed in some great and beneficent power who dwelt behind the clouds, and who gave them the salmon, fruits, roots, etc., who, if they showed themselves ungrateful or unthankful, could, and might, withdraw his gifts from them.

James Teit noted that the Nlaka'pmx observed First Roots ceremonies both before and after the gathering of roots or fruits. He explained that they conducted the former to ensure and increase productivity and the latter to give thanks. Such resources were never taken for granted. Rather, the plants and animals were recognized as active and willing participants in human livelihood. Nevertheless, the tenuousness of these gifts was seen, and for this reason the ceremonies were observed.

Honouring Sacred Plants

Plants were incorporated into First Peoples' ceremonies and ritual lives in many ways and became themselves sacred objects. Bitterroot is a good example: In Nlaka'pmx traditions, bitterroot plants were once human themselves. In conversation relating to these plants, Bob Bandringa, who wrote his master's thesis on the Nlaka'pmx relationship with bitterroot, has recorded phrases such as: "the *lhQuoopen* [*lhqwepn*, bitterroots] are sitting," "they are holding hands," "they talk to one another" and "they are hiding from you."

Madeline Lanaro, Nlaka'pmx elder, explained to Bob that when she was young, children were taught not to misbehave when they went out to dig the bitterroot; they were told, "You are going to make the *lhQuoopen* upset." Madeline also noted that because bitterroot plants often grow in pairs with their roots entwined, couples planning to marry and wishing to stay together forever will find a bitterroot couple and either bury them or place them under their pillow as a symbolic guiding spirit in their own intimacy.

For the Coast Salish, fronds of sword fern *(Polystichum munitum)* were also seen as spiritual helpers, according to Saanich elder Elsie Claxton. In the winter initiation ceremonies for new dancers in the big house, the new dancers dance around the fronds, which are then carefully gathered and placed in a special location where no one should touch them because they have been transformed through the dance to hold special powers.

Balsamroot, or spring sunflower *(Balsamorhiza sagittata)*, also had exceptional spiritual powers that had to be acknowledged and respected through certain ritual observances when the plants were being harvested and prepared. In particular, youths partaking in the first plant harvesting of the season addressed a prayer to the "Sunflower-Root": "I inform thee that I intend to eat thee. May thou always help me to ascend, so that I may always be able to reach the tops of mountains, and may I never be clumsy! I ask this from thee, Sunflower-Root. Thou art greatest of all in mystery." Failure to recite this prayer before eating was said to "make the person partaking of the food lazy." In addition, Nlaka'pmx women painted their faces red, or painted a large black or red spot on each cheek, before harvesting the roots. While digging the roots, they had to abstain from sexual intercourse. They also offered prayers when they went to dig the plants. Men were not to go near the cooking pit while the roots were being cooked. And taboos prevented a bereaved spouse from eating

Nootka wild rose (Rosa nutkana). PHOTO BY ROBERT D. TURNER

balsamroot for a whole year after the bereavement. The leaves were also used in puberty rituals for girls.

First Peoples throughout North America and beyond observed other seasonally based ceremonies. From the North Coast of British Columbia, Haisla (Hanaksiala) elder Gordon Robinson described a special "flower dance" that recognized and welcomed the first flowers of springtime. Around 1907 or 1908, as a child of about three years old, he participated in this dance. Blossoms of wild rose *(Rosa nutkana)*, salmonberry *(Rubus spectabilis)*, blueberries (*Vaccinium* spp.), northern rice-root *(Fritillaria camschatcensis)* and any other plants that were blooming at the time were sewn into the dancers' costumes and made into wreaths that the dancers wore around their heads. When Gordon was very young, he was given a special name meaning "body covered with flowers," a name traditionally given to youths seen to have high status and promising personal potential.

Flowers hold special symbolism for people everywhere. Because their blooming intervals are generally short, they indicate seasonal change and abundance of other life. The flowers of salmonberry are a particularly propitious harbinger of the coming season of growth and productivity. Years when the salmonberry blossoms are plentiful are said by the Nuu-Chah-Nulth and others to hold promise of excellent salmon runs. For the Haisla (Hanaksiala), the blooming of the salmonberry indicates that the edible seaweed *(Porphyra abbottiae)* is ready for picking.

MANY OCCASIONS are accompanied by ceremony. Events such as when the grizzly bear emerges from its den, when the salmon or eulachon start coming up the river, when deer or elk start to rut or when the leaves turn colour in the fall are widely celebrated and are often named in seasonal calendars of indigenous societies in many parts of North America.

For the Iroquois, for example, special ceremonies were observed at each stage of the cultivation of corn *(Zea mays)*, an important food for these people and many others in eastern and southwestern North America. At planting time, the corn kernels are soaked and the woman of the house offers a prayer to the Creator: "In the sky you live, Creator. We are ready to place in the ground the corn upon which we live. We ask for assistance and that we may have a plentiful crop." Ceremonies are addressed to Thunder Man to bring rain, to celebrate when the first cultivating and hoeing are finished and when the corn is ready to harvest, husk, dry and store away. Nearly every family prepares for this occasion by making cornbread and bringing it to the longhouse. Games are played and stories told, thanks is given to the Creator and numerous dances are performed at this festival.

Anishinaabe wild-rice *(Zizania aquatica)* harvesting in Ontario, To-hono O'odham (Papago) harvesting of saguaro cactus *(Carnegiea gigantea)* fruits in Arizona, the Mapuche's harvest of the seeds or piñons of the araucaria or monkey-puzzle *(Araucaria araucana)* tree in Chile: all these are mediated by special ceremonies and festivals that pay tribute to these life-giving resources.

The Blackfoot, too, acknowledge daily the sacredness of their world, and every year all of the clans come together to renew their connections

Laurie Montour (Mohawk–Kahnawàke), making her special cornbread.

with the universe at an event called *ako-katssinn*, "the time of all people camping together." At the centre of the *ako-katssinn* is the *ookaan* cere-mony, which focusses on a woman of virtue who has vowed to be the Holy Woman. The tipi she shares with her partner is set up in the centre of the camp circle, and in it, for four days and four nights, she and her partner fast and pray. They prepare dried buffalo tongues as an offering, and after the two break their fast the people erect a large, circular arbour nearby. In the centre they erect a pole on which they place offerings of cloth so that *Natosi,* the Sun, will hear the people's prayers and give them a good year.

The origin of this ceremony, often referred to as the Sun Dance Ceremony, goes back into the distant history of the people and is illustrated in the story of the woman who married a star and eventually came back to Earth, bringing with her the sacred prairie turnip *(Psoralea esculenta)*.

Different versions of this story exist, but the theme is similar: Two sisters are sleeping outside and the older one falls in love with the Morning Star. She wishes that he could be her husband. Later, as she goes to the river for water, a young man stands in her path, telling her, "I am your husband, Morning Star." He takes her up to the Sky World, helped by Spider with his web. Morning Star's father, the Sun, and his mother, the Moon, welcome her. She is happy in the Sky World, and after a while she has a baby boy. One day, Moon presents her with a digging stick and tells her to dig up any plants she wants, except the prairie turnip; it would bring unhappiness to all of them if she digs these plants. She wonders about this warning and becomes more and more curious about the prairie turnip. Finally she digs around the plant, and when she pulls out the root it leaves a hole through the Sky World. Seeing her old home and her family far below, she becomes lonely and homesick. The Moon and Sun then tell her that she must return home to her people because she will no longer be happy in their country. They give her the digging stick, wrap her with her baby in a painted robe and lower her down through the hole on a spider's web. So she returns home, but she is never happy after that. When she dies, she is taken back to the Sky World to become the Evening Star and to live forever with her husband, Morning Star. Her son grows up and has many adventures. As a young man he returns to the Sky World and his grandfather, the Sun, gives him the sacred knowledge of the Sun Dance, a ceremony of thanks and honour to the Creator.

In honour of the prairie turnip, the Holy Woman of the *ookaan* ceremony traditionally wears a replica of a root-digging stick and sometimes the roots themselves on her ceremonial headdress.

Finally, *iwígara* ties the Rarámuri people to their songs and cere-monies, to their foods and to the land that nourishes them. Enrique Salmón describes a traditional Rarámuri ritual, *yúmari*, in which the women dance in a continual *íwi* (circle), "which represents the fertility of the land, while two male singers and chanters dance within. The songs they sing àsk for the land to be nourished, and for the land, in turn, to nourish the people. The ceremony brings rain to nourish the land."

Almost universally, and perhaps predictably, these ceremonies cele-brating the sacredness of the plants and the significance and meanings underlying them have dwindled in practice and consciousness. They still exist, however, in the hearts and minds of some. Nlaka'pmx bitterroot harvester Madeline Lanaro explained to Bob Bandringa, "I recall prayers happening when the first *lhQuoopen* of the year was picked when I was a little kid, but I don't remember if anybody does it anymore. . . . When we go out now we just do our prayers quietly."

Elders and spiritual leaders still guide youth in their spiritual quests and journeys, and people still practise special symbolic dances that hon-our the spirits of the plants, animals and supernatural creatures that reside in their world. People still symbolically feed the spirits of their ancestors and communicate with them in special ceremonies. Sometimes these cere-monies are undertaken in conformity with Christianity, as in the prayers of thanksgiving to acknowledge food at the time of a meal, but the origi-nal practices still have meaningful ties with people's past traditions and can still raise awareness and strengthen the bonds to the plants, animals, lands and waters of their homelands. These observances foster a sense of responsibility to care for the natural world and a deep concern for its well-being.

Barbara Wilson (K̲ii7lljuus; Haida)
holding a yew-wood digging stick
made by her brother Ron Wilson (Giitsx̲aa).

5

The BALANCE

between Humans

and NATURE

CHIEF JOHNNY AND HELEN CLIFTON,
Gitga'at elders, were recently featured in a film produced by my friend
Robin June Hood and her associate Ben Fox. The film was made at the
Gitga'at spring camp at Kiel *(K'yel)* and focussed on the significance of the
food resources from that region. I was there during the making of the film
and listened while Johnny and Helen talked about their lives and experiences. When Robin asked about their worst experience relating to their
traditional resources, Johnny immediately referred to the loss of the
abalone due to the carelessness and poor understanding of the fisheries
managers, including the federal Department of Fisheries and Oceans
officials, who allowed a commercial abalone harvest. When the subsequent overharvesting ruined the Gitga'at abalone beds on Campania Island and other regions of the North Coast, Johnny, Helen and the other
traditional users of the resource shook their heads in combined despair
and aggravation. If anybody, they said, had bothered to ask the local people for their advice, they could have avoided this disaster.

As a young woman, Helen had learned the proper protocols for harvesting seafood and other resources with her husband and his family. She

remembers well going to the abalone beds with her husband and mother-in-law, Lucille Clifton, and being taught how to behave towards the abalone. She referred to abalone as a prized food, "worth its weight in gold," and her people know it as a very sensitive shellfish that they must treat with tremendous care and deference. People harvested abalone only in the spring, at low tide. They would cut the motors on their boats when they approached the abalone beds, then disembark quietly and walk around softly on the rocks. They would harvest only the biggest abalone, leaving the smaller ones to grow. They talked to the young abalone, reassuring them. They would tell them that they would be back the next year and ask them to be ready for harvesting then. They always thanked the abalone for giving themselves to the people. Lucille told Helen that abalone will move away if they aren't treated properly.

The commercial divers and shellfish harvesters observed none of these practices. They moved into First Peoples' traditional gathering grounds without permission and ruined the abalone beds by harvesting indiscriminately. Helen said these people were like gold diggers; they tried to take as many shellfish as they could. They sent divers down to get the ones in the subtidal zone and they removed entire populations. Within a pitifully short time, beds that were once piled thickly with abalone, two and three deep, were completely cleaned out. More than a decade later, they still haven't come back. Today, everyone along the coast is banned from harvesting abalone.

The Gitga'at people still go to their gathering grounds to see if the abalone have returned; they feel this loss deeply. They contend that if the commercial harvesters had followed the Gitga'at protocols, they would not have destroyed this valuable resource. Helen and Johnny maintained that this situation was predictable, and that Nature is punishing the greed of the unthinking. Sadly, the Gitga'at and other indigenous people who had used and cared for the abalone for countless generations are the ones who bear the brunt of Nature's punishment. This story, unfortunately, is not unique.

Just as the Earth's Blanket metaphor suggested, the sorrow of Earth, reacting to humans' misuse of the environment, is manifesting over and over again. Talking to elders like Helen and Johnny Clifton, Mary Thomas, Daisy Sewid-Smith and Adam Dick, one hears a litany of envi-

Northern abalone (Haliotus kamtschatkana), *a valued seafood whose populations have been severely depleted from overharvesting.*

ronmental change and degradation that is truly frightening. Daisy explained to me how her people's traditional world view contrasted with that of the Europeans and even with those of her people who have followed the dominant culture's scramble for economic gain:

> If you destroy your environment you are destroying yourself.... When we [Kwakwaka'wakw people] took something from the environment ... we were careful just to take what we needed. And that is something that ... is a difference between traditional Kwagiulths and Europeans today. We only took what we personally needed and no more, whereas the Europeans are reaping our resources to supply the rest of the world, and not thinking of the effects, how it's going to affect us in the future.

Nuu-Chah-Nulth elder and cultural specialist Roy Haiyupis echoed, Daisy's words:

> Respect is the very core of our traditions, culture and existence. It is very basic to all we encounter in life. . . . Respect for nature requires a healthy state of stewardship with a healthy attitude. It is wise to respect nature. Respect the Spiritual. . . . It is not human to waste food. It is inhuman to overexploit. "Protect and Conserve" are key values in respect of nature and natural food sources. Never harm or kill for sport. It is degrading to your honour. . . . It challenges your integrity and accountability. *Nature has that shield or protective barrier [that], once broken, will hit back at you.* (Emphasis added.)

Consider this warning, in the light of a recollection from Ditidaht hereditary Chief *Queesto*, Charlie Jones of the Pacheedaht Nation at Port Renfrew, on the west coast of Vancouver Island south of Clayoquot Sound. A 1992 article from the *Ottawa Citizen* reported: "Queesto . . . tells a story of the great Fraser River sockeye run of 1902. There were eleven canneries at Steveston, south of Vancouver, and each would take 200 sockeye, the prize fish, from each fisherman. Any other type of salmon was thrown back, dead. Any sockeye over the 200 taken from each fisherman was thrown back. The tallyman would say, "all right," when there were 200 fish. The dead fish were piled up four feet high in some places. Describing this situation, Queesto, who was 111 years old when this interview was done, remarked, 'That is how Europeans handled things.' "

First Peoples' narratives abound with lessons that teach respect and care, and provide examples of what can happen when this respect is not given. Mary Thomas tells a story that she was told as a little girl about Trembling Aspen (*meltállp*, "shivering plant") and why it is always shaking or moving, even if there is hardly any wind: Long, long ago, when Nature was making all the trees, each one thanked her and acknowledged her. Aspen, however, refused to bow down in thanks and acknowledgement to Mother Nature and so, to teach Aspen a lesson, Nature caused her leaves to shake continuously ever after. Now, children are told this story as a lesson to themselves always to give thanks, appreciation and respect to the Creator.

Retribution and Natural Disasters

I learned from my Haida friend *Kii7lljuus* (Barbara Wilson) a "lesson" story, which is her ancestral story from the village of Cumshewa *(Hlk'in7ul Ilnagaay)* on *Haida Gwaii* (Queen Charlotte Islands). She did me the honour of adopting me into her family and instructing me about the crests I am now permitted to wear and the stories that are part of my new identity as an Eagle with family ties to Cumshewa. The story of *Jilaa kuns*, the Creek Woman of *xawu kuns* (Pallant Creek) on Moresby Island, is a powerful story, a parable with a theme that reminds all of us to respect the life forms around us. There are many different versions of the *Jilaa kuns* story; the version recorded here is the one told to me by *Kii7lljuus*.

Jilaa Kuns, the Creek Woman of Xawu Kuns

Some young Raven boys from *jiigwah* village (on the north shore of Cumshewa Inlet, near McLellan Island) were out fishing. One was wearing a cormorant (*Phalacrocorax auritus, k'yaaluu*) hat [an Eagle crest, one he shouldn't have been wearing], which kept slipping down on his face whenever he tried to catch a fish, and he could not catch any more. They went ashore near *xawu kuns* (a campsite at the mouth of Pallant Creek) and started a fire to cook their fish. A big frog came out of the bushes. One of the boys grabbed the frog and threw it into the fire. It burned and then exploded, and this made the boys laugh. They threw two more frogs into the fire, and as each one exploded they laughed. The next morning, after this incident, the land shook. It was a woman, *Jilaa kuns*, the supernatural woman who guarded the creek. She wanted her children, the frogs. [She had six frog children altogether.] She sang a dirge-like song and asked, "What have you done with my children?" She told the boys that, because they had treated her children so cruelly, every time they passed a point of land as they headed home in their canoe—and she named each point—one of them would die. Only one would be left, and he would tell everyone back at their village what had happened to them, then he, too, would die. They were warned of an earthquake and a raging fire.

The boys died as *Jilaa kuns* had predicted, each as they passed a point of land. The last one reached his village and told his story, and then he, too, died. Strange, bad events started to occur. Flames and ash emerged from the waves and coals fell from the sky. The village became smoky and eventually the whole town started to burn. Only a woman and a little girl survived; they went into a cave [or the cellar-like entrance to a house] and stayed there until the fire stopped. Then they came out and started walking towards the present site of Sandspit. Someone appeared in a canoe and took them to Sandspit, where the girl was adopted. [The girl's name was *hihluu kinganng*.] *Jilaa kuns* came out of the water and sang a mourning song. This is how the people learned to respect all things, no matter how small.

This girl who survived became the mother of the *jiigwah7ahl 'laanaas* and, according to the versions of the story recorded by John Swanton, she became the ancestress of four important Eagle lineages, including the *st'awaas* of *hlk'in7ul* (Cumshewa), the ancestral village of my Haida sister *Kii7lljuus*. Another version of this story is told by Haisla (Hanaksiala) elder Gordon Robinson, who also explained how Chief *Gitwun* of the Haida Eagle Clan presented the "Chilakoons" (*Jilaa kuns*) totem to *Sunahead*, chief of the Haisla Eagle Clan, and his people at Kitamaat as a peace offering at the time when peace was formally established between the two nations, apparently around the 1850s.

The neighbouring Tlingit to the north of Haida Gwaii had a similar story, set near Baranof Island. George Emmons, who recorded the story, noted that "any abuse of a living being, especially needless killing or harming a helpless creature, or insulting an animal or bird, was likely to bring bad luck," as illustrated by the following story:

In 1881, near Hot Springs [Baranof Island], some six Indian women and a boy were starting out after berries. Before they left the beach, one of the women found a frog and she commenced to stone him, abusing him all the time. And after killing him, she threw him in the water. They then went across to the other shore and gathered baskets full of berries. And one woman began to mimic a loon as it calls and crooks its neck. They laughed at her [with her?] and they got in the canoe. The water was [then] very smooth and [the weather fair], when suddenly wind came and upset the canoe. All the women drowned, except one. And the boy got hold of one and tried to save her, but could not. But he reached the shore, came and told the husbands, and they found only one [woman]. The Indians believe they were lost because they killed the frog and mimicked the loon.

This story and the Cumshewa Haida *Jilaa ḵuns* story, both set in specific places, link these peoples with their histories and their homelands. Both are stories with profound lessons about the consequences of wanton destruction and disrespect for small but important animal-beings. Children listening to such stories will hear the lesson loud and clear: Don't ever make fun of something or needlessly harm anything in your environment, or you and all those near you will suffer for it.

In December 2002 I was at Hartley Bay, where the *Jilaa ḵuns* story is known to Helen Clifton because her community, the Gitga'at, have ties to the Haida through marriage. Helen remarked that there used to be thousands and thousands of frogs around Hartley Bay; they were hopping all over the boardwalks, and everyone exclaimed about their loud choruses in the springtime. Today, she said, you hardly ever see a frog. For her, this is a bad omen and a great concern. She attributes the loss of frogs to environmental changes and she worries about everyone's future. She said that frogs were important in the stories of the Gitga'at and other Tsimshian people, and she is afraid that without the frogs the culture will be the poorer.

Declining Species and Lost Habitats

Frogs are not the only animals that have severely diminished in numbers. According to local observers, key species of birds, sea mammals and fish are declining all along the coast. Haida elders Percy Williams, Roy Jones Sr. and Ernie Wilson described some of these losses from their own memories from the vicinity of Skidegate:

> But I know that there were millions of tons of fish, because when they started moving through Burnaby Narrows it sounded like a big rainfall or something, at night time going through the Narrows. And then the sea lions and the killer whales *[Orcinus orca]* right with them, too.

Hear the sea lions roaring all night going through the Narrows after the herring. . . .

It [herring spawn] used to be so thick. Every week it spawned in different places. . . . It used to start spawning in April, May, June, July, still the odd little spawn. That's how many months we used to get spawn. . . .

There used to be a lot of sea lions. Even *k'aalw*—cormorants. There used to be lots on both islands near Skidegate village. In the evenings you'd hear them. You'd hear them plainly. You don't see them now. No feed for them. No herring. . . . Grey cod and tommy cods, they're edible but they're not there now. . . . Sole, that's gradually disappearing too. We used to go out there and get lots . . ., rowing, just outside Balance Rock. . . .

Tsartlip elder Dr. Samuel Sam described his own observations from the Saanich Inlet area:

Killer whales used to go up [Saanich Inlet]. You'd hear them at certain times and the old people would know the chum salmon was coming. Murres by the thousands, now not one. Blue blacks [coho salmon], now there are none; there used to be thousands. Now we don't see flounders or herring spawning. The old people used to get excited and holler "herring" in our language and get ready and lay down branches, and the roe would be about six inches thick and really white. Now there's hardly any and it's yellowy. Cod fish—the old people used to love it.

The land is destroyed. What's left for young people? Whatever we can do to salvage what's left, anything, that's what we should do. The old people told us to watch out, 60 to 70 years ago.

People hold similar concerns about declining plant and animal populations all over North America and in indigenous and local peoples' territories the world over. Fishers on a global scale are "fishing down" the food chain, eliminating a vast proportion of the large predator species such as tuna, swordfish and sharks, as well as the larger individuals of all the seafood species, from abalone to lobster. In Newfoundland, for example, in one short generation, fishers who used to make a good living catching the bountiful Atlantic cod are now unemployed, have switched to a declining lobster fishery or are catching snow crabs. The snow crabs are relatively abundant, but many feel that it is only a matter of time before they, too, will be reduced to unsustainable numbers.

Working with my friends Mary Thomas, Daisy Sewid-Smith, Adam Dick and Kim Recalma-Clutesi, as well as with students and colleagues, we have documented noticeable declines in well over one hundred kinds of plant and animal resources from coastal and interior British Columbia [illegible] Adam and Daisy. All of these people, specialists in traditional foods and culturally important plants, have closely observed their homelands. They have seen the changes more than most who live in urban environments or who move from one location to another over time. Most city dwellers are removed from [illegible] areas and simply have [illegible] noticed the changes that have occurred incrementally and cumulatively. When the observations of many long-resident people in different places around the continent and around the world are combined, an immense and extensive picture builds of dramatic environmental loss taking place almost everywhere, especially since the Industrial Revolution and in particular over the past one hundred years.

Mary Thomas was a keynote speaker at the "Helping the Land Heal" conference on ecological restoration in British Columbia, which took place in Victoria in [illegible]. She shared her worries about her own lands in Secwepemc territory around Salmon Arm:

> I'm one of the elders who was fortunate to grow up and experience the beautiful times, the richness of our Mother Earth. I went with my grandmother, and we did a lot of learning from the way they survived. Their connection to Mother Nature was something beautiful to learn. And I've seen in my eighty-one years, a big change—and I'm afraid not for the best. And I am really worried. . . .
>
> I left the reservation thirty-three years ago. I went to . . . see what is there out there, what is living in a city like. But I always kept calling back, calling back, to where I was born and raised. And every time I came back, I was seeing a lot of difference. That river [the Salmon River] one time used to be just full of sockeye salmon. In the fall, spring

salmon went up, coho salmon went up to spawn. They were getting less and less. And I'd ask why—what is happening? I saw the water going down. My people used to go down that river to torch for fish at night and I'd spearfish. Now, you couldn't even get a boat to go down that river. It's getting less than ever. And not only that, it's the Thompson River. There's just a trickle. I was really concerned about that. . . .

I look around in the areas I was raised and born, the bluebirds (Western bluebird, *Sialia mexicana*) that used to be aplenty. I don't see one bluebird anymore. We used to go down to the mouth of the river with all the plants that our grandparents dug in the spring to feed on: *etsmáts'* [*Sium suave*, water parsnip], *ckwalkwaluls* [*Sagittaria latifolia*, wapato]. There's not one plant left down there, let alone a cattail [*Typha latifolia*] where the birds used to sing beautiful music. You don't hear that anymore. . . .

Mary identified forestry practices as being responsible for severe environmental damage, with repercussions reaching right to the Salmon River estuary and Shuswap Lake:

You take the forestry. I sat in on many of their meetings. And I looked around at what they were doing—and I saw the destruction that was going on. I looked at the streams, where they'd logged right down to the streams, and it didn't hold back the water—it just eroded and filled the little rivers that feed the big rivers. It seemed like it was just a snowball of terrible things happening. . . .

Mary described how her deep concerns for the environment and the dwindling waters in the rivers led her to initiate, with the help of her son, Louis, and her friend Dorothy Argent, who was a city councillor at Salmon Arm, a restoration and monitoring project for the Salmon River. This project brought together people from all parts of the community and all age groups, to focus on the cleanup and monitoring of the entire stretch of the Salmon River—trying to alleviate the pollution, protect the shores from cattle trampling and restore the trees and shrubs along the banks to help filter out pollutants. Further, she determined to work with the foresters of the region to try to develop responsible timber-harvesting

Redwing blackbird (Agelaius phoeniceus) *among the cattails* (Typha latifolia).
PHOTO BY ROBERT D. TURNER

practices that don't deplete the springs and creeks of the mountainsides and that don't destroy the other life forms of the forest.

Even in her late eighties, Mary works tirelessly to share her message with anyone who will listen, about how the streams and rivers have to be protected and how the birch trees *(Betula papyrifera)* and all the berry and hazelnut *(Corylus cornuta)* bushes need special attention. These valuable plants, she stresses, must not be cut down or killed with Roundup or other commercial herbicides, which has been a common industrial forestry practice. As basket-making artists, she and her family understand both practical and ecological values of the birch tree. She says that because of current forestry practices she can hardly find any birch trees any more. She asks, "What have we done to Mother Earth?" Earth must certainly be sorrowful to experience such deterioration of her Blanket.

LESSONS FROM THE BIRCH TREE

Mary Thomas stresses the teachings of her mother, Christine Allen, and the other elders that the birch, trembling aspen and alder are trees that have great value to all the species of the forest. As just one example, she talks about the sapsuckers tapping rows of little holes in the birch, and how the sap oozes out and traps insects that the sapsuckers eat. The hummingbirds and ants feed on the sap, and other birds make their homes in the cavities carved out of the trunk by the sapsuckers. When the birch trees and aspens are cut down, a whole source of nutrients and habitats disappears. Her people understood these ecological connections long before ecology was a recognized science.

Mary remembers her mother explaining to her how the leaves of the birch, falling to the earth in the autumn, provide a nutritious mulch that feeds all the other trees:

I can remember listening to my Elders when the clear-cutting first started. You know, you see these big bald spots up on the mountain. The Elders questioned, "Why are they doing that?" And the effect it has on our environment is devastating. Our creeks are drying up. And they were saying that like, when they want to cut the timber out, "Why don't they just take the timber and leave the rest?" And I wondered, "Why? Why are they [the Elders] so concerned about the leafy trees?" So I asked my mother and another elderly person way up in the Kootenay, the Shuswap-speaking people. I asked them, "Why are we concerned about the leafy trees? Why should they be left there?" And my mother said, "You know, leafy trees hold a lot of sap. The sap comes up in the spring, and goes up, creates leaves, it's collecting sun's energy. The wind, the rain, the sun. In the fall it goes back down, and it feeds other plants. It adds to our streams, it's kept alive." And I thought, "God, there must be a lot of sap to fill a stream. How could that be?"

Mary was convinced that her mother was right, and that the foresters who cut down birch trees as "weeds" to get rid of them and make way for the commercially valuable conifers were wrong. They didn't appreciate the valuable role in the web of life that the birch plays. She found a neighbour who had a three-trunked birch tree, and they tapped one of the trunks, just as one would tap a sugar maple:

We chose a birch tree about . . . [thirty centimetres across]. We tapped it and we put a little spigot in there. I wanted to know, "How much sap does that tree hold?" We put an ice cream bucket under it. Right away, "drip, drip, drip, drip, drip." I was getting a bucket full in the morning, a bucket full at night. And it went on for a whole week. Not to mention the sap that was missing the spigot and just dripping down, making the ground underneath soaking wet. So we mud-packed it, took the spigot out and mud-packed it so it would dry up [and heal].

Mary used this experiment to prove her point to the local foresters and resource managers:

Paper birch (Betula papyrifera). PHOTO BY ROBERT D. TURNER

I said, "Look how much came from this one little tree; for a whole week I got a gallon in the morning, a gallon at night. How much do the other trees, that are close to it—that stand in the whole mountainside—how much do they put back in the soil?" Therefore, feeding our streams, feeding the other plants, feeding rivers and flushing out our lakes.

And I told them about the trees, when you log, . . . you bulldoze everything out. And on top of that, you take what you want for lumber and the rest you bulldoze, you pile it up, and you set it on fire. You burn it. Well what happens when they do that? It'll snow in the winter, and in the spring, the first hot weather the snow will melt. There's nothing to hold it back. It'll just melt and just come down. Nothing left. It all dries up. How can you heal a mountain without water? Everything needs water. Our bodies are two-thirds fluid. We can't live without water. No life on the planet can live without water. . . .

Mary has always talked about the sacred mountain of her people, *Kela7scen* (Mount Ida). For generations, *Kela7scen* provided the Secwepemc with a great variety of resources necessary to their physical and spiritual well-being. The people harvested and hunted plants and animals on the slopes of the mountain, they offered prayers to it and in return received guidance. Extensive logging on *Kela7scen* concerned Mary greatly, as did the disputes taking place in the Salmon Arm community over resource use on the mountain, which she regarded as ominous. Indeed, Mary was not surprised when, in the summer of 1998, a hot fire raged up the western slopes of *Kela7scen,* burning the trees and everything else in its path. Called the Silver Creek Blaze, the fire forced the evacuation of 7,000 people for a day and a night. The destruction is still visible from Salmon Arm, with vast swaths of dead, burned snags covering the slopes. Mary sadly commented that this is what happens when people treat Nature, and each other, with disregard.

Daisy Sewid-Smith expresses similar concerns and sentiments about the clear-cutting of the coastal rain forests:

Clear-cut logging is the most devastating of all the practices. The reason for that is that they clear large areas of forest with no concern of any of the other plants. . . . When they fell a tree, all they're looking at is a tree. And when we try and fight for a particular area, they're just thinking: "the tree." But we are not just thinking of the tree. We are thinking holistically of the whole environmental damage. The plants, the tree that was used for medicine. . . . It's medicine that's our greatest concern. The area where my grandmother used to go to get my medicine, it's not there anymore. The plants have disappeared because of clear-cut logging. . . .

I sympathize with loggers, because it is their job, their employment, and they have families. . . . And yet, if they continue the practices that are going on now there'll be *nothing* left . . . by the removal of the trees, many hillsides are sliding. They're sliding down, damaging more plants. Some of them are sliding into the river, and blocking the rivers, [so] that the salmon can't go up, or destroying spawning grounds. There are so many little things that are happening. And many of them claim, "No, it's not happening," but those that grew up there, those that are more aware of their surroundings than many of the people, can see the changes. We *see* the changes. It's really not very good.

Both Daisy and Mary have drawn the connection between forest practices and the loss and deterioration of water resources. As well, they have both illustrated clearly the associations between forest ecosystems and human societies. Although neither has received formal training in ecology or environmental studies, they have captured in their own observations and thoughts the essence of our interactions with our environment and all its complexities.

ONCE A RIVER, NOW A WASTELAND

A parallel story from the deserts of the southwestern United States is told by ethnobiologist Amadeo M. Rea in his book *At the Desert's Green Edge*. Rea documents similar declines and deteriorating environments in the watershed of the Gila River, Arizona, and describes graphically how the environmental losses have negatively affected a whole way of life for the Pima peoples who have occupied the surrounding lands for thousands of years. It is a story of how a once-healthy, functioning riverine

Clear-cut old-growth forest, Clayoquot Sound, Vancouver Island;
the large western red-cedar at the top left was several hundred years old.

ecosystem was degraded and transformed over time into a dry, impoverished wasteland. The story relates, with many fascinating historical notations and personal accounts, how the ecosystem held a people and their
language and culture in a tight mutual embrace. It tells about a strong,
hard-working group of people who were nourished by a diverse and

healthy diet. Their culture and well-being were built upon the desert ecosystem and the river that ran through it. Then, their lives were altered when the European newcomers wrought changes to their river.

As recounted by Rea, the river died because its resources were over-used: trappers killed off the beaver *(Castor canadensis)* in its upper reaches; loggers and miners denuded the fragile semi-arid uplands of the forest cover that held back the waters from sporadic but torrential rain-storms; ranchers' livestock overgrazed the native grasses and other plants, and farmers diverted the river to irrigate their crops. Today, where once you could hear the redwing blackbird calls reverberating over vast expanses of tule, willow, reed grass and other moisture-loving plants, there is a parched, hardened ground devoid of many of its original plants and animals.

The Gila River Pima have kept their humour and spirit, but they have lost much of their culture and language that were tied to the land. The river was also their economic backbone. Their cultural practices actually increased the productivity and biological diversity of the ecosystems they inhabited. Now, their way of life and their diet have changed markedly. Obesity is a real problem, and today these people have the highest inci-dence of late-onset diabetes of any population in the world. This story has an essential message, which resonates in almost every North Ameri-can environment and indigenous culture and is captured in just one word: overexploitation.

Spirituality and Environmental Loss

Saanich elder Dr. Samuel Sam was warned by his predecessors about the environmental destruction to come, and he identified a lack of respect and a lack of ceremonial acknowledgement as a reason for the decline:

> About fifty years ago, the elders told them to be careful. My grand-father was 105 years old when he died. He paddled up Goldstream even when he was 100. Things were plentiful then, fish. But, they've de-stroyed the spiritual ways of the Indian people. We're losing reverence for Nature because where we used to go has been destroyed, where old people used to go to get spirit songs for winter dances. So now, young

people don't have the same spirit, the same strength as the old people, because nature is destroyed.

There is reverence in the woods, sacredness—every shrub and tree, because it's a part of life. Now we can't find medicines and have to depend on doctors. Doesn't cure like Indian medicine. Devil's club, it's now very rare, but it and other medicines used to be plentiful around the inlet. Now we have to go up island. In the old days, we couldn't take anything without ritual, without thanking the Creator for the item, thanking when we pick it. Things were not just destroyed.

Of course, ecosystems and cultural systems are dynamic; change is to be expected and is a part of natural processes. However, too much change, too quickly, will not allow the species in the complex web of life to adapt. Nor will it allow cultures, even resilient cultures, to maintain their essential elements. Consequently, environmental, community and human health all suffer. This is what Roy Haiyupis was referring to when he warned us, "Nature will hit back at you." The problem is that change is not always reversible. Even in cases where we might be able to reconstruct or restore parts of an ecosystem—for example, re-establish a wetland or replant a particular species—a habitat once destroyed might never come back in its original configuration. Once a particular ecosystem is gone, it will never be the same again.

As humans, we pride ourselves on being knowledgeable and sophisticated, but there is plenty we do not yet understand. For example, we do not know how to do what green plants have done for over a billion years: capture sunlight and convert it to usable, edible chemical energy in the miraculous process called photosynthesis. We still do not have any more than an inkling of the multitudes of interconnections that join flowering plants with their insect pollinators. What power there must be in a flower that produces combinations of colours—some that we cannot even see—and infinitesimally small but potent, scented molecules that attract the attention of the very insects they require to bring them pollen from others of their kind, to send out their own pollen in return, then provide a tasty reward to the insects for their efforts. Think of the amazing array of devices that seeds and fruits have developed to compel birds, mammals and even the wind to transport them from one location to another, allowing them and their progeny to become established far and wide when they themselves have no means of locomotion.

We are only vaguely aware of the role of soil organisms like mycorrhizal fungi in nutrient and water cycling. These microscopic organisms with their threadlike, branching hyphae grow around, and sometimes penetrate, the root hairs of trees and other plants. There are many different kinds, and they occur in the root systems of approximately 80 per cent of the world's plants. They enhance the growth of plants by assisting them to take up nutrients and water. Using radioactive compounds, we have only recently discovered just how quickly nutrients can be absorbed and spread within a tree and from one tree to another, even between different species, at least partly through these fungi that encase and invade their roots.

Add to this void the lack of understanding of the role of humans in the ecosystem, with all of our synthetic pesticides and herbicides and genetic manipulations, burning of fossil fuels and relocating vast volumes of water with our wells and dams. Even if Nature worked like a well-run machine—and we know that it is much more complex than this—we have been demolishing the machine without keeping track of the pieces, or in some cases without even keeping the pieces. Any attempt to rebuild it is bound to be defective.

We need to find better ways of conserving what we have. Rather than destroying vast areas of old-growth forests, wetlands and other ecosystems of our home places and replacing them with poor imitations or with something else entirely, we need to, for the sake of the planet, learn to maintain the richness of these environments, to maintain their ecological integrity. A new paradigm of working *with* Nature and natural processes, rather than trying to conquer Nature, is starting to take hold in policies for resource management. Sometimes it is referred to as ecosystem-based management. Managers and policy-makers are also becoming aware of the importance of listening to and being guided by local resource users, in a new style of planning and decision-making called co-management. There is still much to be learned, however, not only about inclusive decision-making but about techniques and approaches that can help us to enhance many of our resources through traditional ways of caring for the environment.

LEFT TO RIGHT: *Stl'atl'imx elders Sam Mitchell,*
from Xaxl'ep and Baptiste Ritchie, from Mount Currie (Lil'wat).

6

LOOKING *After the* *Lands and* WATERS

"A perfect Eden in the midst of the dreary wilderness of the Northwest Coast," James Douglas, later governor of the Colony of Vancouver Island, wrote to a friend in 1842. He had just set eyes on what is now the city of Victoria on southern Vancouver Island. He had come to search for a site for a Hudson's Bay Company fort, and like many newcomers who came before and after him he assumed that the landscape he was admiring so much was virtually untouched by human hands. In fact, the very place where he sited the new fort, and the entire surrounding area—a magnificent parkland of garry oak *(Quercus garryana)* interspersed with open meadows rich with wildflowers—was actually an anthropogenic landscape, a landscape moulded and developed by Coast Salish practices of burning, clearing and large-scale harvesting over probably 5,000 years or more. It is only one example of how indigenous peoples have tended their home places.

Daisy Sewid-Smith, in her address to the "Helping the Land Heal" conference held in Victoria in November 1998, described the philosophy of caring for their territories and "giving back" to Nature that underlies the practical actions of her people, the Kwakwaka'wakw:

Our survival depended on the sea, the rivers, lakes. We completely depended on nature. The garments that we had, the houses that sheltered us, the foods we ate, the medicines we had—Nature supplied it. And that is the reason why we respected Nature as we did. . . . *Mother Nature does not want you to take from her and not put anything back. . . . Nature will not survive if we just keep taking. . . .* (Emphasis added.)

The Kwakwaka'wakw, Coast Salish and other peoples have looked after their lands and waters and "paid back" Nature for all her gifts in many ways. These range from very specific, focussed activities such as tending, sustaining and promoting the growth and productivity of their resources to managing and caring for particular localities and habitats, to adopting all-encompassing attitudes of respect and conservation that directed, and continue to direct, people's actions and behaviour.

A specific example of how people cared for their environments was shared by Daisy's friend and elder relative, Chief Adam Dick *(Kwaxsistala)*. He spent much of his childhood and youth at Kingcome Inlet on the British Columbia mainland, and he learned both practical and spiritual ways of relating to Nature. *Kwaxsistala* told my friend and colleague Doug Deur and myself about a term in the Kwak'wala language, *q'waq'wala7owkw*, which translates as "keeping it living." This term embodies an entire system of resource maintenance, conservation and enhancement. For example, when it came to harvesting their traditional root vegetables like Pacific silverweed *(Potentilla pacifica)*, springbank clover *(Trifolium wormskjoldii)* and northern rice-root *(Fritillaria camschatcensis)*, people were careful to leave in or return to the ground some portions of the root or edible bulb to allow it to continue to live and grow. In other words, they made sure to "keep it living." It was the same with other plants, berry bushes and trees used for the roots, bark, medicine or food they yielded; wherever possible they harvested only portions of the living plants, leaving the rest to grow.

Conflicting Views of Cultivation and Land Ownership

Q'waq'wala7owkw practices can be termed "cultivation," in the sense of encouraging and promoting the growth of a plant or population of plants.

There are many examples of "cultivating" traditional resources—both plant and animal, terrestrial and aquatic—among North American and other First Peoples. In British Columbia, peoples of both the coast and the interior applied specific strategies to sustain and enhance their plant and animal resources, carefully monitoring and managing these populations to prevent declines in their numbers or their health.

Anthropologist Eugene Anderson, in his book *Ecologies of the Heart*, points out that Northwest Coast peoples had the technologies, in the form of fish traps, nets and weirs, to completely eliminate the thousands of individual stocks of salmon in creeks and rivers up and down the coast. Yet when the Europeans arrived they found thriving populations of all of the different salmon species everywhere they looked. *Not* destroying the salmon populations was a conscious choice—borne out in careful observation and practice and sometimes encoded in ceremony and social sanctions—to ensure that enough salmon returned to spawn each year. People took care to maintain the riverbeds and lake beds to sustain and nurture the young salmon, enabling them to continue the cycle of life. Not only were people looked after by these means, but so were the bears and other animals depending on the salmon cycles. Sometimes the punishment for harming a river was extreme. Ethnographer Thomas McIlwraith describes a position of "River Guardian" in Nuxalk society at Bella Coola; the person who inherited and was trained for this position had tremendous powers in order to keep the river free from pollution or disturbance while the salmon were running up to spawn. Polluting the river at this time was potentially punishable by death.

Other elders from many parts of the coast and interior describe how, formerly, people were appointed to watch the salmon swimming upriver to spawn. They ensured that enough fish got through to keep the populations healthy before people were allowed to start fishing. Earl Claxton Sr., who as a young man participated in the Saanich reef-net fishery, noted that a hole was always built into the far end of the reef net, allowing some of the salmon entering the net to escape. Earl explained that the salmon were thought of as having families, just like human families, and it was a duty of the fishers to make sure that a certain number of members of each salmon family made it through to the spawning grounds to continue the family line. Shellfish beds—like the abalone sites—were also carefully maintained. In some places there are still beaches that people developed as intensive clam "gardens," where large stones were removed and placed along the tide line to help build up the beach, and the shellfish were selectively harvested by size, always leaving enough small ones behind to keep the populations productive.

People also exercised great care in harvesting birds' eggs, waterfowl and game of various kinds.

Far from being simply opportunistic harvesters of naturally occurring wild fish and animals and random pluckers of berries and roots as the commonly used term "hunter-gatherer" would imply, First Peoples of northwestern North America, and of many other regions as well, were astute and sophisticated caretakers of their plant and animal resources. As a result, large numbers of people resided along the Northwest Coast and they developed complex societal structures, institutions and monumental art over thousands of years.

Like James Douglas, however, Europeans arriving to trade and settle on the Northwest Coast did not generally understand these practices and looked upon the indigenous people as primitive and uncivilized. The Europeans' attitude—and their lack of understanding or appreciation of the indigenous peoples' use and tending of their landscapes—had profound consequences, because the Europeans used the First Peoples' apparent lack of any control over their lands to justify taking them over and converting them to "civilized" purpose.

The newcomers discussed and justified their right to assume ownership of indigenous lands, as recorded by pioneer businessman of the Alberni district Gilbert Malcolm Sproat, later to become Indian land commissioner:

> We often talked about our right as strangers to take possession of the district. . . . The American woodmen . . . considered that *any right in the soil which these natives had as occupiers was partial and imperfect as, with the exception of hunting animals in the forests, plucking wild fruits, and cutting a few trees to make canoes and houses, the natives did not, in any civilized sense, occupy the land.* . . . It would be unreasonable to suppose, the Americans said, that a body of civilized men, under the sanc-

tion of their government, could not rightfully settle in a country needing their labours, and peopled only by a fringe of savages on the
coast. . . . (Emphasis added.)

Joseph W. Trutch, chief commissioner of lands and works of British
Columbia, wrote to the British colonial secretary on 20 September 1865:
"I am satisfied from my own observation that the claims of Indians over
tracts of land, on which they assume to exercise ownership, *but of which
they make no real use* [emphasis added], operate very materially to prevent
settlement and cultivation. . . ." Trutch was absolutely determined to
usurp the First Nations' lands and convert them to settlement in the English tradition. He certainly did not make any attempt to understand the indigenous peoples' sophisticated systems of resource management. Even
those Europeans, like James Douglas himself, who considered that the
local indigenous people held some concept of ownership of their lands
still regarded them as "wandering denizens of the forest," without any
real need for most of their lands or any influence upon them.

The beautiful and parklike landscape of southern Vancouver Island
and the surrounding Gulf and San Juan Islands was remarked upon time
and again by the new arrivals. For example, Captain George Vancouver,
on observing the prairies cleared by indigenous peoples' burning along
the shores of Puget Sound, recorded his pleasure at the sight, but obviously had no understanding of how these landscapes came to be:

> I could not possibly believe any uncultivated country had ever been
> discovered exhibiting so rich a picture. Stately forests . . . pleasingly
> clothed its eminences and chequered its vallies; presenting in many
> places, extensive spaces that wore the appearance of having been
> cleared by art . . . [We] had no reason to imagine this country had ever
> been indebted for its decoration to the hand of man.

MANAGING THE LAND WITH FIRE

More recent understandings contradict the original notion of indigenous
hunter-gatherers' limited use of their lands and acknowledge more complex relationships between people who use wild species and the ecosystems

where they occur. Some of the earliest work to indicate peoples' active participation in promoting and maintaining particular ecosystems, with a view to enhancing the growth and productivity of particular plants and animals, was done by ecologists investigating human-generated fire. Pioneering work by Omer Stewart, Henry Lewis, Stephen Pyne, Robert Boyd and others has demonstrated conclusively, for a variety of regions and habitats, that intentional, controlled burning of landscapes by indigenous people played a major role in maintaining grasslands and clearings and reducing brush in woodlands throughout North America, as well as in Australia and other regions of the world.

For most of us, fire is generally regarded as a destructive force that is harmful to forests and other ecosystems. Think of Smokey the Bear, the icon of outdoor fire safety and wildfire prevention. I well remember in my own childhood driving with my family through stark, burned landscapes and being told about terrible forest fires that had swept through them. The image of a signpost near Manning Park, British Columbia, with a giant cigarette hanging from it and the words THE MAN WHO DROPPED THIS SHOULD BE HUNG! is still fresh in my mind. So are the words painted on highway signs all over western North America: PREVENT FOREST FIRES. USE YOUR ASHTRAY.

The damaging effects of a wildfire are undeniable, and the economic losses from burned timber have been immense. However, fire has been a component of ecological evolution for millions of years—long before humans existed as humans—and many species have adapted to withstand or survive fire, at least at certain stages of their life cycles and under certain conditions. We know that some plant species actually require fire to regenerate themselves, just as some seeds must be frozen for a certain length of time to trigger their germination mechanism. For example, lodgepole pine's hard, woody cones mostly remain tightly shut, trapping their enclosed seeds. When the cone scales are heated by fire, they separate and release the seeds. This is why lodgepole pine *(Pinus contorta* var. *latifolia)* stands grow thickly immediately after a blaze. The pines provide a sheltered canopy for the more light-sensitive, shade-tolerant spruces (*Picea* spp.), subalpine fir *(Abies lasiocarpa)* and other species, which will eventually grow up through them and shade them out. Assuming a similar overall climate, the cycle of forest succession will continue over and over, but with variations. Where fire occurs in a regular cycle the forest will usually be made up of a mosaic of recently burned patches, variously aged pine stands and mature stretches where spruce or fir predominate.

Lodgepole pine is not the only species with built-in fire-survival mechanisms. Trembling aspen *(Populus tremuloides)*, like many perennial plants, has a "meristem bank" in various parts of its trunk and roots. Meristem is plant tissue with the potential to generate growth. If a trembling aspen is burned or cut down (or even when it is still standing), the meristem tissue in its roots can generate sprouts that will eventually grow into new trees. This gives aspen a major survival advantage. As long as the tree's roots are not killed, other stems can grow up to take the place of an individual stem that has been destroyed, and the whole organism with its genetic material and capacity for growth and regeneration can survive for long periods of time, in some cases for thousands of years.

Many perennial grasses have a similar regeneration mechanism. If their leaves are burned or grazed, they will quickly grow back, as long as the underground parts remain intact. Deer and other grazing animals often seek the tender new growth that emerges after a burn, a fact that indigenous peoples in many different places must have noticed long ago. Creating new pasture or grazing grounds for both domesticated and wild animals is a major reason that people give for burning their meadows and grasslands.

Just as in the grasslands, fire helps diversify woodlands. Garry oak *(Quercus garryana)* trees, and a number of other oak species, are well known for their ability to regenerate after being burned or cut. In an oak parkland—a mix of oak woods and open meadows—periodic burning may kill individual trees, especially young ones, but chances are that some will sprout new shoots within a year, and if left undisturbed the sprouts will grow into mature trees. Periodic burning can create a sort of shifting equilibrium, a patchwork of areas where some are maintained as meadow, with all the trees and shrubs burned off, others as developing bushlands, with important habitat and food sources for birds and animals, and still others as more mature woodland. All of these habitats sustain people and the grazing animals they hunt, and each provides important foods, materials and medicinal plants. The fires are also said to reduce the numbers of insect pests, which keeps the oaks and other plants healthier.

Garry oaks (Quercus garryana) *in snow,* *Victoria.* PHOTO BY ROBERT D. TURNER

In 'addition, burned areas stimulate the growth of mushrooms, such as morels, which people enjoy eating.

People also sometimes burned individual fruiting bushes, such as Saskatoon berry and hazelnut, to promote their growth and renew their vigour. Daisy Sewid-Smith explained how the Kwakwa̱ka'wakw tended their berry bushes:

Now, another myth is that we did nothing with our berry bushes—they just grew. That is not true, because, berry bushes were pruned, weeded and they also singed them a bit. Just enough. And, it's interesting that the way they cared for the berry plants—what they did with the berry plants was to singe it as I said, so that it would come back and the following year it would have more berries. Now, when our babies are ten months old, we cut the baby's hair, and we singe it as well. And that is because, that baby now at ten months, we call it [a word that means], 'out of danger. It's going to live now.' And we singe the baby's hair so the hair would grow back in abundance. And he will be handsome—or she will be beautiful. So that is similar to what we used to do with the berry bushes.

Franz Boas recorded and translated a Kwakwa̱ka'wakw address to food and medicine plants, which shows that people burned berry bushes, apparently individually, as a management technique. In this address, which a woman would give before she picked berries, the type of berry is not specified; even in the original Kwak'wala language, only a general term for fruit is used:

I have come, Supernatural Ones, you, Long-Life-Makers, that I may take you, for that is the reason why you have come, brought by your creator, that you may come and satisfy me; you Supernatural Ones; *and this, that you do not blame me for what I do to you when I set fire to you the way it is done by my root (ancestor) who set fire to you in his manner when you get old on the ground that you may bear much fruit.* Look! I come now dressed with my large basket and my small basket that you may go into it, Healing-Women; you Supernatural Ones. I mean this, that you may not be evilly disposed towards me, friends. That you may only treat me well. . . . (Emphasis added.)

As well as burning meadows, woodlands and individual plants, some peoples have used fire to renew and maintain wetland ecosystems. In the boreal forests of northern Alberta, the Chipewyan and other peoples set fire to their cattail *(Typha latifolia)* marshes at the end of the season to clear out the old, dead leaves and fruits and to create more areas of open water.

The traditional fires were lit with care and with attention to the weather, topography and timing. Usually, in western North America, people set their fires in the fall, just before the rains started. The fires burned quickly, running along the ground, and seldom spread to the trees. Dennis Martinez, indigenous ecologist and ecocultural restoration expert, calls these "cold fires" because they move through the dead grasses and fallen leaves without really heating up either the soil or the forest canopy.

An account from an article on colonization of Vancouver Island describes this type of fire in the vicinity of Victoria in the days around the time of the gold rush of 1858, when the small fur-trade outpost was being converted into a major city: "Miles of the ground were burnt and smoky, and miles were still burning. The Indians burn the country in order to [promote] . . . more especially, the roots which they eat. The fire runs along at a great pace, and it is the custom here if you are caught to gallop right through it; the grass being short, the flame is very little; and you are through in a second. . . ."

The practice of burning areas to promote the productivity of plant resources is represented in the stories that go back to mythical times. For example, the text of a Nlaka'pmx narrative recorded by James Teit mentions a girl who had four brothers who had "burned a piece of the mountainside so that the *skamitch* [*sk'émec*] root [*Erythronium grandiflorum,* yellow glacier lily] should yield a better crop, and it was here that the little sister went to dig roots."

One of the most interesting and detailed accounts of intentional burning for upland forested areas of southwestern British Columbia is a story told by Lil'wat (Stl'atl'imx, or Pemberton Lillooet) elder Baptiste Ritchie of Mount Currie. His general translation is provided here in its entirety.

Burning Mountainsides for Better Crops

I am telling you about the doings of our forefathers, why they always did well wherever they went for the purpose of picking all the berries and roots like 'potatoes' [*sk'amts,* yellow glacier lily] that they ate. They used to burn one hill and use the other. When there were a lot of bushes ["sticks"; i.e., "when it got bushy"] then the ripe berries disappear and the roots like 'potatoes', *skimuta* [*Lilium columbianum,* tiger lily], *skwenkwina* [*Claytonia lanceolata,* spring beauty, or mountain potato]

Yellow glacier lily (Erythronium grandiflorum). PHOTO BY ROBERT D. TURNER

disappear when it gets too bushy. Then they burned. It was marked out and there one did his own burning. That is what they did so that they could go here and there to pick berries. Each one watched that it was really burnt. All the other bushes were removed. Then the berry bushes grew again. The roots like 'potatoes,' the *skimuta*, the *skwen-kwina*, all those that were eaten by us, that is where they grow.

It was a few years—I guess it was almost around three years—before those things grew there again. Then there were really lots of berries. Everything was all really fertile. They rarely burnt the big trees. Only the small ones, only around the bushes was burned. It was the same with one hill as with another. That is why we see, we who are grownup Indians, that all the hills seem to be burnt, because that was what they did to their own hills. They burned them so that they would get good crops there. They told others who went there, "Do the same at your place, do the same at your place." Their own hills were just like a garden.

But now, because the white man really watches us, we don't burn anything. We realize already, it seems the things that were eaten by our forefathers have disappeared from the places where they burned. It seems that already almost everything has disappeared. Maybe it is because it's weedy. All kinds of things grow and they don't burn. If you go to burn then you get into trouble because the white men want to grow trees. Because they changed our ways they do good for us and we eat the food that the white men use. Then we forget the good food of our earliest forefathers. The roots like 'potatoes,' the *skimuta,* the *skwenkwina,* all of those were good to eat.

Now they have disappeared because the hills grew weedy and no one seems to tend them, no one clears there as our forefathers did so thoroughly.

That is another story for you folks. Why our forefathers burnt. Now you must do it again. Now you know why everything that was near here just disappeared. There we used to go berry picking. There we went berry picking long ago. Now nothing. The food plants have now all gone. They have disappeared. It seems that everything and anything grows on the hills. It has become covered with bushes all over.

Where we used to pick berries, oh, they were really plentiful! Right here where our house is situated now [in Mount Currie], that is where we used to come to pick berries, like gooseberries [*Ribes divaricatum, sxniż*]. Now there are no gooseberries near us. Now the other berries are the same. They have all disappeared. We named other grounds of ours around here; called them 'The Picking Places' because that is where we went to pick berries. Now you will not find one single berry there.

That is my story to you about how those things which our forefathers ate have disappeared. That is all. You will still know, now that I am reminding you folks, what the old fashioned ways were like. I am Baptiste Ritchie here in Mount Currie.

I am *En Chinemqen*. That is all.

Indigenous elders all over British Columbia have noted that their wild root vegetables and berry plants grow more productively after a fire and that the plants will continue to produce well for at least two or three years afterwards. This includes a whole range of plant resources that respond positively to fire: yellow glacier lily, spring beauty, tiger lily, camas (*Camassia* spp.), wild nodding onions *(Allium cernuum)*, strawberries (*Fragaria* spp.), trailing blackberries *(Rubus ursinus)*, blackcaps *(R. leucodermis)*, huckleberries and blueberries (*Vaccinium* spp.) and Saskatoon berries *(Amelanchier alnifolia)*. Secwepemc elder Mary Thomas, for example, recalled traditional burning by her parents and grandparents:

> A lot of people couldn't believe that our people deliberately burned a mountainside when it got so thick nothing else would grow in it. They deliberately burned it, at a certain time of the year when they knew there were rains coming, they'd burn that, and two years, three years after the burn there'd be huckleberries galore and different vegetations would come up that were edible [roots, berries]. . . .

There are still places around British Columbia that the elders identify as having been burned over periodically within their own lifetimes or those of their parents and grandparents. Botanie Valley near Lytton is one such locality, and Neskonlith Meadows near Chase is another. Although it has been a long, long time since people intentionally burned in these places, they are still renowned for their diversity of culturally important species and their productivity. Even on the coast, people used to burn places to promote the growth of berries. Ernie Hill Jr., hereditary Eagle chief of the Gitga'at of Hartley Bay, told me about an island called *Lax Ngwelk*, off the west coast of Banks Island, that was called "burned over continuously" because the people regularly set fire to it to keep it open for blueberry production. Similarly, the elders of the Haida, Nuxalk, Heiltsuk and Nuu-Chah-Nulth Nations recalled places that were burned and where the huckleberries, salal berries *(Gaultheria shallon)* and other kinds of berries were notably abundant as a result.

My friend Arvid Charlie of the Cowichan (Quw'uts'un) Nation was told by his great-grandfather *Lescheem* that people used to burn the coastline meadows in a place to the west of them, possibly Beacon Hill Park in Victoria, to promote the growth of wild strawberries. Bob Akerman, who was born on Saltspring Island in the early 1900s and whose grandmother was Cowichan and a relative of Arvid's, remembered two places on Saltspring Island where the people used to burn the slopes: one just behind Fulford Harbour and one at the base of Mount Maxwell. In particular, he said, they burned to increase the productivity of trailing blackberries, blackcaps, strawberries and camas lilies. The Gulf Islands and the San Juan Islands were well known for their periodic fires, as were the prairies of Puget Sound in western Washington and other valleys such as the Willamette in Oregon. Not only did the burns promote the growth of berries and edible root vegetables such as camas lily and bracken fern *(Pteridium aquilinum)*, they also produced good forage for deer and elk, which in turn aided hunters as well as the wildlife.

Today, within a relatively brief period of time—less than a century—the clearings and meadows of oak parklands are gone from many of their original locations and those remaining have declined significantly in biological diversity, at least of native species. Around Victoria, even the places that have not succumbed to urban development are not the same as they used to be. A photograph of Uplands Park in Oak Bay taken by C.F. Newcombe in 1892 shows big, old, spreading oak trees underlain by grassy wildflower meadows. Today there is dense bush—mostly thickets of native shrubs: snowberry *(Symphoricarpos albus)*, oceanspray *(Holodiscus discolor)*, Indian plum *(Oemleria cerasiformis)* and wild rose *(Rosa nutkana)*—as well as dense growths of introduced Scotch broom *(Cytisus scoparius)*, Himalayan blackberry *(Rubus discolor)* and English ivy *(Hedera helix)*. The grasses in the remaining meadows are almost entirely introduced. The same is true at Cedar Hill Park, Mount Douglas Park and the University of Victoria campus, all areas with vestiges of the original managed oak parkland vegetation but altered significantly at least in part by stopping the fires.

Impressive recent efforts have been made to mimic traditional burning practices and possibly to reintroduce fire to the landscape in places where it used to occur on a regular basis. But prescribed burning is fraught with difficulties. Today's fires usually burn very hot and are highly destructive, in part because they are less frequent than previously and because they usually occur in the hottest, driest part of the year. Because of the higher "fuel load," they often burn off the organic materials in the soil and, jumping into the tree crowns, burn hot and uncontrolled, killing virtually everything in their path. This is the kind of blaze that burned in Yellowstone Park in 1988, in Penticton in 1994, at Mount Ida *(Kela7scen)* near Salmon Arm in 1998, in the vicinity of Kelowna and Kamloops in 2003 and near Lillooet and in the Chilcotin Plateau in 2004. The elders who talk about these fires say they never would have been so hot or so devastating if people had been allowed to practise their traditional burning, every few years, first in one place and then in another.

Recent attempts at traditional burning on Yellow Island in the San Juan Archipelago in Washington State have been promising. Ecologist Peter Dunwiddie, The Nature Conservancy and a crew of interested assistants and volunteers have been studying the effects of fire in the grassy meadows on this island. They have burned areas, using a drip torch and plenty of water sprayers to curb the flames if they become unruly. In these trials, just one year after burning, wildflowers such as western buttercup *(Ranunculus occidentalis)* and blue camas *(Camassia leichtlinii)* were more abundant than ever. Grasses were suppressed, and so were mosses and lichens. However, introduced, weedy species were not curbed and may actually thrive after fires, which is a large concern. Reinstating periodic burning to restore the oak parkland habitats and camas meadows to resemble past conditions is just not that simple. There are still too many unknowns, as my friend Brenda Beckwith, an ethnoecologist who has studied these ecosystems for many years, attests.

Managing Species and Habitats: Environmental Stewardship

Fire is an important but by no means singular tool for maintaining lands and resources. Many other techniques have been applied on both small and large scales, over short spans of time and over generations. Ethnoecologist

Kat Anderson has been a pioneer in our understanding of the sophisticated resource management systems of Native Californians. Her articles and books describe a number of specific techniques for pruning or cutting back shrubs to the ground, called "coppicing," and for thinning and tilling edible root plants, which are known technically as "geophytes." These and related techniques are being increasingly documented as having been used by "hunter-gatherers" in many places. Brenda Beckwith has found in her work on southern Vancouver Island that even the digging and churning up of the soil that is associated with harvesting camas bulbs may create special conditions for holding moisture and nutrients. The small depressions and uneven surfaces that result may be advantageous to the germinating seeds and developing bulbs, and they may help perpetuate the camas populations in an area. These cultivation practices, Brenda maintains, together with fire, likely represented an integrated resource management system in the past.

Paul Minnis, an archaeologist who studies ancient plant remains, and Wayne Elisens, a botanist, recently edited a book called *Biodiversity and Native America* that compiles ways in which indigenous peoples from across North America have protected and promoted their resources. Their examples include indigenous societies of the high deserts and marshes of Nevada, of the Sierra Madre of Mexico, of the dry hillsides and valleys of southern California and of the Interior Plateau of British Columbia. They also extend back some 2,000 years ago to the indigenous pre-Pueblo farming peoples of the Rio del Oso valley near Santa Fe, New Mexico. Surprisingly, there are actually many similarities between how the First Nations in British Columbia tend their berry patches, edible roots and other resources and how the various indigenous peoples, such as the ancient pre-Pueblo farmers of Rio del Oso who are classified as agriculturalists, farm their land.

Indigenous agricultural societies, like "hunter-gatherers," often use an array of strategies to maintain soil fertility and support diverse habitats and populations of wild and domesticated species. They often balance the populations of their domesticated plants with naturally occurring resources in complex systems known as agroecosystems. Such systems are known, in many parts of the world, to be even more biologically diverse than ecosystems without an evident human presence. Agroecologist Janis Alcorn has identified and documented the mixed gardens carefully created and managed by Huastec farmers in Mexico, and anthropologist Eugene Anderson has documented rain-forest management practices in Mexico, particularly in the Mayan community of Quintana Roo. In Amazonia, research by anthropologists Darrell Posey and Bill Balée points to similar indigenous understandings and directed manipulations of forest ecosystems that people developed to provide themselves with a broader, more predictable range of plant and animal resources, at the same time creating more diverse habitats. These systems show that there is often little distinction between the "hunter-gatherer" lifestyle, in which people tend and manage their so-called wild resources, and the diversified agrarian lifestyle, in which people grow several associated crops and mix their use of domesticated species with a range of wild and partially wild resources.

We now recognize not an absolute division at all, but a continuum between hunting and gathering and agriculture, with a complex assortment of strategies that mix and match these methods in various ways. Indigenous peoples, such as those of British Columbia, who managed culturally important native resources usually did so by replicating or enhancing certain naturally occurring conditions. This may result in genetic simplification—reduction of the number of species—in some sites, but often actually increases overall species and habitat diversity by creating more edges and patches of habitats at different stages of ecological succession, all the way from recently cleared areas to dense old-growth forest. Unlike the single-crop fields of modern agriculture, or the clear-cuts and tree plantations of industrial forestry, these human-tended environments retain many diverse, culturally important species that co-exist in companionable associations. At a single location, one can expect to find trees, shrubs and herbaceous species, even epiphytes (plants that grow on other plants), which together provide the raw materials for people's food, technology and medicine. When people made their seasonal rounds, they would often find many useful resources at these culturally modified sites.

In the summer of 2000, I visited one such site with Adam Dick of the Kwakwaka'wakw. What an experience it was to travel by boat with Adam, Johnny Moon from Kingcome, Kim Recalma-Clutesi and Doug

Deur down to the estuary and the tidal flats of Kingcome Inlet, on the mainland coast of British Columbia. As we travelled in the channels among the islands that made up the delta, Adam stood in the boat and extended his arms, exclaiming, "There wasn't one square inch of this that wasn't part of our *t'ekilakw*!" *T'ekilakw* is the Kwak'wala word that means "place of manufactured soil" and pertains to the intensively cultivated root gardens of the tidal flats. Every part of these flats, now overgrown with grasses and sedges but still with patches of the original silverweed, clover and rice-root, was intensively managed in the old days.

Earlier, Adam had recalled tending the wild root vegetables with his mother and grandmother:

> It was all important. That *texwsus* [springbank clover], and the *tliksam* [Pacific silverweed], and the *q'weniỷ* [*Lupinus nootkatensis*, Nootka lupine], and the . . . *xukwem* [northern rice-root]. See, when they go down to the flats, they use little pegs, [which meant] "This is my area." You got your own pegs, in the flats. And then you continue on that, digging the soft ground . . . so it will grow better every year. Well, fertilizing, cultivating, I guess that's . . . the word for it. Every family had pegs, owned their little plots in the flats.

Daisy Sewid-Smith, though too young herself to have experienced these gardening methods, was told about them by her grandmother, Agnes Alfred. She noted how important a group's ownership of its resource-gathering areas was, and she also described how people would use short wooden pegs to mark off their gathering areas, including tidal flats for digging root vegetables, berry patches, clam beds and wild crabapple *(Pyrus fusca)* "orchards." She confirmed, "Anything that's pegged, you know it's someone's."

For the Kwakwa̲ka'wakw, as well as for Heiltsuk, Nuxalk, Haisla, Tsimshian, Haida and others, clans or lineage groups controlled hunting grounds, rivers, eulachon-fishing areas, salmon-fishing sites, crabapple "orchards," patches of many different types of berries—high-bush cranberries *(Viburnum edule)*, salal *(Gaultheria shallon)*, bog cranberries *(Vaccinium oxycoccus)*, red elderberries *(Sambucus racemosa)*, stink currants *(Ribes bracteosum)*, salmonberries *(Rubus spectabilis)* and huckleberries (*Vaccinium* spp.)—eelgrass beds *(Zostera marina)*, productive patches of root vegetables including those mentioned by Adam Dick, as well as sea milkwort *(Glaux maritima)* and "wild carrot" or Pacific hemlock-parsley *(Conioselinum pacificum)* and beds of different shellfish—clams, cockles, abalone, sea urchins, mussels (*Mytilus* spp.) and others. Chief Adam Dick's ancestors, for many generations back, were guardians of the eulachon, or candlefish, at Kingcome Inlet. It was the guardian's duty to keep a close eye on the river and ensure that the eulachon were spawning well before people were allowed to begin catching these fish on their return trip to the ocean.

For looking after their berry patches, Adam Dick described a similar level of attention and care:

A lot of people think we never touched the wild . . . berries. But we did. We cultivated it. We pruned it. . . . Especially that *gwadems* [*Vaccinium parvifolium,* red huckleberries], when they finished picking the *gwadems,* they pruned them. They break the tops off. Salmonberries [*Rubus spectabilis*] too. . . ."

MANAGING THE LAND THROUGH SUSTAINABLE HARVESTING

Another good example of "keeping it living" is from Haida Gwaii, where Sitka spruce *(Picea sitchensis)* roots and other materials are carefully harvested for the hats and tightly woven baskets for which the Haida are famous. My husband, Bob, and I first went to Haida Gwaii in 1970, and for me that was the beginning of a long and immensely satisfying learning journey. Haida Gwaii has always been a special place, the homeland to a people with an independent, creative spirit. Over the intervening years we made many friends among the Haida and other local residents. We stayed over one unforgettable summer with Nonnie Florence Davidson in Masset. We spent hours just watching her, helping as much as we could, as she went on gathering expeditions for berries and spruce roots for basketry, just as her mother, Isabella Edenshaw, had done before her.

We watched as Nonnie Florence and her sisters and daughters pulled the long spruce roots from the mossy forest floor. One of the key lessons we learned is <u>never to take too many roots from any one tree, or it will harm the tree</u>. If you take just a few roots from one tree and a few from another, the trees will recover easily and produce more roots in the following years. Many years later, I learned the same lessons in harvesting red-cedar roots with Lil'wat basket weavers Margaret Lester and Nellie Peters.

Nonnie tied the roots in bundles to "cook" over the campfire, or in the iron-barrel fireplace of her smokehouse. This was an art in itself because she had to be careful not to scorch the bark off, or the roots would be ruined. (The trick is to heat the roots just enough to soften the pitch in them, allowing the bark to peel off easily when the warm root is drawn through a split cedar stake.) Once the bark was removed, she carefully split the root, first dividing it exactly in half, vertically, using the tiny rootlets lined up along the bottom as a gauge for where to place the split. She had a way of holding the lower part of the root in place with her knees, providing just the right amount of tension while she worked her hands. Using her thumbs as guides, she would split the root in half more by feel than by sight. I've since watched this splitting technique of other basket-makers, and I have tried it myself; it is certainly not as easy as Nonnie made it look. Once the roots are split in half, the halves can be split again, and, depending on the size of the root, several other splits can be accomplished. Nonnie bundled the split roots, air-dried them and then stored them away to be soaked later and woven into beautiful, intricately twined hats and baskets.

Florence's daughters and granddaughters and several other families still make these beautiful works of art and, even more importantly, some have become teachers. April Churchill, for example, told the Skidegate people that the art of weaving had originated in their community and so she wanted to return the gift of weaving to the Skidegate people who wished to learn it, through lessons and workshops. Making these baskets and hats requires hundreds of roots, and considering the enormous numbers of baskets each household possessed in former times, the quantities of materials required would have been immense. Kat Anderson and Michelle Stevens have interviewed basket weavers and harvested basket materials in California; their research shows that basket weavers use enormous volumes of materials in their baskets and that tending basketry plants, coppicing and pruning them and continuously harvesting the roots ensured their productivity.

Bob and I also went with Nonnie Florence to harvest cedar bark from both red- and yellow-cedar. She took us to a stand of fairly young, straight-trunked trees with long unbranching sections in their lower trunk. Using a sharp knife, she cut partway around the circumference just below shoulder height, then carefully pried up the cut end of the bark. Once she had enough to grasp, she pulled the bark away from the tree, walking backwards as the strip was detached, becoming narrower and narrower until it made contact with the branches high in the crown. A firm jerk separated the strip and brought it to the ground. Immediately, Nonnie broke and cut off the brittle outer bark, leaving the soft, leathery inner bark appearing like creamy satin streaked with pink. This inner cedar bark can be split into two separate sheets, each of which is bundled and tied for transport. Like the split spruce roots, the cedar bark is dried and stored, to be taken out and used later when there is more time to weave, usually in the fall or winter after the growing season.

Later I went with my friends Barbara Wilson *(Kii7lljuus)*, Captain Gold and others from Skidegate to harvest cedar bark, and I was able to see first-hand the sustainability of the bark harvest. The young tree chosen by Captain Gold to provide a bark strip was standing next to another, still relatively young cedar from which, many years previously, someone had harvested a strip. A long, triangular scar going up the trunk was healing over around the edges, and the tree was obviously continuing to grow. One hundred years from now the tree will have completely concealed the scar, and, with luck, it will live and grow for many more centuries. Some of the big old cedars growing around Spirit Lake above Skidegate have scars indicating that bark sheets were removed, possibly in the mid-1800s, and they are still growing strong. These so-called culturally modified trees, or CMTs, are found up and down the Northwest Coast and are a testament both to the peoples' long-term occupation of these lands and to their care in looking after the trees and other resources which they use and for which they are responsible.

Nonnie let me try making my own basket of yellow-cedar bark. We worked together; she was weaving a flaring cedarbark hat while I

Culturally modified western red-cedar tree (Thuja plicata), *showing where a slab of bark was removed many years ago; Gitga'at Nation, Turtle Point, on the North Coast of British Columbia.*

struggled with my basket. She was patient and kind, helping me get started and showing me how to add strands and how to insert a row of three-stranded twining at the point where the basket bottom turned up to become the sides. The work was wonderful. It was hard on the fingers, and I just could not get the foundation pieces straight; the basket seemed to have a mind of its own. But I felt a beautiful rhythm in the weaving and experienced an intense, unexpected feeling of accomplishment when I finished my basket. I felt sheepish when I compared my crude creation to those of Nonnie and the other master weavers, but nonetheless I was proud of it. Mary Thomas summarized this feeling best. She said, "If you make something with your hands, you appreciate it, you look after it. You don't waste it." The experience was a good reminder that making something, and using your own skill and the materials at hand, can teach a person not just about skills and techniques but also about patience, about our interconnectedness and about the true value of the resources that we often take for granted.

MANAGING THE LAND THROUGH OWNERSHIP AND RESPONSIBILITY

An important aspect of managing resources is having some form of proprietorship over them, so that the time and effort in caring for them are returned to those who make the investment. All of the indigenous peoples of northwestern North America, as in other regions, have specific territories within which they have held the rights to harvest and use their resources. Many variations exist, but in general the rights to use lands and resources go hand in hand with some form of ownership.

For the Haida, the entire coastline of Haida Gwaii, especially the various rivers and streams, was traditionally divided among the different families. Many of these holdings are still recognized and validated. As well as stands of western red-cedar, primary berry-picking patches, root-digging grounds, patches of fireweed *(Epilobium angustifolium)*, fishing weirs, trapping sites and seabird nesting sites were all included as family or clan properties. As with the Kwakwaka'wakw, the boundaries of these different territories were sometimes indicated by placing poles along the perimeter or were denoted by distinctive landforms. Geologist George Dawson, later head of the Geological Survey of Canada, wrote in the 1870s, "Every lonely and wave-washed rock on which these birds [seagulls and other seabirds] deposit their eggs, is known to the [Haida] natives, who have even these, apportioned among the families as hereditary property."

For the Nuu-Chah-Nulth, linguist Edward Sapir described root-digging patches of the Alberni area from the early twentieth century:

A place for roots or berries was called *tlh'ayaqak*. These patches for roots or berries had four cedar stakes marking the boundaries of the area, which were about one acre in extent. The stakes were six feet high and called *tlh'ayaqiyaktlhama*. These posts were changed about every ten years to prevent rotting.

These patches would have been similar to the *t'ekilakw* described by Adam Dick and would have been tended and selectively harvested in a similar manner.

Among the Nuu-Chah-Nulth, chiefs were responsible for the well-being of the plants and animals on their lands as part of the very definition of ownership. Ethnographer Philip Drucker characterized the Nuu-Chah-Nulth concept of ownership as follows:

> The Nootkans [Nuu-Chah-Nulth] carried the concept of ownership to an incredible extreme. Not only rivers and fishing stations close at hand, but the waters of the sea for miles offshore, the land, houses, carvings on a housepost . . . names, songs, dances, medicines, and rituals, all were privately owned.

According to Earl Maquinna George, *hahuulhi* is the word used by hereditary chiefs of the Nuu-Chah-Nulth "for aboriginal right, ownership and territory." He continued, "It's a chief's role to hold that *hahuulhi* as a sacred right. Now today they call it aboriginal right." Chief Maquinna explained, "They had specific areas. They couldn't go beyond their own realm of boundary lines because . . . there were known places that marked off territorial area. There is a fine line between two nations. . . ." Historically, *hahuulhi* authority was passed on as a hereditary privilege. Rivers, fishing areas, hunting areas and plant-harvesting areas all were considered private property. In the past, it would have been unthinkable to violate a chief's *hahuulhi*: all areas, from the peaks and ridges of the Vancouver Island mountain range to the sweeping river valleys and coastal plains, to the west coast beaches and out to the distant halibut-fishing banks, were privately controlled by the chiefs and their representatives.

Hahuulhi means more than ownership, however. Nuu-Chah-Nulth cultural specialist Roy Haiyupis stressed that it carries with it a concept of responsibility: "*Ha hoolthe* [*hahuulhi*] . . . indicates . . . that the hereditary chiefs have the responsibility to take care of the forests, the land and the sea within his *ha hoolthe,* and a responsibility to look after his *mus chum,* or tribal members. . . . Embedded within the *ha hoolthe* initiated from [the chief's] rights to and ownership of tribal territories, lies the key to the

social and cultural practices, tribal membership and property ownership—economic, environmental and resource controls to . . . sustain life
for the tribe today and for generations to come."

These two aspects of land use and occupancy—proprietorship and responsibility—are critical elements within the same overall system. They
cannot be separated. Similar arrangements were in place, with their own
cultural variants, in indigenous societies everywhere. Leaders were indeed given special privileges, but they also bore the responsibility of ensuring continued health and well-being of both their lands and their
peoples.

The Gitxsan chiefs explained their beliefs about land ownership in
their introductory statements to the landmark *Delgamuukw* court case of
1989, in which the Gitxsan and Witsuwit'en peoples of the Skeena River
region of British Columbia defended their right to regain control of their
traditional lands and resources from the Crown:

> For us, the ownership of territory is a marriage of the Chief and the
> land. Each Chief has an ancestor who encountered and acknowledged
> the life of the land. From such encounters come power. The land, the
> plants, the animals and the people all have spirit—they all must be
> shown respect. That is the basis of our law. . . . By following the law,
> the power flows from the land to the people through the Chief; by using
> the wealth of the territory, the House feasts its Chief so he can properly
> fulfill the law. This cycle has been repeated on my land for thousands of
> years.

The Central Coast Salish had a similar system in which the chief, head
of a family or other designated leader held proprietorship of a given area.
Resource sites owned by family groups included camas beds, "wild carrot" patches, bracken fern rhizome sites, wapato patches, bog cranberry
areas, horse clam *(Tresus capax)* and butter clam beds, sites for duck nets
and sturgeon *(Acipenser transmontanus)* fishing, dip-net locations and certain fishing streams. Others might ask to harvest from these sites, but, at
least for the prime producing sites, they had to obtain permission before
they could do so.

Anthropologist Wayne Suttles described how this worked for the Katzie of the Fraser Valley:

> The bog south of the Alouette [River] belonged to all the Katzie; how-
> ever, other important cranberry areas north of Sturgeon Slough and
> along Widgeon Creek belonged specifically to Simon Pierre's father's
> family from Pitt Meadows. Outsiders had to seek permission from the
> owners before gathering cranberries in these locations, although appar-
> ently they were rarely denied permission, and no tribute was re-
> quired. . . . Use by outsiders was closely monitored by the family who
> owned an area. For example, it was the responsibility of Simon Pierre's
> father to watch the cranberry bogs and ensure that no one picked the
> berries until they were fully ripe. . . . At the head of Sturgeon Slough,
> families could establish seasonal claims to wapato plots. These areas
> (which might be several hundred feet long) would be cleared of other
> growth so that the wapato tubers might be more easily gathered.

For the Straits Salish—the Saanich, Samish, Songhees Esquimalt and Sooke—prime camas-harvesting locations were often privately owned and inherited. For example, the camas beds on Mandarte Island in Haro Strait were owned by three people, and the ones on an islet south of Sidney Island were owned by a single person.

Saanich elder Christopher Paul, of Tsartlip, shared his understandings of traditional camas harvest and management with anthropology student Marguerite Babcock in 1967. He said that a family group would establish a claim to a camas bed by clearing it, and once that was done it would "just naturally" become their plot to use. He thought that this clearing activity was done in the fall or spring before the gathering season. He reasoned that in those seasons the soil was soft from the heavy rains but not muddy (or frozen) as it would have been in the winter. Stones, weeds and brush, but not trees, would be removed from the plot, and the stones would be piled up in an area where no camas plants were growing. The brush would be piled to one side and left to rot or to be burned.

Chris Paul said that the bushes were actually uprooted, not just cut back, so that the camas were easy to dig. He himself grew enormous camas bulbs in his garden. He certainly combined his knowledge of gar-

Blue camas (Camassia quamash). PHOTO BY ROBERT D. TURNER

dening European-style with traditional production practices for these valuable bulbs. Until 1960, the Tsartlip people routinely burned areas of their ground, and although the camas are not as plentiful as they once were, they still bloom in abundance around his family's property.

MANAGING THE LAND FOR PRODUCTIVITY

Indigenous peoples consider that their actions are critical to maintaining their lands and resources, as Kat Anderson discovered in her work with Native Californians and anthropologist Kay Fowler learned in her research with the Paiute and Shoshoni peoples of Nevada and adjacent areas. The productivity of the land and the sea was not simply a random occurrence in which humans passively accepted their foods or endured hardship if the resources were not forthcoming. Far from it: In carefully monitoring and looking after their resources, in tending, weeding and burning over root gardens; in burning, pruning and even fertilizing their berry patches; in thinning out their clam beds and patches of basket "grasses"; in keeping their rivers clean and unpolluted, and in linking their lives directly to those of their ancestors and to the spirit world, they were—and are—participating in and contributing to the health and well-being of their territory, all the other life forms and to their own societies. This is a critical notion: giving back to Nature. It is a theme that constantly recurs in conversations with indigenous elders.

Daisy Sewid-Smith summarized the traditional perspective of her people:

> We completely depended on nature. The garments that we had, the house that sheltered us, the foods we ate, the medicines we had—Nature supplied it. And that is the reason why we respected nature as we did. Of course, many people say, "Oh, that's wonderful. You live off Nature and it must be wonderful. You don't have to do a thing—Nature does it all, right?". . . . People think that you don't have to do anything when you remove something from Nature. . . . And that is so far from the truth. Because, when you remove something, you have to put something back to make that plant, animal, fish, live again.

In the Interior Plateau country, the Nlaka'pmx, Okanagan, Stl'atl'imx and Secwepemc peoples held similar beliefs about the importance of tending their lands and resources. One Okanagan elder speaking at an indigenous science conference recalled that his people used to find an area in the hills where two creeks converged, then carefully burn over the area between the creeks, using the water as a firebreak. The first year after the fire there was plenty of fresh green grass and herbage, and the hunters could count on finding deer on the burn. A couple of years later, the berries grew thickly, and people gathered there to pick the fruit and socialize. Then, the young trees grew up and there was a rich mixture of herbaceous plants, shrubs and woodlands, where the people could get their fuel and construction material, and an assortment of other materials, foods and medicines. After a while they burned that spot again, and the whole cycle repeated itself.

These people looked on their harvesting practices as not only sustainable but actually restorative for the plants and animals and their habitats. For the edible roots, burning, digging and tilling the soil and breaking up the sod enhanced their growth and productivity. Sometimes, too, the people moved plants around from one area to another. In his thesis on Nlaka'pmx bitterroot use, Bob Bandringa reported that the roots were taken in baskets to replenish areas that had been depleted or to establish populations in new areas. Other culturally prescribed practices included selecting the edible roots of only the "female" (non-flowering or fruiting) plants of desert parsley *(Lomatium macrocarpum)* and leaving the "male" plants to reproduce; leaving the large "mother" plants of balsamroot *(Balsamorhiza sagittata)* that would produce thirty to fifty flower heads each and selecting only the younger carrot-sized daughter roots; digging glacier lily bulbs only after the leaves had turned yellow and the plants had gone to seed, then selecting only the large double- or triple-headed plants, and breaking off the branches of soapberry periodically to renew its growth over subsequent years. All these practices were said to promote the health of the plant populations and make them even more productive in the future.

Saskatoon berry is a particularly valuable species for the Interior peoples, and the bushes were often carefully tended. Mary Thomas recalled that her mother, Christine Allen, would look up at a tall, unkempt Saskatoon bush and say, "Yes. It's time to cut it back!" Then she would coppice the bush—cutting the thick, branching stems right back, almost to the ground. Mary said that the next year the bushes sprouted long, thin, unbranching shoots that were ideal for the rims of their birchbark baskets. They harvested some of these for this purpose, carefully forming them into hoops and wrapping the ends around to hold them in the right shape. Saskatoon wood, Mary explained, is tough and flexible, and it tends to grow in a spiral, so it is easy to form into a hoop. After a while the wood will keep its hoop shape, then it can be formed to the right size and

Saskatoon berries, or service berries (Amelanchier alnifolia).
PHOTO BY ROBERT D. TURNER

inserted into the top of the birchbark containers to be stitched in place with split cedar roots. This strengthens the basket immensely. (These same Saskatoon withes were used to help train infants, especially baby boys, almost from the time of birth. The sticks were placed into the clasping hands of the baby as it lay on its back, then gently pulled up, with soft, rhythmic, encouraging words: "Ooooh, boy! Ooooh, boy!" The baby, holding onto the stick, would develop its little muscles and become stronger and stronger through this technique.)

About two years after they were cut back, the Saskatoon bushes started to produce fruit again—with large, sweet and juicy, plump berries arranged in dense clusters that were easy to harvest. The bushes remained productive for quite a while after this. Eventually they would grow tall and bushy again, however, and their berry production would fall off; then it was time to cut them back again. Kept in this "young" state, the bushes will keep producing both withes and fruit for generations. Mary said people tended chokecherries *(Prunus virginiana)*, too. She remembers her father assembling a group of men to ride all around the Neskonlith reserve lands to check on the health of the chokecherry bushes, and she recalls the group pruning off or burning the tent caterpillar nests and generally looking after the bushes.

The old people would say that they were taught how to look after the land by the Creator and the Transformers, and all the other supernatural beings and even their human ancestors who used their powers and sacrificed themselves to provide for the people. The ceremonies, the words of praise, the discretion and the respect people have when they harvest their foods, materials and medicines, and the ways in which they tend their plants and salmon streams and talk to the young abalone . . . all of these, ultimately, are a part of the philosophy of Adam, Daisy, Mary, Helen and other indigenous people with traditional training.

Many of these attitudes and practices are being lost and forgotten as children are no longer raised with these experiences or understandings. This is one of the reasons, the elders say, why the productivity of the lands and waters is declining. Today, they say, many people no longer recognize their responsibilities to the land, and they only take from it, without giving back.

Chief Earl Maquinna George, HawiiH of Ahousaht.

PHOTO BY ROBERT D. TURNER

7

Everything

Is ONE

INDIGENOUS UNDERSTANDINGS of the natural world are like a story with many interdependent plots that are so intertwined it is difficult to know where the beginning is, or how to bring the story to a fitting close while recognizing that it continues into the future. For me, the phrase that best encapsulates this idea is the one that became the motto of the Scientific Panel for Sustainable Forest Practices in Clayoquot Sound: *Hishuk ish Ts'awalk,* which translates approximately as "everything is one." This motto reminded the panel of the Nuu-Chah-Nulth understanding that mirrors but is even more comprehensive than the concept of ecology, the interconnectedness of everything around us, cultural and ecological, past and future, and of the profound implications of these linkages and interrelationships.

In the previous chapters, I have used different but related themes to focus on humans' interdependence with the environment and how indigenous peoples in a particular region, northwestern North America, have developed world views, philosophies and approaches that have directed them towards behaviours and practices that respect and sustain the environment. How do all of these ideas fit together? How do they all work? In western society generally, we tend to compartmentalize our thinking and the ways in which we approach our work. We are governed through ministries or departments: the Ministry of Forests, for example, or the Ministry of Human Resources. Similarly, we divide our academic institutions into departments: Biology, Chemistry, Engineering, Political Science, Psychology and so forth. It is, indeed, a natural inclination of humans to divide the world into cognitive parts so that we can think about them more clearly, classify them, then communicate about them, in other words to "get our minds around them." If we try to think about everything together, the world becomes overwhelming and too complicated. The problem is that the world *is* overwhelming and complicated, and if we simplify our knowledge systems too much, without making an effort to recognize them as enduring parts of an enormous whole, we do ourselves and our environments serious harm.

Links between the Forest and the Sea

Western society separates forestry and fisheries into different administrative and academic units. In British Columbia, this compartmentalization has resulted in widespread and ongoing decline of wild salmon populations, at least in part through habitat destruction. In the past, loggers routinely used rivers and creeks to transport cut timber to collection locations along the shoreline. Nuu-Chah-Nulth hereditary Chief Earl Maquinna George, who as a young man worked for a logging company at Tahsis on the west coast of Vancouver Island, remembers well the destruction of the Tahsis River that was then routine:

> At the time, the logging operations at Tahsis were six miles up the Tahsis River. It was one of the places where I found the early evidence of environmental damage to the fish stream. Logs were dragged by a bulldozer along the river bed. For many years the operation used the river as a road. And there was a dump at the bottom end of the river where the logging truck dumped its logs. The road was the river so that anything that went downstream went down the river. . . . The Tahsis sockeye and

chum runs were pretty well ruined by that logging. And you can imagine what little is left there now after over fifty years of operation. . . .

For some reason, the loggers didn't make the connection between their activities and the impacts they had on salmon-spawning creeks, or they concluded that their impact wasn't important in a land of limitless resources. However, similar destruction occurred up and down the coast. The reality was that hundreds of streams and rivers were damaged by logging. Sometimes the loggers mined the gravel from the salmon-spawning beds to use in road construction. Or they felled the trees right to the edge of the water, changing the water temperature and nutrient regime for the young salmon fry. Logs and debris filled the creeks and choked them, making it impossible for the returning salmon to get up the river to spawn. It took many years for the government officials overseeing the forestry and the fisheries to coordinate their efforts and to implement regulations to protect the rivers. By this time, the salmon populations had plummeted.

Along the coast, indigenous people—and many non-indigenous fishers as well—could see the destruction caused by logging; they understood that the salmon streams had to be protected and that you couldn't separate what was done in the forest from what happened in the rivers, or even in the oceans. Kwakwaka'wakw cultural specialist Daisy Sewid-Smith's family, who were fishers, knew well what was happening to the fish due to logging practices. Daisy recalled:

One of the major concerns that they [the old people] had was the removal of trees that grow along the river—the riverbanks. And they said that if they continued to remove those trees along the riverbank, the waters of the river are going to warm up and we are going to lose the salmon. And they said, "Salmon will not go into warm waters." And it's very true. I come from a fishing family, all my life. That's all I knew was fishing. I went out to sea with my father, my brother and eventually my late husband. And when the sockeye was ready to come in, and if it was really, really hot, my father would say to my husband, "Salmon's going to come through the north, not through the west coast." And he was always right. And I'd ask him, "Why, why do you know this?" And he would say, "Because the west coast—it's too hot there. The salmon will not come in if it is too hot." So those were some of the things they said. The removal of the trees is very bad for the rivers. And that is exactly what they've done with a lot of the rivers.

Stanley Sam, Nuu-Chah-Nulth elder with the Clayoquot scientific panel, described a situation in which logging practices had a direct impact on the herring populations:

And we come to a place called *tanaknit* [Steamer Cove, northwest of Flores Island]. . . . And it had a lot of disturbance. Logging was there for a few years. And it was a dumping ground for logging. And herring never goes back in there any more because there was so much bark and different things in the bottom of the ocean. And that destroyed what the spawners . . . spawned on [eelgrass and kelps].

Industrial logging has also been seen as a destructive force against wildlife, as noted by Pacheedaht Chief Charlie Jones in his autobiography, *Queesto:*

Ever since logging came, there's been no more deer or wolf or elk or beaver. They've all disappeared. Maybe they've been killed off, or maybe they've just moved on to somewhere else. We don't know where the animals have gone.

More recently, scientific research has demonstrated the impacts of forest practices and the close links between the forest and the ocean. Gordon Hartman, a fisheries biologist, and Mike Church, a hydrologist, both members of the Clayoquot scientific panel, informed the other panel members about some of the findings of a major research project at Carnation Creek, near Barkley Sound on the west coast of Vancouver Island. Over three decades, their research team studied the effects of logging on fisheries, and Gordon explained how the impacts of forest practices were cumulative over time and space and therefore not easily identified. For example, removing the trees lining the creek caused the water to warm, which initially caused the coho salmon fry to multiply and mature rapidly. The salmon grew quickly, and as young smolts they left their home stream for life in the ocean. It was only after four years, when hardly any of these fry returned to the creek, that the researchers realized something was wrong. Apparently, the fry had grown too fast, had left their home stream and entered the ocean too early, and had not survived the rigours of life in the ocean. If the research hadn't continued over this longer time period, this remote effect would not have been detected.

Another finding was that the fry emerging from a particular section of the creek were all very small. Further investigation showed that larger hatchlings existed, but that the gravel beds were so choked with silt from logging and road-building runoff that the larger fry had been trapped in the gravel and were unable to make their way out into the open water. Again, if the investigators hadn't taken the trouble to dig into the gravel they would not have noticed this indirect impact.

Another fascinating modern confirmation of *Hishuk ish ts'awalk* is the work of Tom Reimchen of the biology department at the University of Victoria. He has demonstrated how many nutrients are moved between the ocean and the giant trees of the coastal temperate rain forests of the central and north coast of British Columbia. While observing bears at night, he saw them catching salmon from spawning streams on Haida Gwaii and along the central and north coast of British Columbia. More importantly, he recorded the bears dragging carcasses of spawning salmon into the forest and leaving them, partially eaten, on the forest floor. These carcasses, he found, were actually helping to nourish the growing trees of the coastal rain forest. He discovered that a heavy nitrogen isotope called ^{15}N, which is usually found only in deepwater marine ecosystems, occurs in their wood. This shows that the forest has benefited from the salmon fertilizer introduced by bears.

Traditionally, First Nations *lived* this interconnectedness between their landscapes and resources, relying fully on all of the components and their associations simultaneously. West coast fishing technology is a good example of how such connections work: To harvest the halibut, black cod and other fish from the ocean a complex array of materials was required, as well as important skills and technologies.

The circle of linkages can start with sword fern *(Polystichum munitum)*, an attractive dark-green fern that grows in clumps in the rich, moist soils of coastal forests. Its coarse, pointed leaflets are arranged along both sides of the central stalk in a featherlike formation, and each leaflet, or *pinna,* is attached to the stalk at a single point at its base. Sword fern is called the *pila pila* plant in several languages around southern Vancouver Island and the adjacent mainland. *Pila* indicates "one," and it refers to a contest whose purpose, as explained to me by Ditidaht elder John Thomas, was to train young men to hold their breath for a long time. The young male contestants were each handed a sword-fern frond. Each participant started at one side of the base of the frond, pulling off the leaflets one at a time and saying "*pila*" with each one. The challenge was to see how many leaflets could be taken from the frond all in one breath.

To be able to hold your breath for a long time was important for those training to be divers. The most successful contestants—the toughest and most hardy—were the ones chosen to dive deep into the ocean to cut the tough, deep-growing stalks of bull kelp *(Nereocystis luetkeana)* from special locations where they grew long and supple. (Fishers used these kelp stems to make their fishing lines. The stems had to be alternately soaked, dried, twisted and rubbed with dogfish or some other kind of oil, until their tissues were completely saturated with oil. This process took as long as a year to produce the best lines.)

The same young men who were trained to hold their breath went out on the whaling canoes, and when a whale was harpooned and killed they dived down into the water to tie the whale's mouth shut so it wouldn't sink when it was being towed to shore. The sword fern, through this unlikely route, therefore helped First Nations obtain the marine food.

Fish hooks and fishing lures also inextricably linked the forest with the sea. There are many different styles of fish hooks, as well as lures, and all were originally fashioned from wood. Pacific yew wood *(Taxus brevifolia)* was commonly used to make fish hooks because it is such a tough material. It was also prized for making bows, root-digging sticks, wedges, halibut clubs and many other implements that would be subjected to stress and pressure. One particularly ingenious style of fish hook, still mimicked in the metal hooks that trollers and halibut fishers use today, is a bentwood hook. These U-shaped hooks were fashioned either from yew wood, moulded and bent into a U, or from the dense knotwood of western hemlock *(Tsuga heterophylla)*, Douglas-fir *(Pseudotsuga men-ziesii)* and other forest trees. Knotwood comes from the trunk of the tree where the wood has grown around the ends of the branches. (Watch a tree in the wind and you will understand the levering pressure to which the bases of branches are subjected; they have to be tough and flexible.) This kind of wood is called, aptly, "stress wood."

My Ditidaht friend and teacher John Thomas demonstrated the hook-making process when we were camped out on the beach at Whyac with him in 1979. This small but important village site at the mouth of Nitinat Lake on the west coast of Vancouver Island is very near Clo-oose, where John was born.

John sought several long, heavy, dagger-like tree knots, each about twenty-five centimetres or longer, from a rotten hemlock log on the forest floor inland from the beach. With his sharp knife he split the dense knots vertically into three or four lengths each, depending on the original size of the knot: the bigger the knot, the more lengths it would yield. He shaved away the extra wood from each piece until it was even in width, rounded on one side and slightly flattened on the other. Then he found a fresh, hollow, bulblike bull-kelp float, and he cut the stipe (the long, hollow stalk) to make an elongated kelp bottle slightly longer than the carved tree-knot lengths. He inserted three knotwood lengths into the kelp bulb, poured in a little water, then sealed the hole at the top with a wooden plug. Then he buried the entire bulb with its contents in the hot sand beside the fire, moving some of the ashes directly overtop. He kept the fire smouldering overnight by banking it with wood. In the morning he removed the kelp, still warm, from the sand and pulled out the moist, warm lengths of knotwood. Properly steamed, the knot-wood lengths were flexible when tested on his knee and could be easily moulded into the proper oxbow shape—like a U but with the ends slightly constricted, then flared out. This bending stage is very tricky; the wood has to be just right—moist, warm and flexible—to bend it to the proper shape. Once bent and allowed to cool and dry, the hook will keep its shape. John explained that the bent piece is fitted with a barb, lashed on with split cedar root or spruce root. Attached to the top is a leader of stinging-nettle twine.

Many people know stinging nettle *(Urtica dioica)* well because of its stinging properties. However, coastal First Peoples also valued it as a supremely useful and versatile plant whose stems yield a tough fibre that has many applications, especially in fishing technology. In fact, indigenous peoples—including indigenous Europeans—have used stinging-nettle fibre for thousands of years to make cordage, fishing line, fishnets and, in Europe, even a linen-like fabric. Stinging nettle grows from branching rhi-zomes, or underground stems, and forms extensive patches, preferring moist, rich soil in partial shade such as at the forest's edge. Stinging nettle is ready for harvesting when it is fully mature in the late summer and early fall—just as the first snows dust the mountaintops. Since people cut the stalks after the seeds are produced, and because the nettle also has the capacity to regenerate from its rhizomes, the crop renews itself every year. (Other materials that people harvest similarly include leaves of slough sedge, or basket sedge *[Carex obnupta]*, for twined baskets; cattail leaves *[Typha latifolia]* and stalks of tule, or round-stem bulrush *[Schoenoplectus acutus;* syn. *Scirpus acutus]*, for mats and mattresses; and, in the Interior, Indian-hemp stems *[Apocynum cannabinum]* for cordage, fabric and fishing nets.) On the Northwest Coast, people tended their stinging-nettle patches and sometimes transplanted stinging nettle from one village site to another, to have access to the best-quality patches.

To make twine, women split the stinging-nettle stems in half and partially dry them, then remove the tough fibrous outer part from the brittle and pithy inner stem. Next, they dry the fibres and work them with their hands or draw them over a wooden paddle until the strands are soft and supple. To produce the basic twine, each rolls the fibres on a bare leg, using deft, repeated movements that bring two strands—each twisted in one direction—together in an opposite twist to yield a two-ply twine so strong that two men can play tug-of-war with it without breaking it. For making nets, the men roll a five-ply twine from single twisted strands that the women prepare. Sometimes women spin the strands together using a hand-held spindle with a plate-like disk slid over the spindle stick to hold the twine as it is produced.

The "leader" of stinging-nettle twine, to which the fish hook is attached, is fastened to a crosspiece of yew wood, balanced at the other end with another fish hook, also attached to a line, and a short central

Stinging nettle (Urtica dioica).

nettle-twine anchor line is attached to a stone weight. The long, flexible kelp line, already cured, is also attached to the centre of the yew wood crosspiece. The entire ingenious device is lowered to the ocean bottom from the cedar canoe—itself a product of the old-growth forest eco-system—and the two hooks, baited with pieces of octopus, are swept sideways or upwards in the current, providing a tasty-looking and -smelling lure for a halibut. For really deep water, fishers could tie two or more lengths of kelp line together using a fisherman's knot. John said that when the halibut or other large fish opens its mouth, it actually draws the baited hook right into its mouth with the vacuum it creates.

The sword-fern/kelp/tree knot/stinging-nettle/halibut connection is just one example of how people creatively merged their resources, drawing from different ecosystems simultaneously to sustain themselves over generations.

The bull kelp was used for more than ocean-oriented activities. Adam Dick described how his people, the Kwakwaka'wakw, buried the long, hollow stalks, or stipes, in the dirt floor of the dance house at the time of their winter ceremonials. One end of the stipe was left exposed outside the wall of the dance house; the other end resurfaced in the centre of the fireplace in the middle of the house. With this arrangement in place, someone could crouch outside the house during the spiritual dances and, by singing or shouting into the kelp mouthpiece, could give the impression of a spirit voice coming from the fire. Obviously this enhanced the drama and impact of the dances for those witnessing them. The Kwakwaka'wakw and other Northwest Coast people are skilled performing artists, and the winter dances, sacred and spiritual as they are, are products of immense theatrical prowess.

People also used bull-kelp stipes, cured with oil or simply allowed to dry, to store eulachon grease or other kinds of fish oil and, later, during the trade era, to store molasses. The stipes, though narrow, can be filled for a considerable length and can hold several litres of liquid. If tied or plugged at the end, the tubular containers can be coiled and hung up with their contents for later use.

From the forest to the ocean, from the ocean to the forest, coastal peoples' lives—both physical and spiritual—were constantly and inextricably intertwined with the lands and waters of their home places. To assume that people could easily live only from the sea or only from a small fragment of their lands was to ignore this primary and fundamental feature of their lives.

Links between the River Bottom and the Mountaintops

Interior peoples' ties to all parts of their territories—from the river valleys to the mountaintops—were extensive and strong. For them, too, everything in their lives was, and still is, interconnected: The different landscapes and waterways that sustained their ancestors are as critical as ever to their well-being and their very survival. The Xaxl'ep community of the Stl'atl'imx, or Lillooet, Nation is a good example. Their homeland, which they call their "survival territory," extends from the Fraser River—where their forebears have fished for spring salmon, sockeye and coho since time immemorial—east and north into the Fountain Valley and the surrounding mountains, as far as the upper reaches of the Hat Creek Valley including territory shared with their Secwepemc neighbours there.

The main Xaxl'ep community is situated at Fountain, a small settlement on a bench above the Fraser River just north of Lillooet. There, the narrow Highway 99 (previously Highway 12) winds along the canyon from Lytton at the confluence of the Thompson and Fraser Rivers (where Simon Fraser and his men were hosted so ceremoniously) to Lillooet, then on to Fountain and Pavilion, and through Marble Canyon to near Cache Creek. It is a modern overlay of the Cariboo Wagon Road, which was built during the gold rush days to transport miners and supplies to the Cariboo goldfields. Long before the gold rush, however, this track was an ancient trade route traversed by the Xaxl'ep and neighbouring peoples for probably thousands of years. Along this same route, between Fountain and Pavilion *(Ts'kw'áylaxw)* where it traverses Keatley Creek, is a major archaeological site, a large and impressive pit-house village occupied probably by distant ancestors of the Xaxl'ep for generations.

We can tell a lot about the ways of life and the beliefs of the Keatley Creek people by looking at what they left behind. Excavations have revealed that they lived in semi-underground houses, called pit houses, that were usually round, with circular, shallow, cone-shaped roofs constructed of logs overlain with a series of smaller-diameter poles, which were covered with pine needles or bunch grass and a layer of Douglas-fir boughs and claylike soil. (This style of winter house was used by the Interior Plateau peoples from all over what is now southern British Columbia, northern Washington and adjacent areas. In fact, anthropologists consider the use of winter pit houses to be a defining characteristic of the Plateau Culture Area. As late as the turn of the twentieth century, people still occupied these houses in some places.) In the centre of the roof was the entranceway, which also served as a smoke hole for the central hearth. A notched log extended down into the living area, where there were platforms for sleeping and sitting and scaffolding for storage along the wall. Further storage was provided by pits dug into the floor of the house and lined with pine needles or sheets of bark, or conveniently located outside the house.

Archaeologist Brian Hayden, with students and colleagues, has done most of the research and excavation work at Keatley Creek, in collaboration with the Ts'kw'áylaxw and Xaxl'ep communities. One of the houses Brian and his team investigated had an inside storage pit in the floor that was full of salmon backbones, probably remains of dried pink salmon, which were approximately 1,200 to 1,500 years old.

Depending upon the size of the house—which reflected in part on the social status and wealth of the owner—several families might dwell in such a structure during the winter months. Although it would have been cramped inside, people would have remained safe and warm in this shelter. They might have ventured out onto the pit-house roof, if the weather allowed, to process their basketry materials or to make their fishing lines and dip nets. There would have been plenty of activity, even in winter— basket-making, visiting back and forth, storytelling and instructing the children. Family groups would have made plans for the coming year and reminisced about past travels and experiences.

At the very hint of spring—when the little shiny yellow sagebrush buttercups *(Ranunculus glaberrimus)* bloomed among the big sagebrush and bunch grasses and patches of snow—people would have started on their seasonal round. This annual pattern of travel would have taken them down to the river to fish for the first spring salmon of the year, then led them up to the mountain peaks to hunt and to seek spiritual guidance and support, with stops at various locations in between. This movement from one resource-rich area to another continued over the entire growing season, ending only when winter set in again around November. Each year the timing of the moves might be different, depending on the weather conditions. People watched for local signs, such as the blooming of the sagebrush buttercup, whose name, *skwexmalus,* translates as "spring salmon eye" (compare with *skwexem,* spring salmon). The eye of the first run of spring salmon is yellowish, like the buttercup, and the buttercup helps remind people about the salmon's arrival. The second run of spring salmon arrives later, when the wild roses are blooming; these fish have a reddish stripe down their side, the colour of the wild rose *(keĺkaż)*, and are called *keĺksulh* after this flower. Still later, the melting of distinctive snow patches or the loud clicking noise of grasshoppers signifies the arrival of other runs of salmon.

Like their descendants, the Keatley Creek people would have named the moons by the different activities and occurrences that took place during the relevant time. Although they might have travelled to a certain place mainly for a particular type of resource—sockeye salmon at the river, spring beauty corms *(Claytonia lanceolata)* in the montane meadows, or huckleberries and blueberries (*Vaccinium membranaceum, V. caespitosum*, dwarf mountain blueberry) among the trees up near the treeline—they would have been harvesting and processing many different important foods, materials and medicines at each place or type of habitat. On the river bench close to the village, they would have found the sweet-tasting bulbs of the mariposa lily *(Calochortus macrocarpus)* and wild nodding onions *(Allium cernuum)*, which still grow today all over the Keatley Creek site. They would also have found prickly-pear cactus (*Opuntia* spp.), which they relished as a green vegetable once the spines were singed off and the stems barbecued for a short time and peeled. Big sagebrush *(Artemisia tridentata)* and its small cousin northern wormwood *(Artemisia frigida)*, which have intensely aromatic essential oils, were valued as medicines, especially for respiratory ailments. The people would have picked Saskatoon berries *(Amelanchier alnifolia)*—usually the first fruits to ripen, beginning in June—around their village and down towards the river, and again later on in the higher country as the fruit ripened there. Men valued Saskatoon wood for their arrow shafts and women, for crafting digging sticks. They also would have harvested such woods as Rocky Mountain juniper *(Juniperus scopulorum)* for bows, Rocky Mountain maple *(Acer glabrum)* for snowshoes, and mock orange *(Philadelphus lewisii)* for mat-making needles. In moister sites along the creek, they would have found the tender green bud stalks and leaf stalks of cow parsnip *(Heracleum lanatum)*, which would be ready to be peeled and eaten fresh, and the birches *(Betula papyrifera)* and cottonwood *(Populus balsamifera* ssp. *trichocarpa)*, whose bark sheets would be ready to cut off and fashion into containers and liners for their storage pits.

Some people would have ventured up into the mountains by late spring, when the inner bark of the lodgepole pine *(Pinus contorta* var. *latifolia)* was ready for harvesting and some of the root vegetables, such as spring beauty *(Claytonia lanceolata)* and balsamroot *(Balsamorhiza sagittata)*, were at their prime for digging. People would have stayed at a harvesting place for many days in order to procure and process their food supplies for the year. They generally chose a camping place at the edge of the woods, next to a creek for a ready water supply. Not only food but medicines and materials—cedar roots and maple bark for basketry, Engelmann spruce *(Picea engelmannii)* and lodgepole-pine pitch and possibly devil's club *(Oplopanax horridum)* and Indian hellebore root *(Veratrum viride)* for medicine—were gathered at each site. They might also fish for trout and hunt grouse and other game. These harvesting expeditions would have been enjoyable times for all and important times for children to observe and practise the skills and techniques they would need for survival.

They would have learned how to start a fire, which fuels to use and which ones to avoid. They would have learned teamwork and co-operation, respect and appreciation, and the pleasure of fulfilling responsibilities and contributing to the well-being of the family and community. The women would have supported each other, helping to look after all the children and enjoying the pleasure and company of their friends and relatives. Elder Edith O'Donaghey, who experienced such a lifestyle in her younger years, looked back on the days she spent camping in the mountains with her own family and other, related families, as the happiest time of her life. She said that each family had its own fireplace, but all were close enough together to keep in constant touch. In the evenings, everyone would congregate at one place or another and tell stories, sometimes the same stories over and over, until all the children knew them by heart.

Different runs of salmon come up the Fraser River over the summer months, so the families would have returned to the river fishing sites before long to take advantage of this important food. There at the river camps the men would have fished with long dip nets fashioned from the sapling wood of Douglas-fir *(Pseudotsuga menziesii)*, with strong netting of Indian-hemp string. The Indian hemp would have been harvested from

Wild-dried salmon from Fraser River near Lillooet.

the moist swales and seepage zones near the river and the fibres processed into string and fashioned into nets during the winter months. The women would have cut the fish along the backbone with deft strokes, removing the insides, carefully setting aside the eggs or milt, and the heads, and leaving the two sides, still with skin on, attached at the tail. First, they scored the flesh right down to but not into the skin using close, parallel cuts, inserted spreading sticks crosswise to prevent the flesh from curling up, then hung the fish to dry in the constant hot summer winds that swept—and still sweep—down the river gorge. They would have built drying shelters, as people still do today, to keep the direct sun from the salmon as it quickly gave up its moisture and dried into deep-red, striated tilelike sheets of concentrated protein. Salmon was worth its weight far more than the gold in the river gravel that people were to struggle after in later centuries. The women would have dried the eggs and milt, and the heads as well, or slowly cooked them with fire-heated rocks in basins hollowed out from the bedrock, until the fish yielded their rich, reddish oil. This oil could be stored in containers made from the salmon skins themselves.

At a much later time, when Simon Fraser and his men came down the river and stopped at various places in the vicinity they were offered, in variation, dried berries, dried roots including onions, and dried salmon and salmon oil.

By midsummer the Keatley Creek people would have travelled back up into the mountains, camping in family groups and picking great numbers of wild raspberries *(Rubus idaeus)*, blackcaps *(R. leucodermis)*, thimbleberries *(R. parviflorus)*, strawberries *(Fragaria* spp.), soapberries *(Shepherdia canadensis)*, gooseberries *(Ribes* spp.) and huckleberries, as well as different varieties of Saskatoon berries. They would also have harvested more spring beauty, onions, tiger lily bulbs and other edible root vegetables. They would have processed and dried the berries and roots right on site because, without horses or other forms of transportation except possibly dogs for carrying some supplies, the produce would have been too heavy and too perishable to bring back fresh to the winter village. By the time the people returned to the village, the chokecherries *(Prunus virginiana)* would have been ripening: two different varieties, one dark and one bright red. Depending on their success at harvesting other berries, the women might also have picked quantities of black hawthorn berries *(Crataegus douglasii)* to knead and dry into cakes. These berries, because of their large seeds and insipid flavour, were not always sought, but the bushes were invariably productive, and so they provided a "backup" in case of a poor year for Saskatoon berries or other fruit. Kinnikinnick berries *(Arctostaphylos uva-ursi)*, too, were useful in times of food scarcity, because the fruit remains on their low-growing plants over the winter. People could find the berries, like the cactus, even under the snow, and they could bring valued sustenance in times of shortage. At other times people enjoyed kinnikinnick berries fried in grease until crispy, as a snack food. They also knew that grouse and bears favoured these berries, so they played an important role in hunting as well.

In the fall, the people would have ventured into the mountains again in search of other products of the high elevations, such as black tree lichen *(Bryoria fremontii)* and white-bark pine seeds *(Pinus albicaulis)*, and to hunt the deer fattened on buckbrush *(Ceanothus velutinus)*, false box *(Paxistima myrsinites)* and other known favourite forage shrubs of the upland ranges. The men would work in small teams, herding the deer into narrow canyons or places where it was difficult for them to manoeuvre. Such places were well known to hunters and were used for many generations; some are still used today.

The occupants of the Keatley Creek village 2,000 to 4,000 years ago probably trod along many of the same pathways as the contemporary Xaxl'ep. Until just a couple of generations ago, their lifeways were similar. For example, the Keatley Creek people processed their food—probably wild nodding onions, balsamroot and other root vegetables—in earth ovens just as the Xaxl'ep people did in the childhood days of my friend Sam Mitchell, who was born on 2 June 1894 near a fishing camp by the Fraser River and raised at *Xaxl'ep*. Sam's son through custom adoption, Art Adolph, still lives in the community with his family. I worked with Sam in the early 1970s, and he was a lively and skilled man, truly a fountain of knowledge as well as a great storyteller. As a young man he drove mule teams along the Cariboo Road, taking supplies to 100 Mile House, Quesnel and other locations up the Fraser River route.

Sam showed me just how the total landscape and the Xaxl'ep people were linked together, from the river bottoms to the mountaintops in the Interior Plateau, for more than 2,500 years. Sam knew all the plants that the Xaxl'ep ate and how to harvest and prepare them. In early May 1977, my friend Adrienne Aikins, a photographer, and I travelled with Sam around the Xaxl'ep territory and he showed us many different plants and how to gather them. He showed us five distinct varieties of Saskatoon berry, which he identified by size, colour, seediness, juiciness and taste, as well as by habitat and size of bush. Each one had a name: the "real/ original" Saskatoon, the "sweet" Saskatoon, the little "white-white" Saskatoon, the "red Saskatoon" and the "rotten Saskatoon." Sam also demonstrated how to peel and eat the bud stalks of the balsamroot, whose insides are sweet and crunchy and somewhat reminiscent of sunflower seeds in flavour. Then he showed us how to pry up the big taproots of the balsamroot and how to pound them to loosen the rough outer "bark," and he told us how people cooked them for a long time in underground pits to make them sweet and edible.

Sam also talked about nodding onions. He called them "barbecuing onions"; their name in the Lillooet language (Stl'atl'imx-ts), *kwelawa 7ul,* translates as "real/original onions." It contrasts with "poison onions," or death camas *(Zigadenus venenosus)*, and "sweet onions," or mariposa lily *(Calochortus macrocarpus)*. Sam described how they dug quantities of nodding onions before they flowered in the spring, braided their leaves together to make long mat-like strings and then laid these in the cooking pit, sometimes over masses of soaked, kneaded black tree lichen (the food originating from Coyote's hair braid in the Okanagan story recounted earlier). This lichen, once properly cooked, resembles black licorice, but without onion or some other kind of flavouring its taste is bland. People all over the Interior Plateau region pit-cooked the lichen, dried it and cut it up into cakes. Then they cooked it in soups and stews in the wintertime.

Sam made me a digging stick, which I still have, a simple but ingenious tool made from a mule deer antler. The largest prong forms the pointed end, and the main stem of the antler is cut off at either end to make a horizontal handle. For countless generations, root harvesters— usually women—used implements like this to pry out and dig up onions, spring beauty, desert parsley *(Lomatium macrocarpum)* and other edible roots. People also fashioned these digging sticks from hard wood, such as Saskatoon wood or oceanspray *(Holodiscus discolor)*, which is actually called "digging-stick plant" in the Stl'atl'imx language. A more recent type of digging stick is made with the tine of an old-fashioned hay rake, fitted with a wooden handle of Saskatoon or some other hard wood. Handles of digging sticks like these, dating back at least 2,500 years, have been found in archaeological sites in the area near Keatley Creek.

Sam took us up to Pavilion Mountain, where he demonstrated how to find and pry out the little brown, spherical corms of the spring beauty, using the digging stick he had made. The lands where he and his family used to camp and dig these roots were, as they are today, part of a big cattle ranch. The ground is trampled by horses and cattle, especially in the moist places, and there are many introduced weeds. The spring beauty and other wild plants do not grow as abundantly or as productively as they used to. Even so, I will never forget seeing the vast meadows, almost as far as the eye could see, covered with blooming spring beauty. They resembled snowfields in winter or a kind of earthly Milky Way. Short weeks after flowering the plants go to seed, and the leaves start to turn

Spring beauty, or mountain potato (Claytonia lanceolata).

yellow and die back so quickly that by midsummer it is hard to know the spring beauty has been there at all.

We also tested the lodgepole pine to see if the cambium—the edible growing layer between the bark and the wood, together with the undeveloped inner bark tissue—was ready to be scraped. Sam explained that there is a period of only a few weeks when the pine's outer bark, when cut through to the wood, comes away easily because the cambium is soft, moist and thick. This is the time of year when the tree is growing the fastest. Using an implement fashioned from a tin can, cut from the curved part of the can with a section of the rim left to hold onto, Sam demonstrated how to scrape off long ribbons of the soft, juicy cambium and inner bark tissue. (The original cambium-harvesting implement was made from the thin shoulder-blade bone of a deer.) Back in his youth and that of Edith O'Donaghey, a Stl'atl'imx elder originally from Shalalth on Seton Lake, this favourite food was still harvested routinely. Edith recalled that her father would sometimes collect a bucketful of inner pine bark while he was hunting. When he arrived home, even if it was midnight, he would make everyone get up and come and eat it, because it has to be eaten fresh. They would sprinkle a little sugar on the whitish, somewhat gelatinous food, then eat it at once so that it did not lose its flavour or start to ferment.

The legacy of Keatley Creek village and its inhabitants remains, although the village site now resembles a congregation of craters—circular pits of various sizes, some overlapping—each defining the original extent of a pit house, long since burned or rotted and collapsed and filled in. This and other ancient village and camping sites provide the people of today with a sense of continuity and oneness with their homelands. Though many things have changed, the original threads are still there. For example, the Xaxl'ep and their neighbours continue to go down to the river every summer to fish for sockeye and the other salmon species, wind-drying the fish on the very sites that have been used for thousands of years since their ancestors moved into the benches near the river after the melting of the glaciers. Nowadays people sometimes freeze or bottle the salmon for winter use, but the wind-dried ones are still the most prized.

Archaeologist Brian Hayden and his students excavated several large hearths or earth ovens between 1986 and 1996. Like the digging-stick handles and rolls of birchbark from this site, they confirmed a continuity of culture and use of the landscape and its resources from around 3,000 or 4,000 years ago up to the twentieth century. Several years ago, my students and I participated in a rebirth of pit-cooking at Xaxl'ep. Elder Maggie Adolph was in her mid-eighties at the time, but as a little girl she had helped her mother gather the large stones used in their cooking pit. Under Maggie's direction, a large pit was dug in the ground near the cemetery at Xaxl'ep. Maggie (who had lived her entire life at Xaxl'ep) told us, as we all—my students and I, and the Xaxl'ep community members—went about preparing the food and assembling the different components of the cooking pit, that the ancestors were there with us, and that they were happy with what we were planning. In fact, we made two pits. One was to be left cooking overnight, for moose meat, deer meat, balsamroots, black tree lichen and other foods that required a longer cooking time. The other we started early the next morning and filled with faster-cooking foods—salmon, nodding onions and potatoes, carrots and other garden foods. We even tried a few less-well-known foods like prickly-pear cactus, which we also roasted over the fire on skewers. Both pits were scheduled to be opened around one o'clock in the afternoon. As we worked, we imagined the ancestors—even those ancient people of the Keatley Creek village—digging their pits, gathering the vegetation to surround the food and heating up the rocks in a hot fire lit right in the pit, just as we were doing. It gave us all a feeling of awe and intense pleasure to think of this.

Several of the Xaxl'ep elders helped, giving us advice, cutting wood for the fire, gathering the wild rose, thimbleberry and fir boughs for the pits and preparing the food. We improvised a little: We wrapped the meat in thimbleberry leaves, and we made a woven tray of inner bark from the Rocky Mountain maple (*Acer glabrum*) to hold some of the food, as Mary Thomas had taught me and others some years previously. Although Mary is a Secwepemc elder, and we were in Stl'atl'imx country, we thought it would be good to use this device. Another young man from the Secwepemc Nation showed us how to fashion a cooking rack for the salmon from a long sucker of maple wood, bent and lashed into a hoop about the size of the webbed end of a tennis racquet. He then wove several twigs across the hoop in each direction to hold the salmon as it cooked. Before long all of us were learning his technique, and we experienced first-hand how skills can be passed from person to person and group to group. We prepared these pits in much the same way as Mary Thomas had done to cook the black tree lichen. Everyone in the community participated in some way. One young man held a post in the centre until the entire pit was filled with the vegetation and food to be cooked; when he drew out the post, we poured water in to generate clouds of steam. Then we quickly covered the entire pit until no steam escaped and left it to cook.

Opening the pits was a truly wonderful experience. Many people came to watch and participate in the feast, the first pit-cooked food to be served in the community since Maggie Adolph was a little girl. The food in both pits was cooked to perfection. As the warm breeze played around the hillside, Sam Mitchell's son, Art Adolph (who was the elected Xaxl'ep chief at the time), and other community members carefully lifted out the food and placed it on trays. We added peeled cow parsnip (*Heracleum lanatum*) shoots harvested from up the valley, and bannock. Maggie said a prayer so moving and heartfelt that many of us were in tears. Then plates of food were taken away as an offering for the ancestors, a long-practised gesture of respect and appreciation to those who had gone before us. The younger people filled the elders' plates with food, then everyone else helped themselves. Once we had had our fill of pit-cooked food, one of the elders showed us how to make a traditional soapberry whipper from maple bark and we whipped soapberries *(Shepherdia canadensis)*, which were served in small cups. Following the meal, the Xaxl'ep singers performed beautiful traditional songs accompanied by drumming: songs that would make the ancestors proud.

The Xaxl'ep still need their lands, just as their ancestors did. Their lands are full of history and crowded with stories, recent and time-honoured. The entire Fountain Valley, its lakes and streams, the mountains surrounding them, the river bench, the sloping canyon walls and the Fraser River itself are all part of these people's identity. It is indeed their survival territory that provides everything they need to live healthy, fulfilling lives. Everything in their territory is connected to them, and if part of it is lost the Xaxl'ep lose part of themselves. They, like so many other indigenous groups, have spent many years and mortgaged their jobs and their lands in their struggle to be recognized as legitimate occupants and caretakers of their territory. Everything—the people and their lands—is one.

The Xaxl'ep have had to buy back some of the lands that were taken from them. Much of their traditional territory is privately controlled: forest companies have clear-cut extensive parts of their forests, ranchers have grazed cattle over their rangelands. The hillsides are now so trampled and degraded that they are eroding and losing their capacity to support the native grasses and wildflowers that used to grow so lush everywhere. For example, *Sxílxel* (Chilhil) Lake in Fountain Valley is named for silverweed *(Potentilla anserina)*, a plant whose roots, James Teit reported, were dug, cooked and eaten "in large quantities." Today, you have to look hard to find any *xílxel* plants; they are small, trampled and barely visible around the shores of the lake that bears their name. Sam Mitchell was a good friend of Baptiste Ritchie and confirmed that the Xaxl'ep people used to burn areas just as Baptiste described, yet they have not been able to do this as they did in the past, so their uplands are becoming dense and bushy and no longer produce the quantities of berries and root vegetables that they once did.

"Everything is one" is a profound yet basic concept. The complex webs that connect the past with the future, the ocean and rivers with the land, the plants with the animals and the people with everything else are breaking down. As they fragment and erode, so does Earth's capacity to sustain us all. In particular, we need to better understand the links between human cultures and environments, between ecological systems and social systems.

The Sandbar Willow Syndrome

Peoples' cultural practices, knowledge and well-being depend completely on their lands and resources; they cannot be maintained without an intact and healthy environment. I am reminded of a time in July 1999 when my family and I went with our friend and ethnobotanist Dick Ford to the Eight Northern Indian Pueblos Arts and Crafts Show near Santa Fe, New Mexico. More than 1,000 Native American artists at over 500 stalls were exhibiting and selling their silverwork, leatherwork, pottery and other arts. I was interested in seeing traditional baskets, and I asked Dick why we weren't seeing many basket weavers at the show. He knew of one stall that was selling baskets, and he took me there. On display were only three or four baskets, all woven from the flexible twigs of sandbar willow *(Salix exigua)*. I decided to purchase one of them, which was made by Pueblo basket weaver Chester Aquino, of San Juan Pueblo, New Mexico. As I was paying for my basket, the woman at the stall commented sadly that it was getting harder and harder to find good willow for their baskets. "Ever since the U.S. Army Corps of Engineers flooded our river," she said, "we haven't been able to find much willow; they ruined our willows." I wondered about the possibility of reinstating the willows at a few sites down the river, and I asked her whether this might be a good approach to bring back the willows. Her response was not what I expected. She said, "Hardly anyone knows how to make the baskets any more."

It finally struck me that when a key habitat and its resources are taken away, either through environmental destruction or restricting access, people lose the knowledge, the *"know-how,"* associated with that place and that resource. Even if the habitat is restored, or access to the resource is reinstated, it is no longer useful once the knowledge about how the resource is harvested, processed and used has disappeared, because no one holds the skills to use it. It is lost to the culture. I call this combination of circumstances "the sandbar willow syndrome," and now that I have identified this obvious "effect and cause" I recognize it over and over again in my work with elders and communities.

In 1977, on my trip to Pavilion Mountain with Sam Mitchell and Adrienne Aikins, we stopped to see a patch of sandbar willow—the same willow used to make baskets by the Pueblo people of the Southwest—along the highway between Fountain (*Xaxl'ep*) and Pavilion, far above the Fraser River. The willows were growing in a dense thicket in a moist ditch. Sam told us that they were called *nexwtín-až* (literally "rope plant"), and that the Stl'atl'imx people used the slender, pink-barked stems to make the tough, flexible ropes for lashing together their pit houses, fishing weirs and drying shelters. They also threaded their fish on these stems for easier carrying. Sam demonstrated the art of making rope: First, while it is still growing, the long, supple branch, bark and all, is twisted and twisted, starting at the upper end and working down towards the base, until the entire length remains twisted, its crosswise fibres broken all the way along. Then it is cut from the plant. If necessary, the bark is peeled off; for rough work, it is simply left in place.

When I revisited that site just a decade later, the sandbar willow was gone. The highway had been resurfaced and widened, and giant ditching machines had simply removed the whole patch of willows. Today, no sandbar willow is evident along this stretch of road, and virtually no one knows about the "rope plant" and its past use. When I heard about the plight of the willow from the Pueblo woman, I could see the similarity of circumstance and vividly remembered Sam's teachings of many years before.

In the early 1920s, shortly after World War I, a complete lake—Sumas Lake or *Sema:th*—in the Fraser Valley of British Columbia near Chilliwack was drained away. About 8,800 hectares in extent, the lake had tremendous value to the local Stó:lō people. They camped around it in the summertime (Hudson's Bay Company employees had reported approximately 300 to 400 people camped along the banks of Sumas Lake in the early 1900s) and had probably done so for hundreds, if not thousands, of years. Draining the lake to create more land for agriculture was called

Peach basket made of sandbar willow (Salix exigua) *made by Chester Aquino of San Juan Pueblo, New Mexico (sandbar willow also in background).*
PHOTO BY ROBERT D. TURNER

"reclamation," and the agriculture-oriented residents of the Fraser Valley heralded the event as progress. Wetlands were drained and diked in many places, and traditional resources drastically changed as a result. In 1918 in *Forests of British Columbia,* H.N. Whitford and R.D. Craig wrote about the lands in the Fraser Valley, including Sumas Lake:

> Though the general policy has been to reserve all the agricultural land for homesteaders, some 115,000 acres have been sold, chiefly under special conditions requiring reclamation by dyking or irrigation. . . . Nearly all the land in the lower Fraser Valley is valuable for agricultural purposes, especially for fruit, vegetables and dairying, and greater efforts should be made to have it cleared and put under cultivation as soon as possible after logging.

Draining the lake, and diverting the Chilliwack River that ran into it, represented a profound loss for the Stó:lō. Gone were a major means of transportation, as well as the traditional resources that the lake provided: beaver, Roosevelt elk *(Cervus elaphus roosevelti)*, moose *(Alces alces)*, muskrat *(Ondatra ʒibethicus)*, sturgeon, Dolly Varden *(Salvelinus malma)* and cutthroat trout *(Oncorhynchus clarki)*, eulachon, sockeye and coho salmon, whistling swan *(Cygnus columbianus)*, Canada goose *(Branta canadensis)*, sandhill crane *(Grus canadensis)* and ducks of various kinds. Basketry materials, too, were lost: cattail, tule, basketry grasses, willows, western red-cedar and bitter cherry *(Prunus emarginata)*. Wapato *(Sagittaria latifolia)*, or "Indian swamp potato," once a staple root vegetable, also grew around the edge of the lake, and vast patches of it were destroyed. Today it is difficult to find wapato in the Fraser Valley, although remnant populations still exist outside the "reclamation" area. Most Stó:lō today do not recognize wapato, let alone know that it was a major food of their ancestors. Very few people know how to make the beautiful coiled cedar-root baskets, decorated with overlain cherry bark and grass stems, that the Stó:lō women traded and sold over the past centuries to sustain their families. My friend Andrea Laforet, an ethnologist and basketry expert, recognizes a correlation between the decline in basketry arts in the Stó:lō region and the loss of western red-cedar and other basketry plants through logging and agricultural conversions in the Fraser Valley.

The Stó:lō are working hard to revitalize their traditional basketry and other elements of their cultural heritage, including their language. They have built an ethnobotanical garden next to the Stó:lō museum at the Coqualeetza Cultural Education Centre, formerly the site of a residential school to which aboriginal children were sent from many parts of British Columbia. One of the features of their beautiful garden is a pond, where they are growing wapato, cattail, willow and other wetland species that used to be so abundant. Through school tours to the garden and museum, and teachings of the elders and others knowledgeable in their traditions, the Stó:lō hope, through their children and youth, to reinstate the cultural knowledge of a lost environment.

It is estimated that 80 per cent of southern Canada's wetlands have been converted to agricultural lands. Similar stories could be told in many places about peoples' loss of their traditional wetlands and the consequences of this loss, not only in ecological terms, but in cultural and even economic terms. Fortunately, there is a growing appreciation for wetlands conservation in Canada, though First Nations have always known the value of wetland habitats.

People are alienated from their traditional resources and practices for many reasons, but in all cases it is very hard, sometimes impossible, to reconnect the pieces and re-establish people's connections to past use and knowledge. Sadly, the residential school system that, over several generations, took indigenous children away from their families and placed them in boarding schools where they were severely punished for speaking their own language and indoctrinated with a negative view of their families' and communities' traditional cultures and lifeways, has had long-lasting repercussions. The abuse, racism and oppression that abounded at residential schools certainly affected the children (and their families) at the time they attended. However, the less obvious consequences of this system—preventing children from spending time with their parents and grandparents at a critical stage of their development—have been even more insidious. Furthermore, because Native children were not allowed to voice their own language many lost the ability or the heart to speak it, even after they returned home. This set up a barrier to communication with their elders, which resulted in a further cultural and generational gap. Not only were the children taught mostly agricultural and domestic skills that were irrelevant to their culture, they were also instructed that the ways of their families and peoples were ignorant and backward. Many of the children were taught to abhor their background and their history and to turn their backs on the environmental and cultural traditions of their parents and grandparents.

The combination of the residential schools, the assimilation policies put in place by the colonial government and subsequently by the Canadian federal government, the reserve system and the environmental destruction that has accompanied the industrialism of the past two centuries has been devastating to indigenous peoples' traditional knowledge and practices, their identity and their connections to the land. The ramifications have extended to the present day.

Fortunately, peoples all over North America have not only survived through this era of cultural and environmental erosion but have retained, restored and renewed their traditional knowledge, values and practices and even, in some cases, their languages. People like Adam Dick, Daisy Sewid-Smith, Richard Atleo, Mary Thomas—elders with the memory of the old ways, a vision of what could be and the knowledge and will to teach—and other culture-holders are the ones who will make a difference to the future. Many, many younger people are eager to learn about their language and culture, eager to rekindle the environmental knowledge and wisdom of their ancestors and to take it with them into the future. No one has illusions that they will revert to a life as it would have been in the old days, but they see a possibility for blending elements of their original cultures with the new ways, using the old ways as a foundation on which to build "new" traditions.

Teachings for the Future

My friend Laurie Montour, a Mohawk biologist and resource specialist who was born and raised at Kahnawàke, recently spoke to my class at the University of Victoria about traditional systems of land and resource management. She began by passing around copies of a Mohawk prayer of thanksgiving. We began the class with it. Instead of reading it aloud herself, she asked each student to read a portion of it. This prayer, translated from the original Mohawk, epitomizes a world view in which everything is one, and it emphasizes our need to recognize and express our appreciation to all the elements of our universe. Laurie said that this prayer, or one similar to it, is recited at any meeting when Mohawk people come together to make decisions or to celebrate some event in their lives, and I myself have heard it spoken at meetings.

Haudenosaunee Thanksgiving Address

Today we have gathered, and as we look around at each other we can see that the cycle of life continues as our Creator intended. We, the people, have been given the duties and responsibility to live in balance and harmony with each other and all living things around us. We now bring our minds together as one, and with one mind we give greetings and thanks to each other as people.

We now turn our heart and mind to our Mother, the Earth. She has been given the duties and responsibilities to support us and all forms of life. She supports our feet as we walk about upon her. She provides us much joy that she still performs these duties and responsibilities that were bestowed upon her by our Creator. When we, as people, complete the tasks here upon the Earth, our bodies will be placed back in her arms for safe-keeping. We now bring our minds together, and with one mind we give greetings and thanks to our Mother Earth.

We now turn our heart and mind to the water. We give thanks to all the waters of the world for performing their duties and responsibilities as given to them by our Creator. We give greetings and thanks to these waters for quenching our thirst and for providing us with strength. We know water in its many forms such as rivers, streams, waterfalls, rain, mist and oceans; and with one mind we send these greetings and thanks to the waters of the world.

We now turn our heart and mind to all the fish life in the water that still carry out their duties and responsibilities to cleanse and purify the water. We also acknowledge that the fish give of themselves in order that we may gain their strength to carry out our responsibilities in their cycle. With one mind we send greetings to the fish life.

We now turn our heart and mind to the plant life. As we look around and about us, we see that the plant life still follow their original instructions given to them by the Creator, so it is with one mind that we now send greetings and thanks to all plant life.

There are many kinds of plants, and we now turn our heart and mind to the food plants. We acknowledge the three sisters (corn, beans and squash), the grains, berries and all the other food plants that they too still carry out their original instructions from the Creator in order that we may draw our strength and health from them. We bring all these foods together, and with one mind send our greetings and thanks to these food plants.

We now turn our heart and mind to all the medicine plants and herbs of the world. These plants were instructed to take away our sickness. These plants are always ready and waiting to perform their original instructions. We are happy that these plants are still among us, and we now bring our minds together as one and send greetings and thanks to these as well as to the keepers of these medicine plants for their knowledge and their ability to care for the plants.

It is now time to turn our heart and mind to the animal life of the world. Many of these animals give themselves as food in the whole cycle of life. Each animal has many things to teach us as well in the preservation and balance of life. We see and hear them near our homes and in the forests. We are grateful that these animals still carry out their original instructions as given to them by our Creator. We now, with one mind, send our greetings and thanks to these animals.

We now turn our heart and mind to the trees. Our Mother is covered with many families of trees: some provide us with fruit, some with syrup, some with nuts, some with medicines, some with roots to bind things, some with boards to build things, some with wood for heat and cooking; and all [the trees] that provide us with clean fresh air to breathe. It is with one mind that we extend our greetings and thanks to the trees, for they too still carry out their original instructions.

We now turn our heart and mind to the birds of the world. They fly about us and bring sweet music to the ear. Each day they remind us of the beauty and simplicity as well as the vastness of the world, for they are the travellers of the world. We send greetings and thanks to these birds that they return to us each year, which also provides us with wonder of the vastness of this world and the creations within. We now bring our minds together and extend our greetings and thanks to the birds of the world.

We now turn our heart and mind to the four winds. We hear the voices of the winds as they pass through the trees and refresh and purify the air we breathe. The winds help to bring the changes in the seasons, and with one mind we send greetings and thanks to the four winds.

We now turn our heart and mind to where our Grandfathers, the Thunder Beings, live. The thunder and lightning bring with them the waters that renew life. We now with one mind send greetings and thanks to the Thunders.

We now turn our heart and mind to our elder brother, the Sun. Each day the sun passes overhead, bringing us a new day which begins a new life cycle. The sun brings us heat and is the source of all fire. With one mind we send thanks and greetings to our eldest brother, the Sun.

We now turn our heart and mind to our Grandmother, the Moon. She provides us with the night-time light. She is the elder of all women and controls women all over the world. With her power she controls the tides that bring new life to the waters of the world. She watches over the planting cycle and harvest of our gardens. She controls the birth of our people, so it is of one mind that we send greetings and thanks to our Grandmother, the Moon.

We now turn our heart and mind to the stars of the sky. They are a wonder as they spread their beauty across the night sky. They humble us with their vastness and extend their life to a far-off place. They help the moon with providing the morning dew which helps our gardens. They provide guidance for our travellers. Let us now bring our minds together and send greetings and thanks to the stars of the universe.

We now turn our heart and mind to our enlightened teachers. It is with their knowledge that we are able to be here today with these thoughts of greeting and thanks that have been passed down through the ages. They remind us of our duties and responsibilities that must be carried out to continue the cycle of life. Let us be of one mind as we give greetings and thanks to our teachers.

Let us now turn our heart and mind to the Creator. It is our Creator who allows us to know life as we do. It is the Creator who gives us all the beauty and all that we spoke of in our Thanksgiving Address and more. It is our Creator that gives us the ability to love. It is now time for us, each of us, to think of anything that was not addressed in our thanksgiving [pause] . . . Let us now gather our thoughts that we had this day as we spoke of this thanksgiving and send that greeting and thanks to the Creator.

Let us now carry on our purpose here, and it is our hope that any decision made here today will benefit the next seven generations without hurting them in any way, shape or form.

Laurie told the students that this prayer belonged to all the Mohawk people. She gladly shared these words with the entire class, regardless of our ethnic background or religion. The students greatly appreciated these words and the rest of Laurie's teachings; many said they were a highlight of the course. What better reminder of the interconnectedness of everything, and of our dependence as humans on all the gifts of the universe?

Verna Miller, Nlaka'pmx cultural specialist,
with her niece Alison Yamest.

8

Finding MEANING
in a CONTEMPORARY
Context

Our environments in British Columbia and around the world have deteri-
orated in many ways over the past
century. Species are disappearing at an ever-increasing pace. We are damaging our habitats and depleting our resources—even those we call
renewable—almost everywhere. We see examples of human impacts
on ecosystems at every turn.

A study published in *Science* in 1998, "Killer Whale Predation on Sea
Otter Linking Oceanic and Nearshore Ecosystems," by J.A. Estes and his
associates, illustrates the cascading effects our actions can have on other
species and habitats. Scientists have documented recent declines in sea
otter populations on the North Pacific coast due to predation by killer
whales, or orcas. Killer whales of the open ocean feed mainly on seals and
sea lions. However, there are fewer seals and sea lions, in part because
fish, like salmon and other species, that have been *their* primary food have
declined. (Industrial offshore fishing and possibly also global warming—
both situations relating to human activities—have killed the fish.) Without the sea otters to feed on them, sea urchins, a major food of sea otters,

have multiplied. Sea urchins graze on kelp, and because there are so many sea urchins the kelp "forest" habitats along the coast are deteriorating. Dwindling kelp habitats, more erosion along the shorelines, and fewer places to feed and shelter young fish and the small invertebrates and larval species they require for food: The end result? This entire system of inshore and open ocean habitats, critical for the well-being of so many species, including humans, is in jeopardy because of our overfishing and climate-changing activities.

How can we restore our habitats and the species we depend upon? We cannot continue such destruction. At least part of the problem, however, is that we do not readily identify ourselves as the cause of environmental damage, because the pathways linking human actions and ultimate results are intricate and uncertain. We may be able to see simple, direct impacts and find ready solutions to counter them, but the most serious environmental problems of our time need to be addressed through complex approaches, including modifying our own behaviour and the ways we treat the earth. Traditional approaches of indigenous societies provide models to follow—models that recognize the interconnectedness of everything, captured in the phrase "everything is one," and models of relationships to foster within our communities, between past, present and future generations, and among all of Earth's species: our relatives.

Three examples from First Nations in British Columbia show the promise and potential for alternative ways of relating to the earth. Situated in different regions, and with different key players, they all share common attributes that, when combined, reveal a framework for positive change.

The Tmixʷ Project: A Nlaka'pmx Lands Initiative

My friend Verna Miller is a Nlaka'pmx woman of great character and wisdom. We have known each other since she was my student—one of those students who have taught me as much as I have ever taught them. As a girl, Verna learned about traditional environmental knowledge from her aunts and grandmothers, and over the years she has become a leader in the Nlaka'pmx community. Through the Nicola Tribal Association, she

Botanie Valley, Nlaka'pmx territory, a cultural landscape.

and her colleagues initiated the Tmixʷ Research Project (*Tmixʷ* means "land"), which encourages developers to apply Nlaka'pmx traditional knowledge in current forest and land management to integrate aboriginal land use with modern, innovative forestry practices. This project brings full circle the teachings of the Nlaka'pmx elders who told James Teit about Earth's Blanket, as well as those shared by Annie York, Mabel Joe and the other Nlaka'pmx elders who, from 1975 to 1990, collaborated in our ethnobotany study with my linguist friends Larry and Terry Thompson (first published in 1990 as *Thompson Ethnobotany*). The Nicola Valley Institute of Technology in Merritt now teaches ethnobotany and traditional knowledge but, more importantly, these issues are considered key components of land use planning and future practice for the Nlaka'pmx of the Thompson and Nicola Valley region.

The work of the Tmixʷ project is still experimental, since techniques used by previous generations for maintaining and enhancing Nlaka'pmx lands need to be relearned. To do this, the project coordinators are seeking help and advice from plant and forestry scientists and ethnobotanists, and more importantly from the elders in their own communities, through a newly established technical advisory panel.

Recognizing that fire played an important role in the past, the Tmixʷ committee has proposed a five-year restoration plan for the Spius Creek watershed (*Ipowsus*), which has been accepted by the Merritt forest district. The Tmixʷ strategy is to work slowly and on a small scale, by first testing and experimenting with traditional methods within a single watershed, to develop a model for using fire as a natural disturbance agent to restore Nlaka'pmx traditional use areas. Initially the Tmixʷ research team will identify and inventory archaeological, fire-history and ecological data in the mid-alpine (Engelmann spruce–subalpine fir) region of the watershed, an area with extensive historical record of use and burning practices by Nlaka'pmx communities. Also incorporated in the plan are education and training for young adults and youth, so that they can take up and carry on with the project as they gain in knowledge and experience.

Using the results of this study, leaders for the Tmixʷ project intend to expand their influence over a broader land base, creating new culturally validated land and resource-management options and silvicultural practices within the Merritt forest district. Their work will reflect the best practices in the fields of ecological restoration and conservation biology, which recognize and incorporate traditional ecological knowledge and traditional land and resource-management systems into land use history, planning and decision-making. Such practices as landscape burning, pruning, selective harvesting and transplanting, which maintain and promote culturally significant resources, are being revived because their general approaches and underlying philosophies are based on Nlaka'pmx values and understandings.

The lands on which the Tmixʷ project researchers are planning to work are the same places their grandparents, great-grandparents and earlier ancestors have harvested and sustained themselves for millennia. The aim of this project is to balance practical strategies for land use with respectful care and recognition of the spiritual values, while also communicating and teaching the associated knowledge and understanding to other members of the community, particularly the youth. By monitoring and documenting their progress, the Tmixʷ team intends to learn from their research and also make the findings available for the benefit of others who may want to access them. To this end, they will present their findings through training programs and workshops for Nlaka'pmx and neighbouring First Nations as well as for foresters, government workers and members of the general public, especially students. The researchers also plan to publish results in academic scientific journals. Their ultimate goal is to foster and rekindle a Nlaka'pmx land ethic that promotes stewardship and respect for the land and all its beings—in short, to protect Earth's Blanket.

Traditional ecological knowledge (and its practice) has much relevance to contemporary efforts by both aboriginal and non-aboriginal people to live sustainably. Fostering a responsible land ethic, as the Tmixʷ project is doing, is an essential component of any formula for sustainability. Fortunately, other indigenous and local communities—and even people in larger, urban communities—are finding ways to maintain, restore and sustain some of the cultural and ecological richness of their home places. Volunteers and community groups throughout North America are working together to restore habitats, including salmon streams, oak parklands, marshes and dryland ecosystems. Some of these initiatives are still embryonic; accomplishing their ultimate goal of restoring environmental and cultural integrity, complexity and wholeness to damaged systems may seem daunting given the prevailing forces of globalization and industrialization. However, the energy, enthusiasm and commitment that people are giving to these efforts is inspiring. I am reminded of anthropologist Margaret Mead's memorable words: "Never doubt that a small group of thoughtful, committed citizens can change the world. In fact, it's the only thing that ever has!"

Many elements need to come together for positive changes to prevail, but three key ingredients are necessary: skilled teachers who hold the cultural knowledge, wisdom and values; willing, interested learners who have the opportunity and desire to become skilled at and practise environmental stewardship, and access to intact, productive environments, or environmental capital, on which to build and practise. If any one of these crucial elements is missing, the system cannot be sustained or sustaining.

Such ecocultural systems will not necessarily remain constant and unchanging, but their constituents will be resilient enough to withstand changes and still retain their essential character and integrity.

Koeye: Restoring a Heiltsuk Treasure

The Heiltsuk of the Central Coast of British Columbia, together with friends and supporters, are undertaking a major restorative project at one of their traditional village sites, at the mouth of the Koeye River. This watershed is a spectacular and diverse area about forty-five kilometres southeast of Waglisla (Bella Bella), which is the main Heiltsuk village and the largest First Nations community on the Central Coast. A key part of Heiltsuk traditional territory, Koeye has a rich history of Heiltsuk occupation over 10,000 years. Recently, however, it was also subjected to outsiders' attempts at economic development: A logging company clear-cut a vast swath of the original forest, and developers constructed a fishing lodge—an eyesore that stands out at the top of the steeply sloping, denuded bluff adjacent to the shoreline. On lands they still retained at the mouth of the river, the Heiltsuk constructed small cabins and a roofed beach shelter, to which they have been bringing children and youth from Heiltsuk and neighbouring First Nations communities for summer camps to learn about their cultural traditions and to spend time on the land.

There was an enormous sadness when the Heiltsuk elders and others visited this part of the territory. The flowing river, the stately trees and the long, clean, sandy beach on one side of the bay were a picture of breathtaking beauty and the trashed, scarred, eroding landscape on the opposite side stood in stark contrast. Fortunately, with the vision and collaboration of the Heiltsuk and their associates, including several nongovernmental organizations (Raincoast Conservation Society, Ecotrust Canada and The Land Conservancy of British Columbia), funds were raised and a 74-hectare parcel of degraded lands was eventually purchased and returned to Heiltsuk ownership in August 2001. Plans began immediately to reintegrate this area as Heiltsuk land and to restore it for

Koeye, Heiltsuk territory, at the mouth of the Koeye River.

its own sake and for the benefit of the Heiltsuk and others. The concept is still unfolding, and there is much work to be done, but the enthusiasm and spirit that is being brought to this project is exciting and promising. The idea is to use the original Kvai (Koeye River) fishing lodge as a healing and education centre—to reinstate balance and harmony to both the land and the communities.

One of the key players in the restoration initiative is my friend Pauline Waterfall *(Hilistis)*, a Heiltsuk woman with extensive knowledge and understanding of Heiltsuk culture and history, and of traditional medicines and healing practices. Another is Larry Jorgenson, who married into the Heiltsuk community and has been supporting Heiltsuk youth, culture and environment in a variety of ways, including organizing films and youth expeditions.

In the spring of 2002, I travelled to Koeye with Pauline Waterfall and her niece Jessie Housty, Karen McAllister and Louise Wilson of the Raincoast Conservation Society, and a few others. Our friend Cyril Carpenter, a Heiltsuk fisher and cultural specialist, generously took us there from Bella Bella in his big fishing boat. It was a wonderful trip, a time for peaceful reflection and for sharing ideas about restoring damaged parts of the Koeye watershed as well as for experiencing the friendship of our companions and the adventure and tranquility offered by the river, forest and beach of the intact part. Looking back on those blissful few days, a deep sadness overcomes me with the realization that Cyril is no longer here, except in his bright, strong spirit. Tragically, he drowned at Bella Bella in the winter of 2002, leaving his wife, Jennifer, an anthropologist who for many years has been director of the Heiltsuk Cultural Education Centre, and his two daughters, Karmyn and Julie, both remarkable young women. Cyril served his community first and foremost. He was always there, helping with the food fishery, offering his boat to take people to Potlatches or other events up and down the coast, hosting and supporting people when they needed it. He loved the Heiltsuk ways; he was proud to be Heiltsuk. His great-grandfather, Captain Carpenter, was a famous artist and master canoe builder, and this is why their family name is Carpenter.

As we travelled down to Koeye, I spent quite a bit of time sitting beside Cyril in the wheelhouse of his boat while he manoeuvred through the passageways between the islands, pointing out the main landmarks, the old village sites and the mountain peaks, valleys and river estuaries where his people's stories were born. I could have listened to him for hours as he talked about Heiltsuk fishing, dances, ancestors.

He told me about his childhood, and about how children learned what they needed to know in their culture. He said that until about the age of eight years a child is simply steeped in the stories, songs and culture. Then, from about eight to twelve years of age, the child starts to show his or her own talents and participates in activities according to those talents, whether it be canoe-making, art, fishing or basketry. In the old days, he said, if a young person really worked hard for about three years he was given a holiday, a chance to participate in a canoe trip, to trade. The Heiltsuk used to travel as far south as Catalina Island in California, taking their dried berries, herring eggs, salmon, halibut, seaweed and other goods to trade for the big California abalone and other products from the south. He said that their large ocean-going canoes—like the ones built by his own forefathers—used to journey about thirty kilometres offshore

Cyril Carpenter, Heiltsuk cultural specialist, in his boat en route to Koeye,
in spring 2002.

where the water is less rough. Each canoe had two large sails set and they
were able to travel amazingly fast.

Cyril also told me, as we sat together, about traditional Heiltsuk
"berry gardens." When he was about ten years old, his grandmother,
Bessie Brown, pointed out to him a wide, bushy ledge beside a waterfall
at Roscoe Inlet in Heiltsuk territory. She told Cyril that in this place
above the village site was a productive berry garden. She said that people
often located such berry gardens beside waterfalls, above a village or
campsite, because mists around the waterfall kept the berry bushes moist,
even in the summertime. In this spot, the gardens were also protected
against the extreme prevailing winds. Up on these ledges, the bushes had
the advantage of periods of warm sunshine, and this was important for

ripening the berries. Long ago, Bessie Brown stated, the hunters and fishers would keep all the remains from cleaning and dressing their salmon, as well as from deer, mink *(Mustela vison)*, otter, wolf and mountain goat. They would dig holes in the ground around the berry bushes and bury these remains there. To help neutralize the acidic soils, people also scattered the ashes from their fireplaces as well as broken clamshells around the berry bushes. This is what made the berries grow so well. She said the Heiltsuk also used to transplant whole berry bushes to these special sites. Cyril confirmed that the blueberries and huckleberries from these sites were healthier, bigger and tastier than any other berries; he said you could harvest them from the branches in handfuls.

Later, he noted, the people also used to fertilize the vegetable gardens, orchards and domesticated berry bushes around their houses using the same methods and nurturing materials. They added seaweed, usually in the fall, just before winter set in and after people had processed their fall runs of salmon. Cyril demonstrated the success of these practices himself, with two cherry trees growing beside his house in Bella Bella: one he fertilized with ashes and fish remains, and it has grown rapidly; the other he left alone, and it has grown far more slowly and produces less fruit.

Pauline Waterfall also described the traditional berry gardens; she had been told about them by her own grandmother, Beatrice Brown, who was Bessie Brown's sister-in-law. During our group's brainstorming session about how to restore the damage at Koeye, we talked about how appropriate it would be to create a "new" traditional berry garden on the scarred slopes below the lodge, a garden that would bear luscious fruit for the people, that would be a tribute to the grandmothers and that would serve as a living lesson in the wisdom of Heiltsuk tradition. Now I believe that such a garden will also be a fitting tribute to Cyril, a kind and generous man who worked hard to keep the Heiltsuk ways alive.

There are many other plans and dreams for Koeye. The lodge could be both a healing centre and retreat for people needing some peace in their lives, and perhaps an education and ecological centre for both Heiltsuk and visitors to the territory. People could stay there, participate in the different restoration projects, learn about Heiltsuk history and traditions and renew their own spirits. Children could help garden, prepare food, propagate and research plants and restore the site. (This kind of participatory activity is called "ecocultural restoration.") Some of the ancient tidal gardens for traditional root vegetables—Pacific silverweed, spring-bank clover and rice-root, for example—could be established in the moister seepage areas, and there could be a crabapple orchard and plant-ings of red elderberry *(Sambucus racemosa),* salmonberry, gray currant *(Ribes bracteosum,* also called stink currant), wild rose and high-bush cranberry. A medicinal garden, too, could be planted, with traditional Heiltsuk healing plants available to be harvested and used by those who need them. A smokehouse and food-processing area could be created, providing children and youth with important opportunities to learn the skills associated with preparing and preserving fish and other traditional foods. An area with a traditional earth oven for pit-cooking vegetables and fish could be incorporated. Elders could participate directly in all as-pects of teaching, including Heiltsuk language, stories, songs and dances, as well as the protocols and philosophies of their culture.

The Koeye Restoration Plan is an ambitious one, and it will require the dedication of many, but its benefits will be immense for all those in-volved. Koeye has already been working its magic. In the summer of 2004, my friend and colleague Duncan Taylor went to Koeye with several Heiltsuk leaders including elder Evelyn Windsor, accompanying a group of seriously ill young people. Their activities at Koeye, including salmon fishing, dancing and playing games, guided by the Heiltsuk, gave them all an exhilarating and unforgettable experience, which from Duncan's ac-count was intensely therapeutic. All of the participants returned from their adventure renewed and invigorated, with a heightened awareness of their place in the world and of the beauty and continuity of life. As the vi-sion for Koeye is realized, this place will continue to be a Heiltsuk treas-ure, a site that nurtures, teaches and inspires all who have the privilege of experiencing its beauty.

Haida Gwaii and Gwaii Haanas

During the two summers my husband, Bob, and I stayed on Haida Gwaii (Queen Charlotte Islands) in the early 1970s, we witnessed terrible envi-ronmental destruction. Often, we saw the lumber companies' massive self-loading barges carrying away millions of board feet of logs—worth millions of dollars—down to the mills on British Columbia's Lower Mainland, or perhaps to be shipped whole and unprocessed to faraway countries like Japan. We saw salmon streams filled with the rubble of forest practices gone awry. Huge stumps washed down from the eroded hillsides onto the beaches, where their roots stretched across the sand like the tentacles of a giant moribund octopus. Entire mountainsides had been clear-cut, and at that time people were already starting to worry about the dwindling numbers of salmon—the result of damage to their spawning beds as well as overfishing.

Deer had been introduced to the islands on more than one occasion. The first time, in 1890, just ten animals were brought to Haida Gwaii, but around 1910 and 1920 more deer were imported to provide game for hunters. By the time we were there—fifty years later—the deer had multiplied beyond control. On one nighttime trip driving from Masset to Skidegate we counted more than fifty deer, just alongside the road. (Recently, on the same route, I counted sixty-three.) The Haida elders said that the deer, and the cattle that had been introduced and had gone wild, were eating up all the traditional foods—the cloudberries (*Rubus chamaemorus*, also known as bakeapple), the currants, the blueberries, the strawberries and the high-bush cranberries—as well as their valued medicinal plants. People were worried about the future of Haida Gwaii. Even those who were employed in the forests or who hunted the deer for food were worried about the impacts. The elders were also deeply concerned that their language and traditions were being eroded and in danger of being lost as the pressures of the global economy and consumer lifestyles took hold.

By this time, the Haida had already endured tremendous changes to their lifeways and losses to their cultural fabric. In particular, the devastating disease epidemics that began here in the 1830s and recurred throughout the nineteenth century swept through the Haida and other Northwest Coast communities and resulted in the deaths of many artists, weavers, fishers and other knowledge-holders, as well as of the children who would learn the traditions and carry them forward. Many masterpieces of Haida monumental art—cedar house posts and mortuary poles, as well as countless other objects of art and utility—had been burned or destroyed in the previous two centuries. The missionaries had discouraged Haida from keeping their totem poles because the church officials assumed, without understanding their symbolism or the history and clan memberships they represented, that these magnificent structures were idols that the people were worshipping. Some other pieces were stolen from village sites, and some were purchased by collectors, often for meagre amounts. These works of art were shipped to museums all over the world, including the Provincial Museum (now Royal British Columbia Museum) in Victoria.

As people perished and their culture was eroded, speakers of the many diverse Haida dialects from the different villages of Haida Gwaii dwindled in numbers. Some people moved north to Prince of Wales Island, Alaska, and those remaining on Haida Gwaii regrouped in the two major centres: Skidegate and Masset. There, as elsewhere, the residential school system took its toll on the children and their parents. Many people felt that for the youth to survive in the modern world they would have to forget their past, their language, their songs and dances and learn instead the ways of the dominant society. The Haida are strong and resourceful people, however, and despite all that has happened, they maintain their resilience and the essence of their strong and vibrant culture.

The concerns the elders expressed in the 1970s still exist today, but a number of developments since that time have brought added optimism and a renewal of spirit. In the 1980s the Haida, increasingly distressed by the continuing destruction of their homeland, took a stand against the effects of the logging on Lyell Island along the east coast of Moresby Island. They set up a roadblock and stood up to those who arrived to cut the trees. Elders like Ada Yovanovich were arrested. But out of their courage and determination a new spirit emerged. Many non-Haida—those residing on the islands and those from outside—admired the courage and fortitude of the Haida defenders who were standing up for their land, and they vowed to help the Haida try to regain control of their lands.

Out of the strife and environmental devastation an alliance was born between the Haida, who were tired of watching the destruction of the forests, salmon streams and other habitats of their homelands, and the environmental community, which recognized the value of this unique ecological and cultural treasure. Certainly differences had to be accommodated and compromises negotiated, but the result was a focus on an extensive region on the southern portion of Moresby Island now known as *Gwaii Haanas,* "island of beauty."

The Haida formalized their approach in a written constitution, which states, in part:

> Our culture, our heritage is the child of respect and intimacy with the land and sea. Like the forests, the roots of our people are intertwined such that the greatest troubles cannot overcome us. We owe our existence to Haida Gwaii. On these islands, our ancestors lived and died, and here too, we will make our homes until called away to join them in the great beyond. The living generation accepts the responsibility to ensure that our heritage is passed on to following generations.

In 1981, the Skidegate Band Council and the Haida Nation initiated the Haida Gwaii Watchmen Program. The Haida were concerned about theft and vandalism at their ancestral villages, and they concluded that the best way to protect these areas from harm was by continuous vigilance, with their own people present at each site. At first groups of Haida volunteers used their own boats to travel to these sites—*K'uuna llnagaay* (Skedans), *T'aanuu llnagaay* (Tanu), *Sgang Gwaay llnagaay* (Anthony Island/Ninstints), *Hlk'yah llnagaay* (Windy Bay), *K'iid* (Burnaby Narrows) and *Gandl K'in Gwaayaay* (Hotspring Island)—where they camped for the summer season, acting as both guardians and protectors of their natural and cultural heritage and as hosts and interpreters to the many visitors who came to view these ancient villages. They shared their knowledge about the history of the sites and their perspectives about the lands and waters of the region.

In 1985, with the authority of the Haida Constitution, the South Moresby area was designated a Haida Heritage Site. This began a series of negotiations and agreements, leading first to the South Moresby Agreement, signed by the governments of British Columbia and Canada in 1988, which designated the area as a National Park Reserve. In 1993 the Gwaii Haanas Agreement was established, setting out the terms of cooperative management of Gwaii Haanas National Park Reserve and Haida Heritage Site between the Haida Nation and the Government of

Canada. The Haida Gwaii Watchmen Program was maintained and formalized as part of the co-management agreement.

The "Watchmen" name comes from an earlier tradition. The original watchmen were the triad of human figures wearing high, ringed hats, situated at the top of many Haida poles. These symbolic figures were intended to alert the owner of the pole to the approach of enemies or to any other significant happenings. Today the Haida Gwaii Watchmen are key participants in both safeguarding Gwaii Haanas's heritage and educating those who come to this spectacular part of the world. People visiting the ancient villages are taught not only about the Haida's past lives and history, but also about the spiritual, cultural and economic life of the Haida today, as they continue to respectfully harvest the region's marine and terrestrial resources and to participate in their time-honoured cultural traditions.

Sgang Gwaay llnagaay, the southernmost Haida village and one of the most famous, is a good example of how a series of concerns and initiatives has brought a renewed sense of focus, empowerment, connection and optimism to the elders and other Haida. In 1957 eleven of Sgang Gwaay's spectacular totem poles had been removed by museum officials and shipped south. The remaining mortuary poles and house frames were threatened by vandalism. Although most non-indigenous people came with respect and deep feelings for the place and its spirits, some saw it only as a forgotten place and had no understanding or appreciation of its sacredness. Although desecrating an archaeological site was strictly prohibited under provincial law, with no one to enforce the laws people ignored them. They took away the artifacts as curios, removing them from their cultural context; they carved their initials in the ancient wood, and they left their garbage behind them.

The need to protect the village from this harm was obvious to many, and in 1981 this remarkable ancient village was declared a World Heritage Site by UNESCO. An *in situ* restoration project was initiated at Sgang Gwaay, and some of the remaining poles were straightened and the surrounding brush and recently grown trees were removed to prolong the period of time before the poles and built structures returned to the earth. A small house, modelled after an old-style longhouse, was built to house the Haida Gwaii Watchmen.

Pole at Cumshewa, Haida Gwaii, early 1970s. PHOTO BY ROBERT D. TURNER

The forests and shorelines around Sgang Gwaay, as elsewhere on Haida Gwaii, had been severely affected by deer. The ecosystems had become simplified and were losing their integrity. The only berry bushes left intact were those growing on the top of tall stumps; the forest floor had been cleaned out. Furthermore, with all the flowers being browsed the numbers of pollinating insects had diminished, and without these insects and without the berries there were fewer songbirds and other native wildlife. Introduced red squirrels *(Tamiasciurus hudsonicus)* and rats *(Rattus norvegicus)* had also reduced the number of birds by preying on them in their nests. North of Sgang Gwaay—on Limestone Island, where deer were present, and on Low Island, where they were not—a long-term ecological monitoring program measured the loss of ecosystem complexity due to deer browsing. An experimental deer removal program through hunting was also initiated on Reef Island, as well as on Sgang Gwaay (Anthony Island) on an ongoing basis. As elsewhere on Haida Gwaii, the deer had overpopulated these islands, devouring virtually all the herbaceous and shrubby browse within their reach.

By 2003, after deer had been mostly absent from Sgang Gwaay for only a few years, the original ecosystems had been noticeably restored and renewed, though there were still a few deer and some signs of their browsing. Visiting Sgang Gwaay is a breathtaking experience for Haida and non-Haida visitors alike, and in a sense this ancient village, still relevant and meaningful today, represents the continuity of a people's ties to their lands and their oneness with Nature and history.

Throughout Haida Gwaii, similar restorative initiatives have been underway. Haida children and youth, and even those of older generations who did not learn Haida in their younger years, are taking courses in the Haida language guided and instructed by those who still speak Haida. These classes are offered in both Masset and Skidegate. Through sharing and discussing, the elders are remembering and relearning a wide range of words—place names, names for special technologies—that reflect the ancient great diversity of the Haida language and the Haida themselves. Traditional dances, songs, naming ceremonies, feasts and commemorative dinners are numerous, and their frequency is increasing. Other classes such as the art of weaving with cedar bark and spruce roots and the traditional knowledge of plants, forest practices and healing herbs have also been offered and eagerly attended. Haida art, made famous more than one hundred years ago by the masterful works of such artists as Tom Price and Charles Edenshaw, but evident in its eloquence and creativity long before then, has continued to be revealed in the younger generations.

The hereditary chiefs and elected leaders in the Council of the Haida Nation have strongly opposed unsustainable fishing and destructive forestry practices in their territories. People across the country are starting to listen, and at each turn the Haida are strengthening the recognition of the rights to their lands. In June 2001 there was a magnificent series of ceremonies as six new poles, carved by six different artists and their assistants and representing the six Potlatched lineages of the Skidegate Haida, were raised, one each day. These poles are now standing on grounds at *Qay'llnagaay* (Sea Lion Town), near the Haida Gwaii Museum, at what will soon be the site of a new multi-use cultural heritage centre. There will be traditional gardens of Haida root vegetables, berries, medicine plants and trees. These gardens will educate people about the importance of these species, and they will provide sources of plant foods, materials and medicines that can be used to prepare feasts and for teaching programs, among other purposes.

More Haida youth are participating in post-secondary education today. When my friend Barbara Wilson (*Kii7lljuus*) went to residential school in the 1950s, she was immediately channelled into a program for domestic work; a university education was not seen as an option for her by the school administrators. Recently, *Kii7lljuus*, now employed by Parks Canada, obtained her Diploma in Heritage Resource Management from the University of Victoria. She is not alone in seeking to upgrade her original education. Many people who left Haida Gwaii for training and education have returned to help their nation to reclaim its land base and control over their resources.

The Haida and other First Nations are gradually rebuilding, blending the strengths of their heritage with new ways of working with other administrations, with their neighbours and with their lands and waters. Although many are frustrated at the slow pace of change, almost all are convinced that the change will happen and that it will be for the better.

The Elements of Ecocultural Renewal and Sustainable Living

What are the real keys to living productively in today's world, maintaining a sense of balance and harmony within one's own life, while supporting the necessary move towards true sustainability? How can it be done?

How can we renew our connections with the other life forms of Earth and allow them the room and resources they need to live out their own lives? How can we support the rich cultural diversity in the world, which, in turn, can help to support and maintain Earth's biodiversity?

These three initiatives—the Tmixʷ Research Project of the Nlaka'pmx, the Koeye Restoration project of the Heiltsuk and the establishment of Gwaii Haanas and related projects of the Haida—and many others like them embody several common approaches and ideas that help to move us in this direction. In all, I have identified eight distinct but related concepts that, applied together, provide significant support for eco-cultural restoration and environmental renewal in a variety of settings. They are not in themselves solutions to our environmental problems, but they exemplify ways in which humans can help to serve Earth and ourselves at the same time.

1. *Humans within Nature.* Most significant among the concepts that these three initiatives reflect is a belief that humans are an integral part of their habitat, their home place, rather than being apart from Nature, or superior to and in control of Nature. This belief is also an element of the Deep Ecology movement, founded by Norwegian explorer and environmentalist Arne Naess and described by environmental philosophers Alan Drengson and Yuichi Inoue in their book *The Deep Ecology Movement: An Introductory Anthology.* This view recognizes explicitly that people rely on Earth and its bounty; it in no way takes these for granted, nor does it assume that the other species and their habitats exist solely for humans' use and enjoyment. It fosters a different understanding of what we really need for our sustenance. By appreciating our ecological place in Earth's precious system of life and the limits to the resources we can sequester, we lower our expectations for material wealth. At the same time, we recognize that, as co-operative players in our habitats, in working *with* Nature and in properly valuing the services Nature bestows, we can actually restore and enhance the processes that provide for our needs.

2. *Rooted Cultures.* The second key concept is that when people's cultural identity is closely linked to their ancestral lands they have a high incentive to care for them. In each of the examples cited, the local people witnessed and experienced environmental degradation and deterioration on lands they knew and loved, and in undertaking the projects they

sought to restore the earth, to help it to heal and to make restitution for bad practices, no matter whose. To truly understand changes in ecosystems and habitats it is essential to know them well, to be familiar with minute details such as the food habits of animals, the locales of all the different plants, the locations of springs and wet places and all the seasonal patterns of weather, light and animal migrations and plant growth. We cannot all be so intimately knowledgeable about all places, but if we are observant and patient we can come to know such details in a few—the ones where we live and spend our time. The longer we stay in a place, observing its rhythms and intricacies day to day and year to year, the greater our chances of recognizing changes when they occur. With time, we develop strong attachments to our dwelling places and our affection for them encourages us to protect them and look after them. This imperative becomes enshrined within a culture as a land ethic.

3. *Elders' Wisdom and Experience.* Also fundamental to each initiative is recognizing the wisdom and experience of community elders. As teachers, advisers and memory-holders, elders have been major participants in these projects from the beginning. Knowing the past is crucial in any restoration effort. For example, in ecological restoration, having a "reference ecosystem" with species, structure and composition attributes to aspire to is essential. In ecocultural restoration projects, which incorporate culture and human history as an integral component of ecosystem restoration, the elders—the people who have lived the longest in a place—are the best sources of such traditional knowledge, oral history, language and cultural protocol. The elders' guidance is therefore vital in developing a sustainable future.

4. *Youth and Education.* Educating young people is another key concept within these projects. Children and youth are cherished participants, especially in the Koeye project, where they are seen as a major focus for the work, because they will carry forward the knowledge and values of the project for future generations. Ecocultural restoration may require continued—even indefinite—monitoring and investment of time, attention and skill. This can only take place if today's youth recognize the value of ongoing involvement; they need to learn how to contribute and to commit themselves to the projects' continuing development and suc-

cess. Through cultural education, young people will learn to apply their own strengths and talents towards improving their community and environment. In turn, they will receive the benefits of increasing confidence, self-esteem and self-reliance, as well as develop pride of accomplishment. In the future, as they mature and become elders in their turn, they will impart their own vision, energy, knowledge and experience to educating the next generations.

5. *Local Languages.* Using local language is an integral component of each initiative, and it is incorporated into each of the plans and visions in significant ways. The Nlaka'pmx term *Tmixʷ* ("land"), for example, symbolically and practically encapsulates for the participants what this project is about. *Koeye* is an ages-old Heiltsuk place name that reinforces and reclaims the Heiltsuk's proprietorship of their historic territory. The Haida name *Gwaii Haanas* ("island of beauty") expresses appreciation for the spectacular region of Haida homeland that has been designated as a co-managed Haida Heritage Site and National Park Reserve. Lessons in language—and in the traditional ecological knowledge mirrored in language—are both a symbolic and a practical way for people to reconnect with their culture and their homelands. Languages mould themselves to a particular place; their vocabulary and cadences harmonize with the surrounding landscapes, often embodying unique nuances and reflecting meanings incapable of translation. This is why it is important and necessary to retain traditional languages. Every time a language ceases to exist, significant knowledge vanishes with it. Ecocultural restoration can both benefit from local languages and help to perpetuate them.

6. *Ceremonial Recognition.* Another significant concept is recognizing in ceremony—songs, rituals, dances, feasts—people's relationships with each other, across families, clans, communities and generations, as well as with their other relatives—the animals, fish, trees and all the other elements of creation. Implicit in this recognition is a sense of gratitude and appreciation for the gifts of the ocean, the land and the ancestors. Ceremonies remind us of the importance of these connections and how critical they are to our survival and well-being. If we never take the time or make the effort to acknowledge our place in the community of Earth, we risk neglecting and abusing the very system that allows us to survive.

7. *Diversity.* Key to the success of each of these projects are the contributions and skills of many people, both within the culture and outside it, to achieve the best possible success. Each initiative welcomed and sought supporters, participants, experts, kindred spirits and fellow travellers from throughout the region. The project initiators and hosts were willing, in return for contributions of time, skills, knowledge and ideas, to share their own knowledge and skills with those who sincerely and respectfully sought to participate and understand. Although many different educational approaches run through them, all of the programs bring together traditional ecological knowledge and wisdom with western academic research and technologies to create a new, even stronger understanding of people and their particular environments.

8. *Patience and Persistence.* Xaxl'ep elder Maggie Adolph used to advise the members of her family and community when they were about to embark on a project or make a decision: "Go slow; make no mistakes." This counsel is particularly relevant in ecocultural restoration. It doesn't mean that one should not take action, but rather should carefully consider all of the aspects and potential pitfalls, and then make the best possible choices. Initiatives that are aimed at enhancing ecocultural systems must anticipate a long time frame, extending far beyond a single lifetime. Benefits of the steps we take today to restore and enhance our ecosystems may not be fully realized for many years, and we have to instill patience and persistence in our outlooks. We also need to be aware that some of our actions may have unforeseen consequences that we will need to take into account by modifying our approaches in the future. Each initiative is a journey—a journey underlain by past experience and tempered and directed by history, memories, longing, wisdom, observation, testing, trying out, deliberating, discussing, consulting, envisioning. Based on many generations of knowledge, these journeys extend themselves far into the future.

I have a poster on my office wall of the late Alice Paul of Hesquiaht, with her words: "The ultimate law of our people is the absolute protection of our offspring, for this is the way we as Nuu-chah-nulth people will survive." A span of centuries is the time frame on which to base decisions, a time interval an order of magnitude greater than most of us consider when we are thinking about our past and future. Another elder and Native American basket weaver, Bruce Miller *(Subiyay)* of the Skokomish tribe in Washington, once spoke at an ethnobiology conference about learning from Nature. He talked about learning from the different animals, and then he told us, "We can also learn from plants, and even from rocks. From them especially we learn patience and persistence."

Mainstream planning processes and projects incorporate some of the concepts embodied in these initiatives. The current thinking in land use and natural resource management in North America is directed towards "ecosystem-based management," which tries to accommodate a more holistic understanding of the ways in which parts of the environment are interrelated. Academics and decision-makers are starting to focus on "systems," complexes of related, interdependent elements organized within a whole, encompassing entity, which means they are paying more attention to the linkages between elements, whereas previously the parts would be addressed separately. "Adaptive management" is another concept that recognizes the need for flexibility and careful ongoing assessment, learning from the results of our activities, and for making allowances and adjustments in our plans if unanticipated effects should occur.

Resilience is another idea, originally developed for the study of ecosystems, that is often used to help us understand changes in social and ecological systems. It is a measure of flexibility and the ability of a system to deal with change. In an unpredictable and uncertain world, building resilience is important in enabling communities to retain their essential identity and character despite stresses imposed on them. A resilient system is one that has diversity and maintains "safety nets" and "backups" that can be put into action in the face of stresses. In the case of ecosystems, having a bank of seeds or underground reproductive structures can help a forest re-establish itself after a major fire, flood or other disturbance. In the case of First Nations communities, having the support of both family members and clan members during a time of crisis can help an individual overcome financial or emotional loss. Similarly, extended families residing in different locations can work together to provide a wider variety of foods and materials than would be available in only one locality; this makes them more resilient to local shortfalls. Given the importance accorded by indigenous peoples to future generations and to the long-term health of their environment, as in the Nuu-Chah-Nulth example, resilience thinking resonates well with indigenous views of the world.

In his commentary on "Resilience in Pre-contact Pacific Northwest Social Ecological Systems," my friend Ron Trosper, forest ecologist, economist and member of the Flathead Tribe, proposes that the Potlatch system of Northwest Coast indigenous societies provided these peoples with a robust capacity for social and ecological resilience. Citing a recent proposal by a group called the Resilience Alliance, which focusses its research on social and ecological resilience, Ron argues that the Potlatch fulfills the three criteria of this concept. The Potlatch gives indigenous groups the ability to buffer (to withstand pressure and maintain equilibrium), the ability to self-organize and the ability to learn. It embodies and reflects property rights, environmental ethics, rules of social organization and leadership, public accountability and a reciprocal exchange system— such as the investment system described previously by Kwakwaka'wakw cultural specialist Daisy Sewid-Smith.

The three initiatives featured in this chapter—the Tmixʷ Research Project, the Koeye Restoration project and Gwaii Haanas—also promote resilience for the participants and their environments because these initiatives enhance their ability both to persist and to adapt. Improving capacity for learning is important for building resilience, as it enables people and communities to adjust to an ever-changing world. Not only do adaptations to change give people and their environments more options, they are important for survival. The success of the adaptations, however, depends largely on whether they are conceived, designed and carried out by those who are affected by them. Thus, the key is to have the community respond through its own means and understandings rather than imposing solutions devised by outsiders, which are unlikely to fulfill the specific needs of each community. Local perspectives can help identify these needs, concerns and actions, and that is what each of these initiatives, in its own way, reflects.

Significantly, each of the initiatives described has the potential for being enacted at different scales. Set against a cyclical time frame of centuries, these projects have been conceived and developed within short seasons, working within the modern time spans dictated by political, bureaucratic and economic cycles. However, the concepts underlying the initiatives can be expanded, both conceptually and practically, from specific sites and regions to broader territories, possibly even to an entire land base in all its complexity. Individuals and whole communities, words and complete languages, single populations of organisms and entire habitats, creek estuaries and whole watersheds—the scales are wide-ranging and the scope is potentially immense.

At the heart of all these initiatives and indigenous views of sustainability is what Ron Trosper has termed "contingent proprietorship." Indigenous peoples in general do not consider themselves to be owners of lands and resources in the European legal sense of land ownership. Rather, they see themselves as caretakers of the land who have the privilege of its use but who bear a responsibility to look after its interests and the interests of future generations of people and other life forms. Instead of assuming that everything is intended just for human use—to change to our own ends, to destroy at whim—these societies reflect in their teachings, traditions and institutions a respect for the environment, past, present and future. This is not to say that mistakes will not be made or that misunderstandings will not occur. However, by and large, this approach is less harsh and damaging to the earth.

In 1991, anthropologists Michael Kew and Julian Griggs published a book chapter entitled "Native Indians of the Fraser Basin: Towards a Model of Sustainable Resource Use." They identified the "ethic of reciprocity":

> The linkage between humans, animals and the spirit world which so characterized the First Nations societies created a complex ethical framework which reinforced the notion of mutual dependency. Humans were not seen as dominant but played a complementary and often subordinate role in the larger ecological system. A key feature here was the concept of reciprocity and the belief that respectful human attitudes towards the resources helped to ensure the availability of future supply. Such an ethic encourages responsible use and supports an imperative of restraint.

They cite other characteristics of sustainable resource use demonstrated by First Nations of the Fraser River region, and they stress the importance of developing not just effective technologies for harvesting and processing resources but "an ideology of themselves and nature which informed and shaped their activities. That is to say, they were skilled in *applied* resource use within a workable *theory* of ecology." Although local differences existed, Kew and Griggs maintain that all First Nations shared this theory of ecology, "in fact before 1800 within the Fraser Basin, their theory and practice *prevailed*." Earth's Blanket would have been part of their common ideology.

Only patience and education will win others over to a gentler treatment of the earth. Individuals like Mary Thomas, Daisy Sewid-Smith and Roy Haiyupis are critical in this endeavour. Mary has shared her knowledge, and her pain, with thousands of people. She has taken foresters on walks through Secwepemc lands and talked to them about the value of birch and other trees that have been removed because they were considered useless competitors with economically important species. She tells stories to the children that gently impart lessons of Nature. She uses her immense capacity for love and empathy to reach the hardest of hearts and to make them understand her own concerns for Mother Nature and her own sense of wonder, appreciation, curiosity and understanding.

Daisy Sewid-Smith was told by her father, James Sewid, not to blame people for their prejudice and lack of understanding of her people's culture or ways of life. He said the only way that people would ever change was if they became educated, if they understood each other. He told Daisy never to hesitate to teach other people about their culture, because this would help them lose their prejudice and racism. Daisy and her friend and relative Kim Recalma-Clutesi have both followed this teaching faithfully. Both have generously shared their knowledge and perspectives with school and university classes, and with academics and others keen to enhance their own understanding of the world and the indigenous peoples of their region. I often quote Kim when I am trying to convey to my students a Kwakwaka'wakw perspective of Nature. She explains concisely and elegantly how important plants are to her people, acknowledging that they are part of a complex, balanced whole, and how underlying values are retained even through ongoing change:

Our well-being—mental, physical and spiritual—is absolutely dependent on the intricate rituals and use of plants as well as our ceremonial or ritual acknowledgement of those precious gifts. It is extremely important to remind ourselves that while plant use is important, it is only one part of a whole system that even at this time has been translated into a modern context using the old value systems.

Roy Haiyupis was another wise and knowledgeable person who was always generous and patient in explaining his Nuu-Chah-Nulth perspective and belief system to those who sought to learn about it, including the scientists on the Clayoquot Scientific Panel.

Nothing is isolated from the other aspects of life surrounding it and within it. This concept is the basis for the respect for nature that our people live with, and also contributed to the value system that promoted the need to be thrifty, not to be wasteful and to be totally conscious of your actual needs in the search for foods. The idea and practices of over-exploitation are deplorable to our people. The practice is outside our realm of values.

Dozens of people with this level of empathy and understanding for Nature are already role models and educators for building more caring and appreciative relationships with the earth. Pioneer American environmentalist Rachel Carson was one such individual: Knowledgeable and sensitive, she believed that for environmental integrity to be returned children should develop a sense of wonder for the natural world. She epitomized this sense of wonder throughout her life, never ceasing in her role as an educator and mentor. Against formidable opposition, she defended the birds, the oceans and all the life forms that human actions were throwing out of balance. British ethologist Jane Goodall is another such individual: Recognized the world over for her research with chimpanzees—in large part because of her sensitivity and respect for them and the other creatures of the world—she summarized the essence of this approach in her personal motto: "Only if we understand can we care. Only if we care will we help. Only if we help shall they be saved."

Although it is difficult to remain positive about the future of the world when we continuously witness so much wanton destruction, it is essential for all of us who cherish the environment in all its fragility and beauty to continue to be optimistic, to continue to completely enjoy the privilege of being part of Earth and its intricate systems. I read in a recent newspaper article that there are measurable differences in physical health, and even lifespan, between people who are happy and optimistic and those who are pessimistic in their outlook. Research revealed that people who consider themselves to be highly optimistic live, on average, seven and a half years longer than pessimists, who suffer from higher levels of most diseases, from heart disease to migraine. "Joy . . . a way of being, a state of mind," the article concludes, "is available to everybody. It is not found in things: it is found in us."

This teaching has to be relevant to people in today's world. Those of us—including the indigenous naturalists on whom this book has focussed—who love the natural world can fill our lives with endless fascination, an endless sense of discovery and a true, deep, penetrating sense of happiness at the wonder of it all. We can feel continuously amazed at the beauty of Nature's systems and cycles, at the immense diversity of life in time and space and at the ways in which Nature's elements are interwoven and interconnected. Honouring and respecting Nature is an obvious outcome of such thinking. If we receive our own identity from our place in this earthly galaxy we will never feel useless, bored or irrelevant. The feelings of supreme awe and appreciation for the privilege of being alive, of being a part of something rare and precious, are worth more than any treasure trove of gold or any number of material possessions.

The words of Bob Bandringa in his study of bitterroot in Nlaka'pmx territory bring us back to Earth's Blanket and the beautiful, stark and generous country of the Nlaka'pmx:

In beholding a population of these plants in flower, one is drawn to the tension found in the delicateness of light pink petals against the often rocky and arduous landscape. For the Nlaka'pmx, it is a picture of balance, a sense of place drawn out like a dance over time. They are the ones who have partaken of the valley's rich volcanic soils, a plant whose root body incarnates past generations. How different would bitterroot and surrounding ecologies be valued if everyone affirmed this heritage rather than the pursuit of a narrowly defined sense of wealth? As [Nlaka'pmx] Chief Leslie Edmonds shared, "If the mighty wheel of progress doesn't take these things into consideration, it will all be lost. . . ."

In the end, each of us must ask ourselves the question, "What constitutes *progress?*" Is progress reflected in the pavement of yet another parking lot, the vast swath of another highway or the colossal cement barrier of another dam? An alternative concept of progress honours and embraces Earth's Blanket, finds exhilaration in the trees, flowers and grasses, celebrates the seasonal cycles, accepts the responsibilities for tending habitats and shows gratitude for the gifts of life, family and community. This concept is grounded in the cultural traditions and wisdom of generations of indigenous peoples of British Columbia and elsewhere around the world, and it can lead all of us to a more sustainable society and a place for those still to come.

Source Notes

Works mentioned in the following notes (except Web sites) are cited in full in the References section, starting on page 262.

PREFACE and ACKNOWLEDGEMENTS

p. 1: Many writings exist that document environmental deterioration on both local and global scales. The Worldwatch Institute's *State of the World* annual book series, edited by Lester Brown, is just one example; see also UNESCO's *Encyclopedia of Life Support Systems* (2004) (Web site: www.eolss.net).

p. 2: My father's perspective on "water witching" is typified by the following statement: "Since dowsing is not based upon any known scientific or empirical laws or forces of nature, it should be considered a type of divination. The dowser tries to locate objects by occult means." From Robert Todd Carroll, *The Skeptic's Dictionary*, under "Dowsing" (Web site: www.skepdic.com/dowsing.html).

p. 2: My work with Christopher Paul and other Saanich elders was incorporated into my honours thesis in biology at the University of Victoria and eventually published (Turner and Bell 1971).

p. 3: Examples of academic writing that highlight the importance and relevance of stories and storytelling and discourse as a means of teaching cultural knowledge include the work of Marlene Atleo (2001), Richard Atleo (1999, 2004), Basso (1996), Boelscher (Ignace) (1988), Brody (1981, 2000), Cajete (1994), Cruikshank (1981) and Cruikshank et al. (1995). Some examples of writings that highlight indigenous peoples' perspectives of the environment include E.N. Anderson (1996a, b), Berkes (1999), Brown (1970), Cajete (1994), Callicott (1989, 1994),

Claxton and Elliott (1994), Ford and Martinez (2000), Gadgil et al. (1993), Gottesfeld (1994b), Nelson (1983), Turner and Atleo (1998) and Wall (1993). Some of
my own, often co-authored, writings in ethnobotany of British Columbia and
neighbouring First Peoples include Kuhnlein and Turner (1991), Turner (1995,
1997a, 1998, 2004), Turner and Efrat (1982) and Turner et al. (1980, 1983, 1990,
2000). Others include Compton (1993), Davis et al. (1994), Gunther (1945), Kari
(1987), 'Ksan, People of (1980), Loewen (1998), Norton (1981), Peacock (1998),
Smith (1998) and Steedman and Teit (1930).

The three main reports from the Scientific Panel for Sustainable Forest Prac-
tices in Clayoquot Sound (hereafter Clayoquot Scientific Panel) are Clayoquot
Scientific Panel (1995a, b, c). The first of these focusses specifically on Nuu-
Chah-Nulth perspectives of forest practices and the environment. Most recently,
Umeek (E.R. Atleo) (2004) elaborates on the Nuu-Chah-Nulth world view in his
book, *Tsawalk: A Nuu-chah-nulth Worldview.*

PROLOGUE: THE LAND AND THE PEOPLES

p. 12: Brown and Hebda (2002) provide a good example of the use of pollen analysis
to gain understanding of ecological change in British Columbia. See also Pielou
(1991) and Hebda and Whitlock (1997). The information on the history of cedar
abundance is from Hebda and Mathewes (1984). For reference to the Kamloops
Lake salmon fossils, see Carlson and Klein (1996).

p. 12: For more detailed information on the major vegetation zones of British Columbia, see Meidinger and Pojar (1991). The Lone Pine Publishing publications on
plants of various regions of British Columbia are excellent guides: Johnson et al.
(1995), MacKinnon et al. (1992), Parish et al. (1996) and Pojar and MacKinnon
(1994).

p. 14: Marianne Ignace (formerly Boelscher), working with Ron Ignace and other
colleagues, has produced a number of language lessons and tapes for Secwepemc
and other languages. These materials are available through the Secwepemc Cultural Education Society (Web site: www.secwepemc.org/orderlang.pdf) and the
First Peoples' Heritage, Language & Culture Council (Web site: www.fphlcc.ca).
Throughout British Columbia, indigenous speakers, teachers and linguists have
been developing language authorities to promote, renew and support the teaching of indigenous languages.

p. 15: For a discussion of the origins and usage of names of different language groups,
refer to Poser (2003) and Duff (1964) for an earlier description. For general information on the languages and cultures of British Columbia First Nations, there are
many good sources; see, for example, the Smithsonian Handbooks for the region:
Helm (1981), Suttles (1990) and Walker (1998). There are many ethnographic

writings relating to the various First Nations, as cited in these sources. Some of the references I have cited in this book include the work of anthropologists Boas (1901, 1921, 1930), Drucker (1951), McIlwraith (1948), Swanton (1905a, b) and Teit (n.d., 1898, 1900, 1906, 1909, 1912).

CH I. WEALTH AND VALUE IN A CHANGING WORLD

p. 19: For more information about James Teit and his life, refer to Campbell (1994), Favrholt (1994), Howes and Lean (1979), Lean and Teit (1995) and Wickwire (1998). Teit's work on Nlaka'pmx (Thompson) plants was eventually published after his death in 1922 (see Steedman and Teit 1930; see also Turner et al. 1990). His original field notes and manuscripts are in the American Philosophical Society Library, with copies in the British Columbia Archives (see Teit n.d.).

p. 20: Turner et al. (1990) provides an overview of the Nlaka'pmx people's attitude towards the environment and their use of plants; see also Teit (1900), Laforet and York (1998), York et al. (1993) and Hanna and Henry (1995).

p. 21: Information on traditional seasonal harvesting rounds and land and resource management of indigenous peoples of British Columbia is provided in Deur and Turner (in press), Gottesfeld (1994a, b), Hayden (1992), Loewen (1998), Peacock (1998), Peacock and Turner (2000), Turner (1999) and Turner et al. (1990).

p. 21–22: The quotations are from Whitford and Craig (1918:1 and 1918:64, respectively). Turner and Brown (2004) provide a discussion of linguistic aspects of landscape change.

pp. 22–23: The commentary on agricultural expansion is from Demerritt (1996:42). Jessie Ann Smith's journals are edited and published by Shewchuk (1989:32); see also Laforet and York (1998) and Lutz (in press) for discussions of aboriginal people working in construction, ranching and farming in the B.C. interior. Mary Thomas's observations are from a personal interview with her in 1994, and her experiences and discussions on traditional values are also recounted in her book (Thomas 2002).

pp. 25–27: Chief Adam Dick has shared his thoughts about wealth on several occasions in interviews (e.g., November 1996, November 1997); see also Turner and Peacock (in press) for a more detailed discussion of the implications of environmental deterioration and the loss of access to traditional lands and resources. For further information on the resources of the Kwakwa̲ka'wakw, see Turner (1995, 1998) and U'mista Cultural Society et al. (1998).

p. 26: There are plenty of studies on the topic of wealth, affluence and happiness, including a recent film called *Affluenza* (Web site: www.pbs.org/kcts/affluenza/show/show.html); see also Durning (1992) and Wachtel (1989). For a discussion of this topic as it relates to an indigenous community, see Andre et al. (2003).

pp. 28–30: For a description of Nlaka'pmx territory, see the introduction to Turner et al. (1990).

pp. 29–32: Information on bitterroot is from elders like Selina Timoyakin, Annie York, Mary Thomas and Nellie Taylor (pers. comm.); written sources are Bandringa (1999), Davidson (1916:135–136), Turner (1997a) and Turner et al. (1980, 1990). Quotations from Annie York are from Turner et al. (1990:33, 243). The words of Chief Leslie Edmonds are from an interview with Bandringa (1999:96–99).

pp. 32–33: Information on other culturally important plants of the Nlaka'pmx, including the quotation from Annie York, is from Turner et al. (1990).

p. 34: Susan Allison's journals have been edited and published by Margaret Ormsby (1976:13). In the lower Nicola Valley where Susan's husband grazed some of his cattle, the bunch grass grew three metres high in places in the 1860s, but the continued grazing caused it to become shorter and shorter. Later, Susan noted: "[Okanagan Lake] We rode silently through wild rye grass [*Elymus cinereus*] that was up to our shoulders on horseback, then we came out on our meadow at the harbour" (Ormsby 1976:41). Later still, General Sherman and his troops came over the border, and Susan wrote: "We had plenty of oats that we bought at Keremeos but no hay; but the big bunch-grass field . . . was then flourishing, knee-deep in grass . . . General Sherman and his troops used it for their horses. . . ." (Ormsby 1976:67). Jessie Ann Smith's observations are from Shewchuk (1989:32). See also Demerritt (1996).

pp. 34–35: Information on the recent state of bitterroot is from Bandringa (1999), as well as from conversations with Marianne Ignace about her experiences in harvesting bitterroot in the vicinity of Bonaparte with Secwepemc elder Nellie Taylor.

p. 35–36: Regarding recovery of overgrazed grasslands, see McLean and Tisdale (1972). Alfred Crosby wrote a book on the topic of introduced species, called *Ecological Imperialism: The Biological Expansion of Europe, 900–1900* (1986). ·

pp. 36–38: Landscape change and its impacts are discussed in many publications; see, for example, Carlson (1997) and Laforet and York (1998:29). For information on the Drynoch Slide and its history, see VanDine (1983). The mythological narratives about landslides are from Teit (1912). Ryder and Church (1986) also discuss the history of slides in the Fraser drainage. The Hells Gate Slide of the early 1900s is described by Laforet and York (1998) and by newspaper columnist Stephen Hume (2000:10). James Paul Xixne7 of Spuzzum is quoted in Laforet and York (1998:100).

pp. 38: Smohalla's words were originally quoted by Mooney (1896:721) and are cited in Hunn and Selam (1990:83).

pp. 39: There are numerous examples of conservation concepts and practices embodied in traditional land and resource management among indigenous and local communities in many parts of the world; see, for example, Alcorn (1984, 1993, 1996), E.N. Anderson (1996a), Baker (1999), Baker et al. (2001), Balée (1994), Bennett (1992), Berkes (1999), Freeman and Carbyn (1988), Johnson (1997), Minnis and Elisens (2000), Nazarea (1999), Peña (1999), Posey (1990), Posey and Balée (1989) and Young et al. (1991), to name just a few.

CH 2. LAND-BASED STORIES OF PEOPLES AND HOME PLACES

pp. 42–43: Christopher Paul and I went to look at the whale on ȽÁUWELṈEW̱ in 1969. Elsie Claxton and Violet Williams told me their stories during interviews from 1987 to 1993. The symposium at Dunsmuir Lodge, at which Philip Paul spoke and shared the story of Mount Newton, ȽÁUWELṈEW̱, was in the summer of 1992.

pp. 44: See "The Origin of Daylight" (Bouchard and Kennedy 2002:153). Tom Sampson is quoted in Simonsen et al. (1997) from an interview on 30 July 1996.

pp. 45–47: The Nlaka'pmx narrative "Old One and the Earth, Sun, and People," in various versions, is from Teit (1912:321).

p. 47: Mistreatment of the earth, the theme of personification of Earth and the metaphor of water as blood are widespread. For example, Gene Anderson introduces his book *Ecologies of the Heart: Emotion, Belief, and the Environment* (Eugene N. Anderson 1996a) with the Chinese metaphor of springs of water being the veins of a dragon. Loftin (1991) notes that the Zuñi and Hopi also perceive Earth as their mother. Some believe that a steel plow will tear her skin; that is why they use a digging stick in their gardens. The Gaia hypothesis is described by James Lovelock (1979) in his book *Gaia: A New Look at Life on Earth.*

pp. 47–50: For the Saanich story "Origin of Salmon," see Jenness (ca. 1930:94). For a description of the different species of Pacific salmon and their characteristics and ecological features, see Clarke et al. (1995) and Groot and Margolis (1991).

pp. 48: For information on the importance of qex̱mín (*Lomatium nudicaule*), see Turner (1997a, 1998) and Turner et al. (1990). Many of my indigenous friends, including Earl Claxton, Gordon DeFrane, Daisy Sewid-Smith and Kim Recalma-Clutesi, know this plant well and consider it to be sacred.

p. 50–51: Diamond Jenness's recorded version of the Saanich Flood is from Jenness (ca. 1930:73). Philip Paul shared this version when he was talking about Mount Newton, ȽÁUWELṈEW̱, in 1992.

p. 51–52: Edward Thomas's words about the Malahat and the flood are from Simonsen et al. (1997; interviewed 29 July 1996). The information on the flooding event evident from sediment core samples taken from the bottom of the inlet in August 1996 by the international Ocean Drilling Program vessel *JOIDES Resolution* was shared with me by my friend Dr. Richard Hebda, who participated in this research.

pp. 52–54: For further details on Daisy's ancestor čəqaməy̓ and the Great Flood, see Sewid-Smith et al. (1998).

p. 54: For a discussion of the personification of trees, and their special sacred qualities in human cultures, see Fife (1994).

pp. 54–55: The Saanich story "How Douglas-Fir Got Its Pitch" is from Jenness (ca. 1930:63). I have been told other versions of this story by Arvid Charlie and others; see also Bouchard and Kennedy (2002).

pp. 55–56: Many people, including Florence Davidson, Christine Joseph *(Wata)*, Edith O'Donaghey, Mary Thomas and Annie York have talked about the medicinal values of tree pitch (see Turner 1988; Turner et al. 1990). Tina Robinson from the Gitga'at Nation demonstrated how to make spruce-pitch medicine at the Gitga'at seaweed-halibut camp at Kiel, Princess Royal Island, in May 2002; this was demonstrated in the film *Gitga'ata Spring Harvest* (Coasts Under Stress and Gitga'at Nation 2003).

p. 56–57: The story of the Yellow-Cedar Sisters was told by Alice Paul of Hesquiaht (see Turner and Efrat 1982). A description of how yellow-cedar bark is used can be found in Turner (1998).

pp. 58: The Nuxalk (Bella Coola) story of the origin of soapberries ("buffalo berries") is from McIlwraith (1948:188); see also Turner (1973, 1981).

pp. 60–62: The story of the black huckleberry, the mountain goat brothers and Eagle is from the Sinixt (Lakes) tradition (see also Turner et al. 1980; Pearkes 2002:22–23). For the other information on black huckleberries, see Turner (1973, 1974, 1995, 1997a); Turner et al. (1980, 1990). The information from Mary Thomas is from interviews with her (pers. comm. 2000).

P. 62–64: The story "How Coyote . . . Happened to Make the Black Moss Food" is from Mourning Dove (1933:120–25). Mary Thomas's story about learning from her mother how to cook black tree lichen she has recounted on several occasions (pers. comm. 1994, 2000). For further information on black tree lichen, see Turner (1997a) and Turner et al. (1980, 1990).

pp. 64–65: For further information about the irritant properties of skunk cabbage and other plants in the family Araceae, see Turner and Szczawinski (1991). The Kathlamet narrative "Myth of the Salmon" is from Boas (1901:50).

p. 66: For further information on eulachon (*Thaleichtys pacificus*), see Drake and Wilson (1991): *Eulachon: A Fish to Cure Humanity*. The Tlingit story on the origin of basketry is from Frances Paul (1944:9). The Nuxalk stories on the origin of fishing nets are from McIlwraith (1948 I:648); see McIlwraith (II:535–36) for a description of making nettle twine.

CH 3. A KINCENTRIC APPROACH TO NATURE

p. 69: In *Cosmos* (1980) Carl Sagan wrote: "We are a way for the universe to know itself. Some part of our being knows this is where we came from. We long to return. And we can, because the Cosmos is also within us. We're made of star stuff." Dr. Nancy C. Maryboy was speaking with her colleague Dr. David Begay, both Diné (Navajo) educators and cultural specialists, at a conference of the Society for Ethnobiology in spring 1997.

pp. 70–72: For further information on the concept of *iwígara*, see Salmón (2000a, b). The example from Laguna Pueblo is from Salmón (2000a:1327), citing Laguna author and poet Leslie Marmon Silko. The quotations are from Salmón (2000a: 1328).

pp. 70–71: As well as Enrique Salmón's writings (see Salmón 1996), the works of Armstrong (1996), Basso (1996:100–01) and Davidson-Hunt (2003) all highlight the critical importance of language in understanding indigenous perspectives of the land and environment.

pp. 72–73: Richard Atleo and Roy Haiyupis shared their insights on *hishuk ish ts'awalk* as recorded in Clayoquot Scientific Panel (1995a); see also Craig and Smith (1997), Smith (1997), Turner and Atleo (1998:107, 111) and *Umeek* (Atleo) (2004).

p. 74–75: Arvid Charlie recalled Leschím's teachings in an interview with Trevor Lantz and me in December 1999.

p. 75–76: Theresa Thorne is quoted from Simonsen et al. (1997; interviewed 30 July 1996). Kim Recalma-Clutesi wrote this perspective on Kwakwa̱ka'wakw relationships with resources when she was a student at the University of Victoria in 1993, and it is included here with her permission.

pp. 76: The story about the Salmon People is from an interview with Daisy Sewid-Smith, Chief Adam Dick and Kim Recalma-Clutesi in November 1997.

pp. 76–78: Mary Thomas's recollections of walking along the riverbank of the Salmon River with her grandmother are from an interview in 1997. Her grandmother's recounting of the salmon life cycle is from Mary's book (Thomas 2002) as well as from travels with Mary from 1994 to 2003.

pp. 78–81: For further information on "the bear's own berries," see Turner (1997b), and on yellow glacier lily and its use by grizzlies, see Loewen (1998). Information on *nkéxw* is from Laforet et al. (1993), Turner et al. (1990) and Turner (1997a). The Nlaka'pmx story of the animals' preference for *nkéxw* and other human foods is in Teit (1912:219, 221, 233). The stories "The Goat People" and "The Hunter and the Goats" are recorded in Teit (1912:258–64).

p. 81: Ida Matthew's recollections are from an interview with Marianne Ignace (see Turner, Ignace and Ignace 2000).

pp. 81–82: The quotation from Charles Hill-Tout is from Maud (1978b:117). Information on the Tlingit world view is from Emmons (1991:102–03). Helen Clifton shared her people's views on wolves and respect for other life forms in May 2002 at the Gitga'at seaweed camp.

pp. 83: The Nuu-Chah-Nulth celebration attended by Richard Atleo, my husband Bob and myself was in the fall of 2002 at Coombs in honour of the wedding anniversary of Earl Maquinna George and Josephine George.

pp. 83–85: Violet Williams told the story of the wolves in an interview, together with Elsie Claxton, on 23 September 1988. The story "The Woman Who Befriended a Wolf" is from McIlwraith (1948, 1:191–92). "The Hunter and the Wolf" is from Teit (1912:378); for more information on irritant properties of buttercups, see Turner (1984); Selina Timoyakin was warned not to handle buttercups (Turner et al. 1980).

p. 85: The Blackfoot information on learning from wolves is from the Blackfoot Gallery Committee (2001:12).

pp. 85–86: Regarding the special traits of animals see, for example, Teit (1912:227). The Nlaka'pmx story of Beaver and fire recorded by Charles Hill-Tout is from Maud (1978a:101–02).

pp. 87–88: Vi Williams and Elsie Claxton's story about Swainson's thrush was shared in an interview (pers. comm. 9 June 1989).

pp. 88–91: This version of the story of Coyote's wives is from Teit (1912:223). Note that in this version cottonwood is named as the second wife, but the Nlaka'pmx term provided indicates that the tree was actually trembling aspen. Tom Sampson talked about the Giant People who were turned into trees, at a symposium at Dunsmuir Lodge in 1991 sponsored by University Extension, University of Victoria. The words of Ernie Rice are from Simonsen et al. (1997; interview 30 July 1996). Mountain people of the Nuxalk are described by McIlwraith (1948 I:305, 598–600). Information about the Malahat is from Elsie Claxton (pers. comm. 1989), and Earl Claxton Sr. shared the story about Mount Tolmie in an interview in August 2002. Selina Timoyakin's classification of the different communities of beings is described in Turner (1974) and Turner et al. (1980).

pp. 91–92: This "prayer" was recorded and translated by Franz Boas in *The Religion of the Kwakiutl Indians* (1930:237–38). Several of Boas's publications (cf. Boas 1921, 1930) refer to "prayers," which are interpreted here, following Daisy Sewid-Smith's advice (Sewid-Smith et al. 1998, footnote), as "words of praise." Daisy has explained this meaning on several occasions to my classes in ethnobotany at the University of Victoria. Words of praise to the salmonberry and the medicine made from this shrub are from Boas (1930:218). Information on harvesting medicines, as well as food products and materials, from living trees and other plants is provided in Turner and Peacock (in press), and other chapters in the book *"Keeping it Living,"* edited by Deur and Turner (in press). Theresa Sam's words are from Simonsen et al. (1997; interviewed 13 March 1996).

p. 93: The information on Blackfoot teachings on the environment is from the Blackfoot exhibit at the Glenbow Museum, which I visited in November 2002, and from the book that accompanies this exhibit (Blackfoot Gallery Committee 2001:8).

CH 4. HONOURING NATURE THROUGH CEREMONY AND RITUAL

pp. 95–96: My conversations with Mary Thomas about her mother, Christine Allen, took place on many occasions from about 1992 to 2003. Mary often talked about her mother, who was one of her primary teachers, especially at the time when Mary was middle-aged and her mother was quite elderly (see also Thomas 2002).

pp. 96: The citation for Priscilla Russell's work in Alaska is Russell (1991:6). Helen Clifton's instructions for harvesting devil's club (*Oplopanax horridus*) medicine were given during my visit to Hartley Bay in June 2004. See also Lantz et al. (2004) for a discussion on cultural aspects of devil's club use.

pp. 97: I interviewed Earl Claxton Sr. about the Saanich environmental perspectives in the summer of 2002. He has also spoken about this topic to my classes at the University of Victoria (spring 2003). See also his and John Elliott's book on the Saanich reef-net fishery (Claxton and Elliott 1994).

pp. 97–99: Simon Fraser's journal was edited and annotated by archivist and historian W. Kaye Lamb (1960:86–88). Oral traditions of the Nlaka'pmx people's encounters with Simon Fraser are recounted in Teit (1912:414–15); see also Hanna and Henry (1995), Laforet and York (1998) and Wickwire (1994). A good description of the Transformers and their work is in York et al. (1993).

p. 99: Relating to the Douglas Treaties, the text of the treaties and letters regarding them are found in *Papers Connected with the Indian Land Question. 1850–1875* (British Columbia 1987:5–11). The treaties and the relationships between First Nations and the European newcomers are discussed by Arnett (1999), Duff (1969), Elliott and Poth (1990), Fisher (1992) and Harris (1999, 2002), among many other sources.

pp. 100–01: The Saanich people's spiritual relationship with the Malahat mountain and other traditional lands and waters has been referred to by many Saanich elders in speeches and discussions, such as by Philip Paul and Tom Sampson in symposia sponsored by the University of Victoria (1992 and 1993), Elsie Claxton on many occasions in interviews and on outings with me, Earl Claxton Sr. and John Elliott in discussions and course lectures and field trips (summer 2001, spring 2003), as well as in a comprehensive report, available on the Web from a background research report on a potential housing development at Bamberton on Saanich Inlet (Simonsen et al. 1997). The words quoted from Ernie Rice are from this report, from an interview on 29 July 1996.

pp. 101–02: Roy Haiyupis, as part of his participation in the Clayoquot Scientific Panel, wrote several documents about different aspects of Nuu-Chah-Nulth perspectives of land and culture. He is quoted on many occasions in the "First Nations' Perspectives of Forest Practices in Clayoquot Sound" document (Clayoquot Scientific Panel 1995a), and the quotations are drawn from this work and from personal communications with him from 1993 to 1995.

pp. 102–03: Chief Earl Maquinna George, hereditary chief of Ahousaht, was an undergraduate and then graduate student at the University of Victoria. As an elder in his seventies he completed his master's degree, and I had the privilege of being his academic co-supervisor. Later, his thesis, based on his own experiences and teachings of elders in his community, was published as a book (George 2003). Between 1997 and 2000 he shared his reminiscences, which were recorded and transcribed into print. The quotations here are from that work.

pp. 103–04: The information on Saanich relationships to the land is from Claxton and Elliott (1994:15).

pp. 104–05: George Clutesi provides the information on the Nuu-Chah-Nulth Potlatch in his book *Potlatch* (Clutesi 1969:35); see also Turner and Atleo (1998).

pp. 105–09: Information on the letters in "The Potlatch Papers" is from a binder of copies of the letters and documents in the possession of Flora Dawson of Kingcome Village, and also discussed by Bracken (1997). The amended version of the Indian Act, continuing the outlawing of the Potlatch, is in Revised Statutes of Canada 1927, vol. II, chap. 98, no. 140, p. 2218. See also Codere (1966), Daly (n.d., 1988), Sewid-Smith (1979) for further discussions on the Potlatch, including legal, social, cultural and economic aspects.

pp. 110–11: The information from Daisy Sewid-Smith on the Kwakwaka'wakw investment system and Sacred Cedar Bark Ceremony is from Sewid-Smith et al. (1998).

pp. 111–13: The description by Charles Hill-Tout of a Halkomelem girl's puberty rites is from Maud (1978c:55). Puberty rites and the importance of ceremonial cleansing are also discussed by Teit (1900, 1906, 1909) and in Jilek (1982). See also Kew (1990). The quotations from Richard Atleo and Roy Haiyupis on Nuu-Chah-Nulth sacred areas and ritual bathing and prayers are from Clayoquot Scientific Panel (1995a:21, 23); see also Atleo (1999), Emmons (1991:202) and *Umeek* (Atleo) (2004).

p. 114: Mary Thomas explained her perspective on the Secwepemc relationship to mountains and remote places when we were on Mount Revelstoke in the summer of 1995. Saanich elder Edward Thomas is quoted by Simonsen et al. (1997) from an interview on 29 July 1996. The words of Tom Sampson are also from Simonsen et al. (1997).

pp. 115–17: The quotation about the Saanich First Salmon Ceremony is from Claxton and Elliott (1994:13). The Chehalis sockeye and First Shoots ceremonies described by Charles Hill-Tout are cited in Maud (1978c:115). Ernie Hill told me about giving a gift to the young person who brings him the first salmonberry in a conversation in December 2002 at Hartley Bay, and he explained this tradition at a school and community gathering in June 2004. Earl Maquinna George talked about Nuu-Chah-Nulth foods and recalled harvesting the spring shoots from his childhood during conversations from 1995 to 1997 at the University of Victoria. See also George (2003).

pp. 118–19: Hill-Tout's discussions about indigenous peoples' relationships with other life forms are from Maud (1978c:115) and on the Nlaka'pmx First Foods ceremonies from Maud (1978a:46). James Teit's observations are from Steedman and Teit (1930:453); see also Kennedy and Bouchard (1992).

p. 120: The information on the sacred aspects of bitterroot, and the quotations from Madeline Lanaro, are from Bandringa (1999:53–56). The importance of sword ferns in the winter initiation rites was explained by Elsie Claxton in an interview in 1993.

pp. 120–22: The Nlaka'pmx quotations about balsamroot are from Teit (1906) and are also cited in Peacock (1998). Gordon Robinson's experiences relating to the Flower Dance of the Haisla (Hanaksiala) are cited in Compton (1993:197), and the special role of flowers as ecological indicators is also described by Davis et al. (1994) and Lantz and Turner (2003).

p. 122: The Iroquois Corn ceremonies are described by Herrick (1995), and other types of Iroquois seasonal ceremonies are cited in Wall (1993). There is also an excellent film on the cultural and spiritual role of corn in Iroquoian and other indigenous cultures (National Film Board 1988). Anishinaabe ceremonies relating to the wild-rice (*Ziẓania aquatica*) harvest are described by Davidson-Hunt (2003). Tohono O'odham (Papago) harvesting of saguaro cactus (*Carnegiea gigantea*) fruits in Arizona and their association with the rain festival was explained by elder Danny Lopez during a Society of Ethnobiology field trip to his home community in 1995 (see also Nabhan 1985). Descriptions of the Mapuche piñon harvest and ceremonial relationships to the araucaria or monkey-puzzle tree (*Araucaria araucana*) in Chile are from Nesti (1999).

pp. 122–25: Information on the Blackfoot ceremonial life is in the museum exhibit book of the Blackfoot Gallery Committee (2001). The story of the sacred prairie turnip (*Psoralea esculenta*) is illustrated in a book called *Star Boy* (Goble 1983); see also Thompson's chapter in Dundes (1965); Thompson discusses versions of this story in the context of many of similar theme, known collectively as "The Star Husband Tale." Salmón (2000a, b) discusses the *yúmari* ritual as one of the key ceremonial aspects of Rarámuri life. Madeline Lanaro's words about bitter-root are recorded by Bandringa (1999:55).

CH 5. THE BALANCE BETWEEN HUMANS AND NATURE

pp. 127–30: Helen and Chief Johnny Clifton talked about the abalone (*Haliotis kamtschatkana*) when I was spending time with them at the Gitga'at spring camp at Kiel, on Princess Royal Island, in May 2001 and again in May 2002, when they were featured in a film, *Gitga'ata Spring Harvest* (Coasts Under Stress and Gitga'at Nation 2003). In this film, they identify the loss of abalone as one of their major concerns about the environment. Daisy Sewid-Smith's words are from an interview with her in 1995. Roy Haiyupis is quoted from Clayoquot Scientific Panel (1995a). *Queesto,* Chief Charlie Jones, is quoted from the *Ottawa Citizen* (5 September 1987, p. F2). Mary Thomas told me the story about the trembling aspen when we were in Utah together in 1997, on the occasion of her receiving the Seacology Foundation's Indigenous Conservationist of the Year Award. She also told it to my students and me in July 2003.

pp. 131–33: *Kii7lljuus* told me this story in 2003. Enrico (1995:159–70) provides Haida versions and English translations of the *Jilaa kuns* story originally recorded by Swanton (1905a, b). One of these (Swanton 1905a:316–17) was told to anthropologist Franz Boas by Charles Edenshaw, who was the father of Florence Davidson of Masset (Blackman 1982). The variations referred to are found in Swanton (1905a:317, 1905b:96ff). The Haisla version is published in Robinson (1956:27–30). The Tlingit version was recorded by Emmons (1991:203). Helen Clifton has talked about the disappearance of frogs around Hartley Bay on several occasions, including in December 2002 and June 2004.

pp. 132–35: The observations of Percy Williams, Roy Jones Sr. and Ernie Wilson are quoted in Jones (2000:205). Dr. Samuel Sam's observations are quoted in Simonsen et al. (1997), in an interview from 28 January 1997. References relating to "fishing down" the food chain include UBC Fisheries researchers Tony Pitcher and colleagues (Pitcher et al. 1998); see also Brown (1998) and Murray and Neis (2004). Observations of declining resources are also discussed in a video by Barb Cranmer and Cari Green (1995), *Laxwesa Wa: Strength of the River*.

pp. 135–36: Observations about environmental deterioration from Mary Thomas, Dr. Daisy Sewid-Smith, Chief Adam Dick and Kim Recalma-Clutesi are recorded in Turner and Peacock (in press); Thomas et al. (in prep.) and Turner, Ignace and Ignace (2000). The "Helping the Land Heal" Conference on Ecological Restoration took place in Victoria in 1998, sponsored by the University of Victoria Restoration of Natural Systems Program (co-chairs R. Hebda and N. Turner).

pp. 136–40: The restoration project initiated by Mary Thomas, Louis Thomas and Dorothy Argent is described in the film *Voices of the River* (Salmon River Restoration Committee 1993). Some of Mary's thoughts about birch and the web of life are expressed in her book, based on her lectures at the University of Victoria (Thomas 2002), as well as in interviews with me and my students over the past ten or more years (see also her film, Thomas 1996). Her experiments with measuring birch sap production are from Thomas (2002). A description of the Silver Creek Blaze at Salmon Arm is provided in Keller (2002).

pp. 140–41: The words of Daisy Sewid-Smith were recorded in an interview in November 1994 and cited in Sewid-Smith et al. (1998).

pp. 141–43: Amadeo Rea's book is *At the Desert's Green Edge: An Ethnobotany of the Gila River Pima* (Rea 1997).

pp. 143–44: Dr. Samuel Sam is quoted by Simonsen et al. (1997; interviewed 28 January 1997). Many other observations and testimonies of environmental deterioration and loss of resources are presented by Simonsen et al. (1997).

pp. 144–45: An interesting book that describes some of Nature's inventions and our human attempts to emulate them is *Biomimicry: Innovation Inspired by Nature,* by Benyus (1998). Maser's (1994) *Forest Primeval: The Natural History of an Ancient Forest* is another wonderful account of the complexities of Nature, including soil mycorrhizae.

CH 6. LOOKING AFTER THE LANDS AND WATERS

p. 147: For more on James Douglas's views of the Victoria region, and the background to Fort Victoria, see Arnett (1999), Beckwith (in prep.), Deur and Turner (in press), Fisher (1992) and Scholefield (1914).

p. 148: Daisy Sewid-Smith's words are from her address at the "Helping the Land Heal" conference (Sewid-Smith 1998). Chief Adam Dick has spoken about the "keeping it living" concept on a number of occasions, both to myself (pers. comm. 1998) and to my colleague and collaborator Dr. Douglas Deur (2000, 2001). We were so interested and impressed by this concept that we used the term as a title for our co-edited book (Deur and Turner, in press).

pp. 148–50: For examples of stewardship practices for salmon in Northwest Coast societies, see Eugene N. Anderson's *Ecologies of the Heart* (1996a), particularly chap. 4, entitled "Learning from the Land Otter: Religious Representation of Traditional Resource Management" (pp. 54–72). See also "The Northwest Coast," pt. 1, chap. 2 of *Bird of Paradox*, edited by Eugene N. Anderson (1996b). A master's thesis by Jim Jones (2002), based on detailed interviews with a number of Heiltsuk fishers and fisheries experts, also details many different practices relating to "looking after" the salmon streams. The film *Laxwesa Wa: Strength of the River* (Cranmer and Green 1995), featuring Heiltsuk elder Edwin Newman and Kwakwaka'wakw elder Agnes Cranmer, also discusses salmon stewardship. McIlwraith's description of the Nuxalk "River Guardian" is in vol. I, pp. 262–64, of his 1948 publication. Simonsen et al. (1997) provide information on stewardship and "cultivation" of both salmon and shellfish. See also Deur (2000, 2001), Deur and Turner (in press) and examples from Fowler (1992), Fowler and Turner (1999), Minnis and Elisens (2000) and Thomas (2002). Many elders featured in this book—Earl Claxton Sr., Elsie Claxton, Helen and Johnny Clifton, Adam Dick, Earl George and Mary Thomas, to name just a few, have talked about care for different types of resources (clam beds, abalone, nesting-bird colonies, deer, salmon, and various types of plants) using practices of selective and seasonal harvesting, monitoring and proprietorship. See also Claxton and Elliott (1994) and Harper (2003).

pp. 150–51: A discussion of the term "hunter-gatherer" and its implications is provided in the introduction (chap. 1) of Deur and Turner (in press). Gilbert Malcolm Sproat's writings, originally published in 1868, are from Lillard's edited version, Introduction (Sproat 1987:8). Joseph Trutch's letter is from British Columbia (1987:30). The reference of James Douglas to First Peoples as "wandering denizens of the forest" is from a letter written by him on 14 March 1859 to Sir E.B. Lytton, secretary of state to the colonies (British Columbia 1987). For quotes from Captain George Vancouver, see Newcombe (1923:116–17) and Vancouver (1801). For a discussion of the European newcomers' impressions of Victoria, see Lutz (1995); Berhold Seeman sailed on HMS *Herald*, under Captain Henry Kellett, D.B., in the expedition of 1845–51, and recorded his impressions in a journal. His words are from his journal of 27 June 1846 (Scholefield 1914:483). For quotes from Captain George Vancouver, see Lutz (1995), Newcombe (1923:116–17) and Vancouver (1801).

pp. 152–54: For more information on humans, fire and their influence on ecosystems, see Boyd (1999), Gottesfeld (1994a), Kimmerer and Lake (2001), Lewis (1982), Lewis and Ferguson (1988), Pyne (1995) and Stewart (1956). I made the trip through the fire zone in Manning Park in 1959. For an excellent discussion of the role of fire in ecological history, see Pyne (2002). Morels (*Morchella* spp.) are well known to flourish in recently burned areas. In British Columbia and elsewhere they have been a major non-timber forest product. For example, in 2004, members of the Ktunaxa (Kootenay) Nation of southeast British Columbia have undertaken a small-scale development project picking and drying morels; my friend Michael Keefer has been helping in this enterprise.

pp. 154–55: Daisy Sewid-Smith is quoted from her address at the "Helping the Land Heal" conference in Victoria (1998). Boas's Kwak'wala "prayer" to the berries is from *The Religion of the Kwakiutl Indians* (1930:203). Accounts of boreal forest landscape burning are from Lewis (1982) and Lewis and Ferguson (1988).

p. 156: Dennis Martinez has talked about the practice of landscape burning on many occasions, including at the "Helping the Land Heal" conference in Victoria (1998) and at the International Garry Oak Symposium the following year (1999). The citation for the newspaper account of aboriginal burning from the time of the gold rush is: Anonymous (1849:18–19). The Nlaka'pmx story is from Teit (1898:72–74).

pp. 156–59: Baptiste Ritchie's account, given originally in Stl'atl'imx in December 1969, was translated by him for Salishan linguist Leo Swoboda, and later for Salishan linguist Randy Bouchard and anthropologist Dorothy Kennedy. The original text in Stl'atl'imx, together with a word-by-word translation, is given in Swoboda (1971:182–91).

pp. 159–60: Mary Thomas's words about fire are from an interview in 1994. Ernie Hill told me about the island that was burned for berries in May 2002. See also Turner (1999) for a discussion of burning practices. Arvid Charlie's information on burning was shared in an interview with myself and Trevor Lantz in December 1999. Bob Akerman's information is from an interview with him, together with Brenda Beckwith, in 1999. See also Beckwith (2002) and Lutz (1995). Newcombe's 1892 photo of Uplands Park is published in Szczawinski and Harrison (1972, p. x).

p. 162: Kat Anderson's work is published in M. Kat Anderson, (1996, 1997), Blackburn and Anderson (1993) and in her upcoming book (Anderson, in press). Brenda Beckwith participated in the burn on Yellow Island with Peter Dunwiddie and The Nature Conservancy (see Dunwiddie 2002). Her work is reported in Beckwith (2002). Minnis and Elisens's book *Biodiversity and Native America* was published in 2000. Ford's chapter in this volume (Ford 2000) describes the ancient agroecology system of the Rio del Oso valley.

p. 163: For information on Janis Alcorn's work, see Alcorn (1993, 1996); for Gene Anderson's, see Eugene N. Anderson (1996a:73–84, chap. 5, "Managing the

Rainforest: Maya Agriculture in the Town of the Wild Plums"), as well as his most recent ethnobotany (Anderson 2003). References to Amazonian traditional management systems include Balée (1994: chap. 6, "Indigenous Forest Management," pp. 116–65), Berkes (1999), Posey (1989, 1990); and Posey and Balée (1989). For further discussions on the continuums of management between hunters and gatherers, cultivators and agriculturalists, see Ford (1985), Harris (1989), Peacock (1998) and the first chapters of Deur and Turner (in press).

pp. 164–65: Adam Dick talked about traditional gardening on the tidal flats at King-come Inlet on many occasions, including in interviews in November 1996 and November 1997. Then, in 2000, Doug Deur and I went to Kingcome with Adam and Kim Recalma-Clutesi and saw for ourselves the extent of the original root beds at the Kingcome River estuary and experienced, with Adam, the amazing environment there but also the changes that had occurred since the days of his childhood. We have also written about these root gardens in Deur (2000, 2001) and Deur and Turner (in press). Daisy Sewid-Smith talked about the root gardens on many occasions, such as during an interview in November 1997 and at the "Helping the Land Heal" conference in 1998. Edwards (1979) provides a description of similar practices for the Nuxalk of the Bella Coola area. The role of Adam's ancestors as guardians of the eulachon was discussed by Adam Dick in an interview in November 1997. See also Drake and Wilson (1991). Information about pruning the berry bushes is from an interview with Adam Dick in November 1996 (see also Turner and Peacock, in press).

pp. 165–69: For descriptions of harvesting and using basketry materials by Florence Davidson, see Blackman (1982), Nelson (1983) and Turner (1998, 2004). Information on California Native American basketry materials is from M. Kat Anderson (1996, in press) and Stevens (1999). For information on culturally modified trees (CMTs) and their significance, see British Columbia, Ministry of Forests (1997) and Garrick (1998). Mary Thomas's words inspired the title "Making It with Your Hands" in our University of Victoria ethnobotany class book (Turner 1997b).

pp. 169–70: References to resource ownership practices of Northwest Coast peoples are from Boas (1921), Blackman (1990), Drucker (1951) and Richardson (1982) and are summarized in Turner, Smith and Jones (in press). The quote from George Dawson is from his journal of 1878, which was edited by Cole and Lockner (1993:134b). Edward Sapir (1913–1914) recorded the information on Nuu-Chah-Nulth root patches in his journal. See also Arima et al. (1991:190–91). Philip Drucker's observations on Nuu-Chah-Nulth ownership are from Drucker (1951:247).

pp. 170–71: For further discussion of *hahuulhi*, see Turner, Smith and Jones (in press), as well as Earl George's book (George 2003). Roy Haiyupis is quoted in Clayoquot Scientific Panel (1995a:9).

pp. 171–73: Words on ownership from the *Delgamuukw* court case are from Gisday'wa and Delgamuukw (1989:7–8). Coast Salish resource ownership is discussed by Jenness (n.d., ca. 1930), Suttles (1987) and Turner, Smith and Jones (in press). The quote on Katzie ownership is from Suttles (1955:26–27). The material on camas ownership is from Christopher Paul (pers. comm. to Marguerite Babcock 1967, p. 5 in her notes). Personal knowledge of burning on the Tsartlip reserve in 1960 is provided by Dr. G. Brent Ingram (2003) and by Kevin Paul (pers. comm. 2004).

pp. 173–77: Kat Anderson's work with Native Californians is found in many publications and will be summarized in her upcoming book (Anderson, in press). Kay Fowler's research with the Paiute and Shoshoni peoples of Nevada is described in Fowler (1992), Fowler and Turner (1999) and Fowler (2000), in Minnis and Elisens (2000). Daisy's words are from her address at the "Helping the Land Heal" conference (1998). The Okanagan elder spoke at the Fourth Annual Canadian Aboriginal Science and Technology Society Conference, in Richmond, B.C. (September 1996). See Bandringa (1999:92) for the reference to bitterroot. Caring for plant resources by interior peoples of British Columbia is described by Loewen (1998), Peacock (1998), Peacock and Turner (2000) and Turner et al. (1990), including personal interviews with many elders, especially Dr. Mary Thomas, Annie York, Sam Mitchell and Mabel Joe. Information about tending the Saskatoon bushes is from interviews with Mary Thomas (1994–2002) and from her book (Thomas 2002).

CH 7. EVERYTHING IS ONE

p. 179: *Hishuk ish ts'awalk* is discussed in the "First Nations' Perspectives" document, Clayoquot Scientific Panel (1995a); see also Craig and Smith (1997), Smith (1997) and *Umeek* (Atleo) (2004).

pp. 180–82: Earl Maquinna George's recollections are from his master's thesis and his book based on this thesis (George 2003). The Clayoquot Scientific Panel reports (1995a, b, c) document some of the impacts of forest practices on fisheries; see also Hartman and Scrivener (1990) and Smith (1997). Daisy Sewid-Smith's comments are quoted from her address at the "Helping the Land Heal" conference (1998). Stanley Sam's words are quoted in the Clayoquot Scientific Panel report (1995a). The words of Chief Charlie Jones of the Ditidaht Nation are from his autobiography, *Queesto* (Jones and Bosustow 1981:38).

pp. 182–83: For a description of some of the impacts of logging on fish populations, see Clayoquot Scientific Panel (1995b, c) and Hartman and Scrivener (1990). Tom Reimchen's work is highlighted in David Suzuki's CBC *The Nature of Things* documentary "The Salmon Forest" (2001). Another ecological work highlighting the forest-sea connections is Maser and Sedell (1994).

pp. 183–85: For an overview of west coast fishing technologies, see Stewart's (1977) *Indian Fishing: Early Methods on the Northwest Coast*, as well as the information in Turner et al. (1983), from which this example with John Thomas is drawn. Information on sword fern and bull kelp is from these sources and Turner (1998). The many applications of Pacific yew and other tough woods are discussed in Stewart (1977, 1984), Turner (1998) and Turner et al. (1983).

pp. 185–88: Stinging nettle and the other fibrous plants mentioned (slough sedge, cattail, tule and Indian hemp) are described in Turner (1998), and the transplanting and management of populations of these species are discussed by Peacock and Turner (2000) and Turner and Peacock (in press). The halibut-fishing gear is described by Stewart (1977) and Turner et al. (1983). Adam Dick described the use of kelp for special effects in the winter dance in interviews in November 1997 and in presentations to my classes at the University of Victoria (2001, 2003).

pp. 189–200: Information on the Xaxl'ep community is from Sam Mitchell and his adopted son Art Adolph, former elected chief of the Xaxl'ep Band, who kindly checked this section for me in spring 2003. Art also shared the information on the ecological indicators for the various runs of salmon. Other elders including Edith O'Donaghey, Desmond Peters Sr., Bill Edwards and Maggie Adolph also contributed some of this information and shared their experiences with me (see also Turner 1992). Art noted, incidentally, that the change from Highway 12 to Highway 99, connecting with the Vancouver–Pemberton–Duffey Lake route, was recent.

pp. 189–98: For discussions of the traditional pit houses and other technologies of the Xaxl'ep, see Kennedy and Bouchard (1998). The Keatley Creek archaeological site and its findings are described in detail in Hayden (1992) and other works by Hayden and his colleagues. A discussion of ethnobotanical findings is provided by Lepofsky (2002). Descriptions of the various plants mentioned in this discussion of Xaxl'ep use of the landscape are in Turner (1992, 1997a, 1998); see also Hunn et al. (1998) and Turner et al. (1990). Edith O'Donaghey's recollections are reported in Turner (1992).

pp. 198–200: Fladmark (1986) notes that antler handles for digging sticks are found in archaeological sites dating from the last 2,500 or so years. The workshop on traditional pit-cooking was organized by Kimberlee Chambers, then an ethnobotany master's student working with the Xaxl'ep on balsamroot and its potential for cultivation. Others who participated from the University of Victoria were Dr. Sandra Peacock, Kate Leslie and Bernadette Louisier (now Letchford). The information on silverweed, or "cinquefoil" as it is called, is from Teit (1906:222).

pp. 202–05: Sam Mitchell's use of sandbar willow to make rope is described in Turner (1998). Information on the history and loss of Sumas Lake is from Carlson (1997, 2001; see also Spurgeon 2001), as well as from personal observations. The Whitford and Craig quotation is from *Forests of British Columbia* (1918:104). Andrea Laforet is writing a book on basketry in British Columbia (see also Laforet 1990, 1992). See Suttles (1955) for a discussion on the importance of wapato and bog cranberries in the Fraser Valley region. The statistics on loss of wetlands are from National Research Council (1995). For information on the impacts of residential schools, see Haig-Brown (1988:29, 27) and Prentice and Houston (1975:220).

pp. 205–09: Mohawk elder and basket weaver Cecilia Mitchell is a good example of one who has retained her traditional values and teachings. I met her on a couple of occasions and also read her interview in Wall's (1993) book, *Wisdom's Daughters: Conversations with Women Elders of Native America*. Taiaiake Alfred's book *Peace, Power, Righteousness: An Indigenous Manifesto* (1999) draws on traditional ceremonial teachings as a framework for recovery and restoration of Mohawk traditions of leadership and governance. Laurie Montour has shared her teachings with my classes at the University of Victoria and at conferences and elsewhere over the past decade or so. In October 2003 I attended a symposium on traditional food and health at the Centre for Indigenous Peoples' Nutrition and Environment at McGill University in which the Mohawk Thanksgiving Address was used to open the proceedings, setting the stage for a positive and productive session.

CH 8. FINDING MEANING IN A CONTEMPORARY CONTEXT

pp. 211–12: Fisheries ecologist John Volpe provided the example of the Estes et al. (1998) publication and noted that it was only through chance that the researchers working on different components of this study were able to combine their results and to gain an understanding of the complex linkages between inshore and offshore ecosystems described in this paper.

pp. 212–15: Verna Miller recently spoke about the Tmixʷ project in a FORREX workshop (Miller 2003). She also spoke about this work at the Society of Ethnobiology twenty-fourth Annual Conference in Durango, Colorado (March 2001). Jennifer Morrison has been a project coordinator for Tmixʷ, and the project is sponsored by the Nicola Tribal Association.

pp. 216–21: Koeye is sometimes written "Kvai." The watershed is also traditionally used by the neighbouring Oweekeno. As well as Pauline Waterfall and Larry Jorgenson, many others, both Heiltsuk and non-Heiltsuk, including Larry's daughter

Jessie Housty, Heiltsuk archaeologist and youth leader Elroy White, biologist Karen McAllister and Louise Wilson of the Raincoast Conservation Society, and geographer and environmental journalist Briony Penn, have been active participants in the Koeye project. The Kvai Lodge (Koeye) was transferred back to the Heiltsuk Nation on 11 August 2001. Information on the Koeye project can be found on the Heiltsuk Web site: www.heiltsuk.com/news_heiltsukwinkoeye.htm. Information on the Heiltsuk berry gardens from Cyril Carpenter and Pauline Waterfall and their grandmothers is also included in Turner and Peacock (in press); Jennifer Carpenter showed me the cherry trees in their yard, one much larger than the other. Duncan Taylor was participating in an event sponsored by a non-profit organization called Power To Be Adventure Therapy Society (Web site: www.powr2b.com), whose goal is to combine environmental initiatives and outdoor recreation in programs for youth and adults living with disabilities.

pp. 221–28: For further information on the ecology and impacts of logging on Haida Gwaii, see Broadhead (1984) and *Gwaganad* (1990). The Web site of the Haida Gwaii Watchmen (2002), http://pc.gc.ca/pn-np/bc/gwaiihaanas/edu/index_e.asp, describes this program and the history of the development of Gwaii Haanas National Park Reserve and Haida Heritage Site. See Stockton et al. (2001) and Vila et al. (2001) for examples of research outcomes on the impacts of deer browsing on ecosystems of Haida Gwaii. Many researchers have been involved in this research, particularly the Laskeek Bay Conservation Society and the Research Group on Introduced Species. Information on impacts of deer on native plant resources is cited in Turner (2004).

p. 233: Bruce Miller (*Subiyay*), of the Skokomish tribe in Washington State, spoke at the Society for Ethnobiology annual meetings in Seattle in March 2003.

pp. 233–36: Ecosystem-based management (or "ecosystem management") as a concept was described by Grumbine (1994) and discussed in the Clayoquot Scientific Panel documents (1995a, c), where further references are provided. For more information about the concept of resilience, see Resilience Alliance (Web site www.resalliance.org) and discussions in the various chapters of Berkes and Folke (1998) and Berkes et al. (2003). The concept of resilience was originally applied to ecosystem dynamics (Holling 1973). Ron Trosper's "Resilience in Pre-contact Pacific Northwest Social Ecological Systems" was published in *Conservation Ecology* in 2003. For a discussion of contingent proprietorship, see Trosper (1998). The "ethic of reciprocity" is discussed in Dew and Griggs (1991).

pp. 236–37: Mary Thomas has shared her experiences, wisdom and perspectives with many people in her talks and workshops (cf. Thomas 2002). Daisy Sewid-Smith, Kim Recalma-Clutesi and Chief Adam Dick have given lectures in many classes

at the University of Victoria, including my own course, Plants and Human Cultures (Environmental Studies 416). Both Mary Thomas and Daisy Sewid-Smith
have received honorary doctorate degrees from the University of Victoria. Roy
Haiyupis shared his knowledge with the members of the Clayoquot Scientific
Panel (1995a) on many occasions between 1993 and 1995.

p. 237: Rachel Carson's book *Silent Spring* (2002), originally published in 1962, is a
classic. *Under the Sea-Wind* was published in 1941 and *The Sense of Wonder* was
published posthumously in 1965, although she had written it years earlier. Jane
Goodall's words are from the Web page of the Jane Goodall Foundation:
www.janegoodall.org.

p. 238–39: For the citation of the *Vancouver Sun* article on happiness, see Lanton
(2003). Bob Bandringa's and Chief Leslie Edmonds's word are from Bandringa
(1999:99).

References

Alcorn, Janis. 1984. *Huastec Mayan Ethnobotany*. Austin: University of Texas Press.

———. 1993. "Indigenous Peoples and Conservation." *Conservation Biology* 7(2):424–26.

———. 1996. "Is Biodiversity Conserved by Indigenous Peoples?" In *Ethnobiology in Human Welfare*, ed. S.K. Jain. New Delhi: Deep Publications, pp. 234–38.

Alfred, Taiaiake. 1999. *Peace, Power, Righteousness: An Indigenous Manifesto*. Don Mills, ON: Oxford University Press Canada.

Anderson, Eugene N. 1996a. *Ecologies of the Heart: Emotion, Belief, and the Environment*. New York: Oxford University Press.

———. 1996b. "The Northwest Coast." Part 1, chapter 2 in *Bird of Paradox*, ed. E.N. Anderson. Surrey, BC and Blaine, WA: Hancock House, pp. 24–44.

Anderson, Eugene N. et al. 2003. *Those Who Bring the Flowers: Maya Ethnobotany in Quintana Roo, Mexico*. Chiapas, Mexico: ECOSUR, El Colegio de la Frontera Sur Carretera Panamericana y Periférico Sur s/n Barrio de Maria Auxiliadora, San Cristóbal de las Casas.

Anderson, M. Kat. 1996. "Tending the Wilderness." *Restoration and Management Notes* 14(2):154–66.

———. 1997. "From Tillage to Table: The Indigenous Cultivation of Geophytes for Food in California." *Journal of Ethnobiology* 17:149–69.

———. In press. *Tending the Wild: Indigenous Management of California's Natural Resources and Biodiversity*. Berkeley, CA: University of California Press.

Andre, Alestine, Ruth Welsh and Nancy J. Turner. 2003. "Looking After Our Elders: Healthcare and Well-being of the Elderly from the Perspective of Gwich'in and Other First Nations of Canada." In *Alternative Medicine and the Elderly*, ed. E. Paul Cherniack, MD. Bronx, NY: Springer-Verlag, pp. 287–300.

Anonymous. 1849. "Colonization of Vancouver Island." London, UK: *Times*, 4 May 1849, pp. 18–19.

Arima, E.Y., Denis St. Claire, Louise Clamhouse, Joshua Edgar, Charles Jones and John Thomas. 1991. *Between Ports Alberni and Renfrew: Notes on West Coast Peoples*. Canadian Ethnology Service, Mercury Series Paper 121, Canadian Museum of Civilization, Ottawa.

Armstrong, Jeanette. 1996. "Sharing One Skin." In *The Case Against the Global Economy*, ed. Jerry Mander and Edward Goldsmith. San Francisco, CA: Sierra Club Books, pp. 466–67.

Arnett, Chris. 1999. *Terror of the Coast: Land Alienation & Colonial War on Vancouver Island and the Gulf Islands, 1849–1863*. Vancouver, BC: Talonbooks.

Atleo, Marlene R. 2001. *Learning Models in the Umeek Narratives: Identifying an Educational Framework through Storywork with First Nations Elders*. Ph.D. dissertation, Department of Educational Studies, University of British Columbia, Vancouver, BC.

Atleo, Richard. 1999. "A First Nations Perspective on Ecosystem Management." *Ecoforestry* 14(4):8–11.

———. 2004. (see *Umeek* 2004)

Babcock, M. 1967–69. *Camas—Descriptions of Getting and Preparing—From Informants of Tsartlip Reserve (W. Saanich), Vancouver Island*. Unpublished manuscript, cited with permission of author; copy in possession of N. Turner.

Baker, Richard. 1999. *Land Is Life: From Bush to Town—The Story of the Yanyuwa People*. Sydney, Australia: Allen & Unwin.

Baker, Richard, Jocelyn Davies and Elspeth Young, eds. 2001. *Working on Country: Contemporary Indigenous Management of Australia's Lands and Coastal Regions*. Melbourne, Australia: Oxford University Press, pp. 116–64.

Balée, William. 1994. "Indigenous Forest Management." In *Footprints of the Forest. Ka'apor Ethnobotany—the Historical Ecology of Plant Utilization by an Amazonian People*. New York: Columbia University Press.

Bandringa, Robert W. 1999. *The Ethnobotany and Descriptive Ecology of Bitterroot, Lewisia rediviva Pursh (Portulacaceae), in the Lower Thompson River Valley, British Columbia: A Salient Root Food of the Nlaka'pamux First Nation*. M.Sc. thesis, Department of Resource Management and Environmental Studies, University of British Columbia, Vancouver, BC.

Basso, Keith H. 1996. *Wisdom Sits in Places: Landscape and Language among the Western Apache.* Albuquerque, NM: University of New Mexico Press.

Beckwith, Brenda R. 2002. "Colonial Eden or Indigenous Cultivated Landscape: Reconstructing Nineteenth Century Camas Meadows on Southern Vancouver Island." In *Garry Oak Ecosystem Restoration: Progress and Prognosis,* ed. P.J. Burton. Proceedings of the Third Annual Meeting of the B.C. Chapter of the Society for Ecological Restoration, 27–29 April 2002, University of Victoria, Victoria, BC, pp. 64–72.

———. In prep. *The Queen Root of This Clime: Ethnoecological Investigations of Blue Camas (*Camassia quamash, C. leichtlinii; *Liliaceae) Landscapes on Southern Vancouver Island, British Columbia.* Ph.D. dissertation, Department of Biology, University of Victoria, Victoria, BC.

Bennett, Bradley. 1992. "Plants and People of the Amazonian Rainforests: The Role of Ethnobotany in Sustainable Development." *Bioscience* 42:599–607.

Benyus, Janine M. 1998. *Biomimicry: Innovation Inspired by Nature.* New York: William Morrow & Co.

Berkes, Fikret. 1999. *Sacred Ecology: Traditional Ecological Knowledge and Resource Management.* Philadelphia, PA: Taylor & Francis.

Berkes, Fikret, Johann Colding and Carl Folke, eds. 2003. *Navigating Social-Ecological Systems: Building Resilience for Complexity and Change.* Cambridge, UK: Cambridge University Press.

Berkes, Fikret, and Carl Folke, eds. 1998. *Linking Social and Ecological Systems: Management Practices and Social Mechanisms for Building Resilience.* Cambridge, UK: Cambridge University Press.

Blackburn, Thomas C., and Kat Anderson, eds. 1993. *Before the Wilderness: Environmental Management by Native Californians.* Menlo Park, CA: Ballena Press.

Blackfoot Gallery Committee. 2001. *Nisitapiisinni: The Story of the Blackfoot People.* Exhibit guide for the Glenbow Museum. Toronto, ON: Key Porter Books.

Blackman, Margaret B. 1982. *During My Time: Florence Edenshaw Davidson, A Haida Woman.* Seattle, WA and London, UK: University of Washington Press.

———. 1990. "Haida Traditional Culture." In *Handbook of North American Indians.* Vol. 7, *Northwest Coast,* ed. Wayne Suttles. Washington, DC: Smithsonian Institution, pp. 240–60.

Boas, Franz. 1901. *Kathlamet Texts.* Bureau of American Ethnology, Bulletin 26. Washington, DC: Smithsonian Institution.

———. 1921. *Ethnology of the Kwakiutl.* Bureau of American Ethnology 35th Annual Report, parts 1 and 2. Washington, DC: Smithsonian Institution.

———. 1930. *The Religion of the Kwakiutl Indians.* New York: Columbia University Press. (Reprinted in 1969 by AMS Press Inc., New York.)

Boelscher, Marianne. 1988. *The Curtain Within: Haida Social and Mythical Discourse.* Vancouver, BC: UBC Press.

Bouchard, Randy, and Dorothy Kennedy, eds. 2002. *Indian Myths and Legends from the North Pacific Coast of America.* (A translation of Franz Boas's 1895 edition of *Indianische Sagen von der Nord-Pacifischen Küste Amerikas.*) Vancouver, BC: Talonbooks.

Boyd, Robert. 1999. *Indians, Fire and the Land in the Pacific Northwest.* Corvallis, OR: Oregon State University Press.

Bracken, Christopher. 1997. *The Potlatch Papers: A Colonial Case History.* Chicago, IL: University of Chicago Press.

British Columbia. 1987. *Papers Connected with the Indian Land Question. 1850–1875.* Victoria, BC (orig. publ. 1875, Government Printing Office, Victoria).

British Columbia. Ministry of Forests. 1997. *Culturally Modified Trees of British Columbia: A Handbook for the Identification and Recording of Culturally Modified Trees.* Victoria, BC.

Broadhead, John, ed. 1984. *Islands at the Edge: Preserving the Queen Charlotte Islands Heritage.* Skidegate, Haida Gwaii, BC: Island Protections Society and Vancouver, BC: Douglas & McIntyre.

Brody, Hugh. 1981. *Maps and Dreams: Indians and the British Columbia Frontier.* Vancouver, BC: Douglas & McIntyre.

———. 2000. *The Other Side of Eden: Hunters, Farmers and the Shaping of the World.* Vancouver, BC: Douglas & McIntyre.

Brown, Joseph Epes. 1970. *The Spiritual Legacy of the American Indian.* Lebanon, PA: Sowers Printing Co.

Brown, Kendrick, and Richard J. Hebda. 2002. "Ancient Fires on Southern Vancouver Island, British Columbia, Canada: A Change in Causal Mechanisms at about 2,000 ybp." *Environmental Archaeology: The Journal of Human Palaeoecology,* Volume 7 (October 2002), pp. 1–12.

Brown, Lester R., ed. 1998. *State of the World.* Worldwatch Institute. (Web site: www.worldwatch.org).

Cajete, Gregory. 1994. *Look to the Mountain: An Ecology of Indigenous Education.* Durango, CO: Kivaki Press.

Callicott, J. Baird. 1989. *In Defense of the Land Ethic: Essays in Environmental Philosophy.* Albany, NY: State University of New York Press.

———. 1994. *Earth's Insights: A Multicultural Survey of Ecological Ethics from the Mediterranean Basin to the Australian Outback.* Berkeley, CA: University of California Press.

Campbell, Peter. 1994. "Not as a White Man, Not as a Sojourner: James A. Teit and the Fight for Native Rights in British Columbia, 1884–1922." *left history* 2 (2):37–57.

Carlson, Catherine C., and Kenneth Klein. 1996. "Late Pleistocene Salmon of Kamloops Lake." In *Life in Stone: A Natural History of British Columbia's Fossils*, ed. Rolf Ludvigsen. Vancouver, BC: UBC Press, pp. 274–80.

Carlson, Keith Thor, ed. 1997. *You Are Asked to Witness: The Stó:lō in Canada's Pacific Coast History*. Chilliwack, BC: Stó:lō Heritage Trust.

———, ed. 2001. *A Stó:lō Coast Salish Historical Atlas*. Vancouver, BC: Douglas & McIntyre; Seattle, WA: University of Washington Press, and Chilliwack, BC: Stó:lō Heritage Trust.

Carson, Rachel L. 1941. *Under the Sea Wind*. New York: Oxford University Press.

———. 1965. *The Sense of Wonder*. New York: Harper & Row.

———. 2002. *Silent Spring*. Boston, MA: Houghton Mifflin Company.

Clarke, W. Craig, Cornelis Groot and Leo Margolis, eds. 1995. *Physiological Ecology of Pacific Salmon*. Vancouver, BC: UBC Press.

Claxton, Earl Sr., and John Elliott Sr. 1994. *Reef Net Technology of the Saltwater People*. Brentwood Bay, BC: Saanich Indian School Board.

Clayoquot Scientific Panel (Scientific Panel for Sustainable Forest Practices in Clayoquot Sound). 1995a. *First Nations' Perspectives on Forest Practices in Clayoquot Sound*. Report 3, Victoria, BC.

———. 1995b. *A Vision and Its Context: Global Context for Forest Practices in Clayoquot Sound*. Report 4, Victoria, BC.

———. 1995c. *Sustainable Ecosystem Management in Clayoquot Sound*. Report 5, Victoria, BC.

Clutesi, George. 1969. *Potlatch*. Sidney, BC: Gray's Publishing.

Coasts Under Stress, and Gitga'at Nation. 2003. *Gitga'ata Spring Harvest*. Victoria, BC. <video>

Codere, Helen. 1966. "Daniel Cranmer's Potlatch." In *Indians of the North Pacific Coast*, ed. Tom McFeat. Seattle, WA: University of Washington Press.

Cole, Douglas, and Bradley Lockner. 1993. *To the Charlottes: George Dawson's 1878 Survey of the Queen Charlotte Islands*. Vancouver, BC: UBC Press.

Compton, Brian D. 1993. *Upper North Wakashan and Southern Tsimshian Ethnobotany: The Knowledge and Usage of Plants and Fungi among the Oweekeno, Hanaksiala (Kitlope and Kemano), Haisla (Kitamaat) and Kitasoo Peoples of the Central and North Coasts of British Columbia*. Ph.D. dissertation, Department of Botany, University of British Columbia, Vancouver, BC.

Craig, Juliet, and Robin Smith. 1997. *"A Rich Forest": Traditional Knowledge, Inventory and Restoration of Culturally Important Plants and Habitats in the Atleo River Watershed*. Final Report of the Ahousaht Ethnobotany Project, 1996. Ahousaht, BC: Ahousaht Band Council and Tofino, BC: Long Beach Model Forest.

Cranmer, Barb, and Cari Green. 1995. *Laxwesa Wa: Strength of the River*. Montreal:

Nimpkish Wind Productions Inc. and National Film Board of Canada. <video>

Crosby, Alfred W. 1986. *Ecological Imperialism: The Biological Expansion of Europe, 900–1900*. Cambridge, UK: Cambridge University Press.

Cruikshank, Julie. 1981. "Legend and Landscape: Convergence of Oral and Scientific Traditions in the Yukon Territory." *Arctic Anthropology* 18(2):67–93.

Cruikshank, Julie, Angela Sidney, Kitty Smith and Annie Ned. 1995. *Life Lived Like a Story*. Vancouver, BC: UBC Press.

Daly, Richard. n.d. *Pure Gifts and Impure Thoughts*. Oslo, Norway. (Web site: www.ebdn.ac.uk/chaps9/1daly.html).

———. 1988. "Anthropological Opinion on the Nature of the Gitksan and Wetsuwet'en Economy." Report submitted as opinion evidence in *Delgamuukw v. The Queen*. Copy at Gitxsan Land Title Office Library, Hazelton, BC.

Davidson, John. 1916. *Third Annual Report of the Botanical Office*. Vancouver, BC.

Davidson-Hunt, Iain J. 2003. *Journeys, Plants and Dreams: Adaptive Learning and Social-Ecological Resilience*. Ph.D. dissertation, Natural Resources Institute, University of Manitoba, Winnipeg, MB.

Davis, Alison, Bea Wilson and Brian D. Compton. 1994. *Salmonberry Blossoms in the New Year: Some Culturally Significant Plants of the Haisla Known to Occur within the Greater Kitlope Ecosystem*. Portland, OR: Ecotrust.

Demerritt, David. 1996. "Visions of Agriculture in British Columbia." *BC Studies* 108 (Winter 1995–96):42.

Deur, Douglas. 2000. *A Domesticated Landscape: Native American Plant Cultivation on the Northwest Coast of North America*. Ph.D. dissertation, Department of Geography and Anthropology, Louisiana State University, Baton Rouge, LA.

———. 2001. "Plant Cultivation on the Northwest Coast: A Reassessment." *Journal of Cultural Geography* 19(1):24–43.

Deur, Douglas, and Nancy J. Turner, eds. In press. *"Keeping It Living": Indigenous Plant Management on the Northwest Coast*. Seattle, WA: University of Washington Press.

Drake, Allene, and Lyle Wilson. 1991. *Eulachon: A Fish to Cure Humanity*. Museum Note No. 32, University of British Columbia Museum of Anthropology, Vancouver, BC.

Drengson, Alan, and Yuichi Inoue. 1995. *The Deep Ecology Movement: An Introductory Anthology*. Berkeley, CA: North Atlantic Books.

Drucker, Philip. 1951. *The Northern and Central Nootkan Tribes*. Bureau of American Ethnology, Bulletin No. 144. Washington, DC: Smithsonian Institution.

Duff, Wilson. 1964. *The Indian History of British Columbia*. Vol. 1, *The Impact of the White Man*. Anthropology in British Columbia Memoir No. 5. Provincial Museum of Natural History and Anthropology, Victoria, BC.

————. 1969. "The Fort Victoria Treaties." *BC Studies* 3:3–57.

Dundes, Alan. 1965. *The Study of Folklore*. Englewood Cliffs, NJ: Prentice-Hall, Inc.

Dunwiddie, Peter W. 2002. "Management and Restoration of Grasslands on Yellow Island, San Juan Islands, Washington, USA." In *Garry Oak Ecosystem Restoration: Progress and Prognosis*, ed. P.J. Burton. Proceedings of the Third Annual Meeting of the B.C. Chapter of the Society for Ecological Restoration, 27–29 April 2002, University of Victoria, BC, pp. 78–87.

Durning, Alan. 1992. *How Much Is Enough?* New York: Norton.

Edwards, G.T. 1979. "Indian Spaghetti" [springbank clover]. *The Beaver* (Autumn): 4–11.

Elliott, Dave, and Janet Poth, eds. 1990. *Saltwater People*. Saanich, BC, School District 6.

Elmendorf, William. 1935–36. *Field Notes of Lakes Indian Culture and Ethnography Recorded from Lakes Informant Nancy Wynecoop*. B.C. Archives Accession No. 934888, Victoria, BC.

Emmons, George T. 1991. *The Tlingit Indians*. Edited with additions by F. de Laguna. Seattle, WA: University of Washington Press and New York: American Museum of Natural History.

Enrico, John. 1995. *Skidegate Haida Myths and Stories, Recorded by John R. Swanton*. Ed. and trans. John Enrico. Skidegate, Haida Gwaii, BC: Queen Charlotte Islands Press.

Estes, J.A., M.T. Tinker, T.M. Williams and D.F. Doak. 1998. "Killer Whale Predation on Sea Otter Linking Oceanic and Nearshore Ecosystems." *Science* 282:473–76.

Favrholdt, Ken. 1994. "Spences Bridge The Extraordinary James Teit." In *Reflections: Thompson Valley Histories*, ed. Wayne Norton and Wilf Schmidt. Kamloops, BC: Plateau Press, pp. 14–19

Fife, Hugh. 1994. *Warriors and Guardians: Native Highland Trees*. Glendaruel, UK: Argyll Publishing.

Fisher, Robin. 1992. *Contact and Conflict: Indian-European Relations in British Columbia, 1774–1890*. 2nd ed. Vancouver, BC: UBC Press.

Fladmark, Knut R. 1986. *The Prehistory of British Columbia*. National Museum of Man [now National Museum of Civilization, Hull, QC], Canadian Prehistory Series, National Museums of Canada, Ottawa, ON.

Ford, Jesse, and Dennis R. Martinez, eds. 2000. *Ecological Applications* 10(5). Special issue on Traditional Ecological Knowledge, Ecosystem Science and Environmental Management.

Ford, Richard I., ed. 1985. *Prehistoric Food Production in North America*. University of Michigan Anthropology Series, No. 75, Ann Arbor, MI.

————. 2000. "Human Disturbance and Biodiversity: A Case Study from Northern New Mexico." In *Biodiversity and Native America*, ed. Paul E. Minnis and Wayne J. Elisens. Norman, OK: University of Oklahoma Press, pp. 207–22.

Fowler, Catherine S. 1992. *In the Shadow of Fox Pear: An Ethnography of the Cattail-Eater Northern Paiute People of Stillwater Marsh*. Cultural Resources Series, No. 5. Portland, OR: U.S. Fish and Wildlife Service.

————. 2000. "Great Basin Utilization of Plants, Animals. . . . " In *Biodiversity and Native America*, ed. Paul E. Minnis and Wayne J. Elisens. Norman, OK: University of Oklahoma Press.

Fowler, Catherine S., and Nancy J. Turner. 1999. "Ecological/cosmological Knowledge and Land Management among Hunter-gatherers." In *The Cambridge Encyclopedia of Hunters and Gatherers,* ed. Richard B. Lee and Richard Daly. Cambridge, UK: Cambridge University Press, pp. 419–25.

Freeman, Milton M.R., and Ludwig N. Carbyn. 1988. *Traditional Knowledge and Renewable Resource Management in Northern Regions*. Edmonton, AB: International Union for the Conservation of Nature (IUCN) Commission on Ecology and the Boreal Institute for Northern Studies.

Gadgil, Madav, Fikret Berkes and Carl Folke. 1993. "Indigenous Knowledge for Biodiversity Conservation." *Ambio: A Journal of the Human Environment* 22(2–3):151–56.

Garrick, David. 1998. *Shaped Cedars and Cedar Shaping (Hanson Island, B.C.)*. Vancouver, BC: Western Canada Wilderness Committee.

Gaston, A.J., T.E. Golumbia, J.L. Martin and S.T. Sharpe, eds. 2004. *Lessons from the Islands: Introduced Species and What They Tell Us About How Ecosystems Work*. Proceedings from the Research Group on Introduced Species 2002 Conference, Queen Charlotte City, BC. Canadian Wildlife Service Occasional Paper.

George, Earl Maquinna. 2003. *Living on the Edge: Nuu-Chah-Nulth History from an Ahousaht Chief's Perspective*. Winlaw, BC: Sono Nis Press.

Gisday'wa and Delgamuukw. 1989. "The Spirit in the Land." The Opening Statement of the Gitksan and Wets'uwit'en Hereditary Chiefs in the Supreme Court of British Columbia, 11 May 1987. Gabriola, BC: Reflections.

Goble, Paul. 1983. *Star Boy*. New York: Simon & Schuster.

Gottesfeld, Leslie M. Johnson. 1994a. "Aboriginal Burning for Vegetation Management in Northwest British Columbia." *Human Ecology* 22(2):171–88.

————. 1994b. "Conservation, Territory, and Traditional Beliefs: An Analysis of Gitksan and Wet'suwet'en Subsistence, Northwest British Columbia, Canada." *Human Ecology* 22(4):443–65.

Groot, Cornelius, and Leo Margolis, eds. 1991. *Pacific Salmon Life Histories*. Vancouver, BC: UBC Press.

Grumbine, R. Edward. 1994. "What Is Ecosystem Management?" *Conservation Biology* 8(1):27–38.

Gunther, Erna. 1945 (revised 1973). *Ethnobotany of Western Washington*. Seattle, WA: University of Washington Press.

Gwaganad (Diane Brown). 1990. "Speaking in the Haida Way." In *Home! A Bioregional Reader*, ed. C. Van Andruss, J. Plant and E. Wright. Gabriola Island, BC: New Society.

Haig-Brown, Celia. 1988. *Resistance and Renewal: Surviving the Indian Residential School*. Vancouver, BC: Tillacum Library.

Halliday, William. 1910. *1909 Annual Report: Kwagiulth Agency*. Department of Indian Affairs. Unpublished manuscript on microfilm, British Columbia Provincial Museum. Ottawa, ON: Canada Department of Indian Affairs.

Hanna, Darwin, and Mamie Henry, eds. 1995. *Our Tellings: Interior Salish Stories of the Nlha7kapmx People*. Vancouver, BC: UBC Press.

Harper, John. 2003. "The Clam Gardens of the Broughton Archipelago—Case for Pre-contact, Large-scale Mariculture in Queen Charlotte Strait." Presentation to Centre for Earth and Ocean Research (CEOR) seminar series, University of Victoria, 5 November 2003.

Harris, Cole. 1999. *The Resettlement of British Columbia: Essays on Colonialism and Geographical Change*. Vancouver, BC: UBC Press.

———. 2002. *Making Native Space: Colonialism, Resistance, and Reserves in British Columbia*. Vancouver, BC: UBC Press.

Harris, David R. 1989. "An Evolutionary Continuum of People-Plant Interaction." In *Foraging and Farming: The Evolution of Plant Exploitation*, ed. David R. Harris and Gordon C. Hillman. London, UK: Unwin Hyman, pp. 11–26.

Hartman, Gordon F., and J.C. Scrivener. 1990. *Impacts of Forest Practices on a Coastal Stream Ecosystem: Carnation Creek, British Columbia*. Canadian Bulletin of Fisheries Aquatic Sciences 223.

Hayden, Brian. 1992. *A Complex Culture of the British Columbia Plateau: Traditional Stl'átl'imx Resource Use*. Vancouver, BC: UBC Press.

Hebda, Richard J., and Rolf W. Mathewes. 1984. "Holocene History of Cedar and Native Indian Cultures of the North American Pacific Coast." *Science* 225:711–13.

Hebda, Richard J., and C. Whitlock. 1997. "Environmental History." In *The Rainforest of Home: Profile of a North America Bioregion*, ed. P.K. Schoonmaker, P. von Hagen and E.C. Wolf. Covelo, CA: Island Press.

Helm, June, ed. 1981. *Handbook of North American Indians*. Vol. 6, *Subarctic* (William C. Sturtevant, gen. ed.). Washington, DC: Smithsonian Institution.

Herrick, J.W. 1995. *Iroquois Medical Botany*. New York: Syracuse University Press.

Holling, C.S. 1973. "Resilience and Stability of Ecological Systems." *Annual Review of Ecology and Systematics* 4:2–23.

Howes, Katharine, and Pat Lean. 1979. "An Interview with Inga Teit Perkin, Daughter of Noted Ethnologist James A. Teit." *Nicola Valley Historical Quarterly* 2(2):1–2.

Hume, Stephen. 2000. "At Hells Gate the River Defeats the Mountains." *Vancouver Sun*, 1 November 2000, section C, p. 10.

Hunn, Eugene S. with James Selam. 1990. *Nch'i-Wana: The Big River, Mid-Columbia Indians and their Land*. Seattle, WA: University of Washington Press.

Hunn, Eugene S., Nancy J. Turner and David H. French. 1998. "Ethnobiology and Subsistence." In *Handbook of North American Indians*. Vol 12, *Plateau*, ed. Deward E. Walker. Washington, DC: Smithsonian Institution, pp. 525–45.

Ingram, G. Brent. 2003. *Fields or Forest? Aboriginal Food Production Landscapes, Unsolved Legacies and Contemporary Ecosystem Management of Garry Oak Woodlands in Southwestern British Columbia*. International Conference on the Forest and Environmental History of the British Empire and Commonwealth, University of Sussex, Falmer, Brighton, UK, 19–21 March 2003.

Jenness, Diamond. n.d. [ca. 1900]. *Coast Salish Field Notes*. Unpublished original manuscript (No. 1103.6) in Ethnology Archives, National Museum of Civilization, Ottawa, ON.

———. n.d. [ca. 1930]. "The Saanich Indians of Vancouver Island." Unpublished manuscript, Royal British Columbia Museum, pp. 1–10.

Jilek, Wolfgang. 1982. *Indian Healing: Shamanic Ceremonialism in the Pacific Northwest Today*. Surrey, BC: Hancock House.

Johnson, Derek, Linda Kershaw, Andy MacKinnon and Jim Pojar. 1995. *Plants of the Western Boreal Forest and Aspen Parkland*. Edmonton, AB and Vancouver, BC: Lone Pine Publishing.

Johnson, Leslie Main. 1997. *Health, Wholeness, and the Land: Gitksan Traditional Plant Use and Healing*. Ph.D. dissertation, Department of Anthropology, University of Alberta, Edmonton, AB.

Jones, Charles, and Steven Bosustow. 1981. *Queesto: Pacheenaht Chief by Birthright*. Penticton, BC: Theytus Books.

Jones, James. 2002. *"We looked after all the salmon streams." Traditional Heiltsuk Cultural Stewardship of Salmon and Salmon Streams: A Preliminary Study*. Master's thesis, School of Environmental Studies, University of Victoria, Victoria, BC.

Jones, Russ. 2000. "The Herring Fishery of Haida Gwaii: An Ethical Analysis." In *Just Fish: Ethics and Canadian Marine Fisheries*, ed. Harold Coward, Rosemary Ommer and Tony Pitcher. Social and Economic Papers No. 23. Institute of Social and Economic Research, Memorial University of Newfoundland, St. John's, NF, pp. 201–24.

Kari, Priscilla R. 1987. *Tanaina Plantlore: Dena'ina K'et'una: An Ethnobotany of the Dena'ina Indians of Southcentral Alaska*. Anchorage, AK: National Park Service, Alaska Region.

Keller, Keith. 2002. *Wildfire Wars: Frontline Stories of BC's Worst Forest Fires*. Madeira Park, BC: Harbour Publishing.

Kennedy, Dorothy I.D., and R. Bouchard. 1992. "Stl'átl'imx (Fraser River Lillooet) Fishing." In *A Complex Culture of the British Columbia Plateau. Traditional Stl'átl'imx Resource Use*, ed. Brian Hayden. Vancouver: UBC Press, pp. 266–354.

———. 1998. "Fraser River Lillooet." In *Handbook of North American Indians*. Vol. 12, *Plateau*, ed. Deward E. Walker. Washington, DC: Smithsonian Institution, pp. 174–90.

Kew, J.E. Michael. 1990. "Central and Southern Coast Salish Ceremonies Since 1900." In *Handbook of North American Indians*. Vol. 7, *Northwest Coast*, ed. Wayne Suttles. Washington, DC: Smithsonian Institution.

Kew, J.E. Michael, and Julian R. Griggs, 1991. "Native Indians of the Fraser Basin: Towards a Model of Sustainable Resource Use." In *Perspectives on Sustainable Development in Water Management: Towards Agreement in the Fraser River Basin*, ed. H.J. Dorcey. Westwater Research Centre, University of British Columbia, Vancouver, BC, pp. 17–47.

Kimmerer, Robin W., and Frank K. Lake. 2001. "The Role of Indigenous Burning in Land Management." *Journal of Forestry* (November) 36–41.

'Ksan, People of. 1980. *Gathering What the Great Nature Provided: Food Traditions of the Gitksan*. Vancouver, BC: Douglas & McIntyre and Seattle, WA: University of Washington Press.

Kuhnlein, Harriet V., and Nancy J. Turner. 1991. *Traditional Plant Foods of Canadian Indigenous Peoples: Nutrition, Botany and Use*. Vol. 8 of *Food and Nutrition in History and Anthropology*, ed. Solomon Katz. Philadelphia, PA: Gordon & Breach Science Publishers.

Laforet, A. 1990. "Regional and Personal Style in Northwest Coast basketry." In *The Art of Native American Basketry. A Living Legacy*, ed. F.W. Porter III. Contributions to the Study of Anthropology, Number 5. New York: Greenwood Press, pp. 281–98.

———. 1992. "Windows on Diversity: Northwest Coast Baskets in the Pitt Rivers Collection." In *Basketmakers: Meaning and Form in Native American Baskets*, ed. L. Mowat, H. Murphy and P. Dransart. Monograph 5. Oxford, UK: Pitt Rivers Museum, University of Oxford.

Laforet, Andrea, Nancy J. Turner and Annie York. 1993. "Traditional Foods of the Fraser Canyon Nle7képmx." In *American Indian Linguistics and Ethnography in Honor of Laurence C. Thompson*, ed. Timothy Montler and Anthony Mattina. Festschrift Occasional Papers in Linguistics, No. 10. Missoula, MT: University of Montana Press, pp. 191–213.

Laforet, Andrea, and Annie York. 1998. *Spuẕẕum: Fraser Canyon Histories, 1808–1939*. Ottawa, ON: Canadian Museum of Civilization and Vancouver, BC: UBC Press.

Lamb, W. Kaye, ed. 1960. *Simon Fraser Letters & Journals, 1806–1808*. Totonto, ON: The Macmillan Company of Canada Limited.

Lanton, Barbara. 2003. "The Happy Truth: Optimists Live Longer." *Vancouver Sun*, 14 January 2003, section A, pp. 1, 2.

Lantz, Trevor, and Nancy J. Turner. 2003. "Traditional Phenological Knowledge (TPK) of Aboriginal Peoples in British Columbia." *Journal of Ethnobiology*, 23(2):236–86.

Lantz, Trevor, Kristina Swerhun and Nancy J. Turner. 2004. "Devil's Club (*Oplopanax horridus*): An Ethnobotanical Review." *Herbalgram* 62 (Spring): 33–48.

Lean, Pat, and Sigurd Teit. 1995. "Introduction." *Teit Times* I (Summer):3–6.

Lepofsky, D. 2002. "Plants and Pithouses: Archaeobotany and Site Formation Processes at the Keatley Creek Village Site," In *Hunter-gatherer Archaeobotany: Perspectives from the Northern Temperate Zone*, ed. Sarah L.R. Mason and Jon G. Hather. London, UK: Institute of Archaeology, University College of London, pp. 62–73.

Lewis, Henry T. 1982. *A Time for Burning*. Occasional Publication No. 17, Boreal Institute for Northern Studies. Edmonton, AB: University of Alberta.

Lewis, Henry T., and Theresa A. Ferguson. 1988. "Yards, Corridors, and Mosaics: How to Burn a Boreal Forest." *Human Ecology* 16(1):57–77 (reprinted in Boyd 1999).

Lillard, Charles. 1987. Introduction to *The Nootka: Scenes and Studies of Savage Life*, G.M. Sproat, ed. C. Lillard. Victoria, BC: Sono Nis Press.

Loewen, Dawn. 1998. *Ecological, Ethnobotanical, and Nutritional Aspects of Yellow Glacier Lily*, Erythronium grandiflorum *Pursh (Liliaceae) in Western Canada*. M.Sc. thesis, Department of Biology, University of Victoria, Victoria, BC.

Loftin, John D. 1991. *Religion and Hopi Life in the Twentieth Century*. Bloomington, IN: Indiana University Press.

Lovelock, James E. 1979. *The Gaia Theory of Life on Earth*. Oxford, UK: Oxford University Press.

Lutz, John 1995. "Preparing Eden: Aboriginal Land Use and European Settlement." Paper presented to the 1995 meeting of the Canadian Historical Association, Université de Québec à Montréal, QC.

————. In press. *Makuk: Work and Welfare in Aboriginal, Non Aboriginal Relationships.* Vancouver, BC: UBC Press.

McIlwraith, T.F. 1948. *The Bella Coola Indians.* 2 vols. Toronto, ON: University of Toronto Press.

MacKinnon, A., J. Pojar and R. Coupé, eds. 1992. *Plants of Northern British Columbia.* Vancouver, BC and Edmonton, AB: Lone Pine Publishing.

McLean, A., and E.W. Tisdale. 1972. "Recovery Rate of Depleted Range Sites under Protection from Grazing." *Journal of Range Management* 25:178–84.

Maser, Chris. 1994. *Forest Primeval: The Natural History of an Ancient Forest.* San Francisco, CA: Sierra Club Books.

Maser, Chris, and James R. Sedell. 1994. *From the Forest to the Sea: The Ecology of Wood in Streams, Rivers, Estuaries, and Oceans.* Florida: Saint Lucie Press.

Maud, Ralph, ed. 1978a. *The Salish People. The Local Contribution of Charles Hill-Tout.* Vol. 1, *The Thompson and the Okanagan.* Vancouver, BC: Talonbooks.

————. ed. 1978b. *The Salish People. The Local Contribution of Charles Hill-Tout.* Vol. 2, *The Squamish and the Lillooet.* Vancouver, BC: Talonbooks.

————. ed. 1978c. *The Salish People. The Local Contribution of Charles Hill-Tout.* Vol. 3, *The Mainland Halkomelem.* Vancouver, BC: Talonbooks.

Meidinger, Del, and Jim Pojar, eds. 1991. *Ecosystems of British Columbia.* Victoria, BC: Ministry of Forests.

Miller, Verna (Tmixʷ Research Project, Nicola Tribal Association). 2003. *Filling the Gaps: A Process for Amalgamating/Integrating Occidental Science and Indigenous Science.* In Natural Resources Information Management Forum, FORREX (Forest Research Extension Partnership), "Putting Knowledge to Work" (February 2003), Richmond, BC.

Minnis, Paul E., and Wayne J. Elisens, eds. 2000. *Biodiversity and Native America.* Norman, OK: University of Oklahoma Press.

Mooney, James. 1896. "The Ghost-Dance Religion and the Sioux Outbreak of 1890." *Fourteenth Annual Report of the Bureau of American Ethnology,* part 2, pp. 641–1136.

Mourning Dove. 1933. *Coyote Stories.* Idaho: Claxton Press. Republished 1990, Lincoln, NE: University of Nebraska Press.

Murray, Grant, and Barbara Neis. 2004. *Lessons Learned from Reconstructing Interactions between Local Ecological Knowledge, Fisheries Science and Fisheries Management in the Commercial Fisheries of Newfoundland and Labrador, Canada.* Paper presented at the International Association for the Study of Common Property Resources (IASCPR) Conference, Oaxaca, Mexico, August 2004.

Nabhan, Gary Paul. 1985. *Gathering the Desert*. Tucson, AZ: University of Arizona Press.

National Film Board. 1998. *The Gift*. Ottawa, ON. <video>

National Research Council. 1995. *Wetlands: Characteristics and Boundaries*. Washington, DC: National Academy Press.

Nazarea, Virginia D., ed. 1999. *Ethnoecology: Situated Knowledge/Located Lives*. Tucson, AZ: University of Arizona Press.

Nelson, J. 1983. *The Weavers: A Queen Charlotte Islands Reader*. Vancouver, BC: Pacific Educational Press.

Nelson, Richard K. 1983. *Make Prayers to the Raven: A Koyukon View of the Northern Forest*. Chicago, IL: University of Chicago Press.

Nesti, Lorenzo. 1999. *Indigenous Peoples' Right to Land: International Standards and Possible Developments. The Cultural Value of Land and the Link with the Protection of the Environment. The Perspective in the Case of Mapuche-Pehuenche*. European master's degree in Human Rights and Democratization, University of Padua, Italy and University of Duesto, Spain.

Newcombe, C.F., ed. 1923. *Menzies' Journal of Vancouver's Voyage April to October, 1792*. Victoria, BC: William H. Cullin.

Norton, Helen H. 1981. "Plant Use in Kaigani Haida Culture: Correction of an Ethnohistorical Oversight." *Economic Botany* 35:434–49.

Ormsby, Margaret, ed. 1976. *A Pioneer Gentlewoman in British Columbia: The Recollections of Susan Allison*. Vancouver, BC: UBC Press.

Parish, Roberta, Ray Coupé and Dennis Lloyd, eds. 1996. *Plants of the Southern Interior, British Columbia*. Vancouver, BC and Edmonton, AB: Lone Pine Publishing.

Paul, Frances. 1944. *Spruce Root Basketry of the Alaska Tlingit*. Sitka, AK: Sheldon Jackson Museum. (Second reprint edition 1991.)

Peacock, Sandra L. 1998. *Putting Down Roots: The Emergence of Wild Plant Food Production on the Canadian Plateau*. Ph.D. dissertation, School of Environmental Studies and Department of Geography, University of Victoria, Victoria, BC.

Peacock, Sandra L., and Nancy J. Turner. 2000. " 'Just Like a Garden': Traditional Plant Resource Management and Biodiversity Conservation on the British Columbia Plateau." In *Biodiversity and Native North America*, ed. Paul Minnis and Wayne Elisens. Norman, OK: University of Oklahoma Press, pp. 133–79.

Pearkes, Eileen Delehanty. 2002. *The Geography of Memory: Recovering Stories of a Landscape's First People*. Nelson, BC: Kutenai House Press.

Peña, Devon G. 1999. "Cultural Landscapes and Biodiversity: The Ethnoecology of an Upper Rio Grande Watershed Commons." In *Ethnoecology: Situated Knowledge/Located Lives*, ed. Virginia D. Nazarea. Tucson, AZ: University of Arizona Press, pp. 107–32.

Pielou, E.C. 1991. *After the Ice Age: The Return of Life to Glaciated North America.* Chicago, IL: University of Chicago Press.

Pitcher, Tony J., Paul Hart and Daniel Pauly. 1998. Preface to *Reinventing Fisheries Management.* London, UK: Kluwer Academic Publishers.

Pojar, Jim, and Andy MacKinnon, eds. 1994. *Plants of Coastal British Columbia Including Washington, Oregon and Alaska.* Vancouver, BC and Edmonton, AB: Lone Pine Publishing.

Poser, William J. 2003. The Names of the First Nations Languages in British Columbia. (Web site: www.cis.upenn.edu/~wjposer/.downloads/bclgnames.pdf).

Posey, Darrell A. 1989. "Alternatives to Forest Destruction: Lessons from the Mêbêngokre Indians." *The Ecologist* 19:241–44.

———. 1990. "The Science of the Mêbêngôkre." *Orion Nature Quarterly* 9 (3):16–23.

Posey, Darrell A., and William Balée, eds. 1989. *Resource Management in Amazonia.* Vol. 7 of *Advances in Economic Botany.* New York: New York Botanical Garden.

Prentice, Alison L., and Susan E. Houston. 1975. *Family, School and Society in Nineteenth-Century Canada.* Toronto, ON: Oxford University Press.

Pyne, Stephen J. 1995. *World Fire: The Culture of Fire on Earth.* New York: Henry Holt & Co.

———. 2002. *Fire: A Brief History.* Seattle, WA: University of Washington Press.

Rea, Amadeo M. 1997. *At the Desert's Green Edge: An Ethnobotany of the Gila River Pima.* Tucson, AZ: University of Arizona Press.

Richardson, A. 1982. "The Control of Productive Resources on the Northwest Coast of North America." In *Resource Managers: North American and Australian Hunter-gatherers,* ed. N.M. Williams and E.S. Hunn. American Association for the Advancement of Science Symposium No. 67. ed. Boulder, CO: Westview Press, pp. 93–120.

Robinson, G. 1956. *Tales of Kitimaat.* Kitimat, BC: Northern Sentinel Press.

Rowe, J. Stan. 1990. *Home Place: Essays on Ecology.* Edmonton, AB: NeWest Publishers.

Russell, Priscilla N. 1991. *English Bay and Port Graham Alutiiq Plantlore: An Ethnobotany of the Peoples of English Bay and Port Graham, Kenai Peninsula, Alaska.* Homer, AK: Pratt Museum and Anchorage, AK: Chugach Heritage Foundation and Alaska Native Plant Society.

Ryder, June M., and Michael Church. 1986. "The Lillooet Terraces of Fraser River: Paleo-environmental Inquiry." *Canadian Journal of Earth Sciences* 23:869–84.

Sagan, Carl. 1980. *Cosmos.* New York: Random House.

Salmón, Enrique. 1996. "Language Affects Knowledge." *Winds of Change* (Summer): 70–72.

————. 2000a. "Kincentric Ecology: Indigenous Perceptions of the Human-Nature Relationship." *Ecological Applications* 10(5):1327–32.

————. 2000b. "*Iwígara*. A Rarámuri Cognitive Model of Biodiversity and Its Effects on Land Management." In *Biodiversity and Native America,* ed. Paul E. Minnis and Wayne J. Elisens. Norman, OK: University of Oklahoma Press, pp. 180–203.

Salmon River Restoration Committee. 1993. *Voices of the River,* or *Return of the River: A Community's Participation in Streambank Restoration.* Salmon Arm, BC: Fred Bird & Associates Ltd. <video>.

Sapir, E. 1913–14. Unpublished notes: Nootka, Notebook 17, p. 23a, December 1913–January 1914, Roll 23. Microfilm from American Philosophical Society. Copy in possession of Denis St. Clair, Victoria, BC.

Scholefield, E.O.S. 1914. *British Columbia. From the Earliest Times to the Present.* Vols. 1 and 2. Vancouver, BC: S.J. Clarke Publishing Company.

Scientific Panel for Sustainable Forest Practices in Clayoquot Sound. (see Clayoquot Scientific Panel)

Sewid-Smith, Daisy (*My-yah-nelth*). 1979. *Prosecution or Persecution?* Cape Mudge, BC: Nu-yum-balees Society.

————. 1998. Address at "Helping the Land Heal" conference. Ecological Restoration in British Columbia. Restoration of Natural Systems Program, University of Victoria, BC.

Sewid-Smith, Daisy, and Chief A. Dick, interviewed by N.J. Turner. 1998. "The Sacred Cedar Tree of the Kwakwaka'wakw People." In *Stars Above, Earth Below: Native Americans and Nature,* ed. M. Bol. Pittsburgh, PA: The Carnegie Museum of Natural History, pp. 189–209.

Shewchuk, Murphy, ed. 1989. *Widow Smith of Spence's Bridge.* Merritt, BC: Shewchuk, Sonotek Publishing.

Simonsen, Bjorn O., Sandra Peacock, James Haggerty, Jonathan Secter and Frank Duerden. 1997. *Report of the First Nations Cultural Heritage Impact Assessment and Consultation, Bamberton Town Development Project.* Report submitted to Environmental Assessment Office, Province of B.C. and Greystone Properties Ltd. First Nations Management Committee, Bamberton Project Cultural Heritage Component, Victoria, BC. (Web site: www.eco.gov.bc.ca/epic/output/html/deploy/epic_project_home_129.html)

Smith, Harlan I. 1998. *Ethnobotany of the Gitksan Indians of British Columbia,* ed. Brian D. Compton, Bruce Rigsby and Marie-Lucie Tarpent. National Museum of Civilization, Mercury Series, Ottawa.

Smith, Robin Y. 1997. *Hishuk ish ts'awalk—All Things Are One: Traditional Ecological Knowledge and Forest Practices of Ahousaht First Nations' Traditional Territory,*

Clayoquot Sound, B.C. M.Sc. thesis, Canadian Heritage and Development Studies, Trent University, Peterborough, ON.

Sproat, Gilbert Malcolm. 1987. *The Nootka: Scenes and Studies of Savage Life,* ed. C. Lillard. Victoria, BC: Sono Nis Press. (Originally published 1868 by Smith, Elder, and Co., London, UK.)

Spurgeon, Terry. 2001. *Wapato* (Sagittaria latifolia) *in Katzie Traditional Territory, Pitt Meadows, British Columbia.* M.A. thesis, Department of Archaeology, Simon Fraser University, Burnaby, BC.

Steedman, Elsie V., and James A. Teit. 1930. *Ethnobotany of the Thompson Indians of British Columbia.* Bureau of American Ethnology 45th Annual Report, 1927–28. Washington, DC: Smithsonian Institution, pp. 441–522.

Stevens, Michelle. 1999. *The Ethnoecology and Autecology of White Root* (Carex barbarae *Dewey*): *Implications for Restoration.* Ph.D. dissertation, Ecosystems and Landscape Ecology, University of California, Davis, CA.

Stewart, Hilary. 1977. *Indian Fishing: Early Methods on the Northwest Coast.* Seattle, WA: University of Washington Press.

———. 1984. *Cedar: Tree of Life to the Northwest Coast Indians.* Vancouver, BC: Douglas & McIntyre and Seattle, WA: University of Washington Press.

Stewart, Omer C. 1956. "Fire as the First Great Force Employed by Man." In *Man's Role in Changing the Face of the Earth,* ed. W.L. Thomas. Chicago, IL: University of Chicago Press, pp. 115–33.

Stockton, Steve, Anthony J. Gaston and Jean-Louis Martin. 2001. "Where Have All the Flowers Gone? The Impact of Introduced Black-tailed Deer on the Shoreline Vegetation of Haida Gwaii, British Columbia." In *Laskeek Bay Research, 1999–2000.* No. 10, Laskeek Bay Conservation Society, Annual Scientific Reports, 1999 and 2000, ed. Anthony J. Gaston. Queen Charlotte City, BC, March 2001, pp. 31–40.

Suttles, Wayne P. 1955. *Katzie Ethnographic Notes.* Anthropology in British Columbia, Memoir No. 2, Victoria, BC.

———. 1987. *Coast Salish Essays.* Vancouver, BC: Talonbooks and Seattle, WA: University of Washington Press.

———, ed. 1990. *Handbook of North American Indians.* Vol. 7, *Northwest Coast.* (William C. Sturtevant, gen. ed.). Washington, DC: Smithsonian Institution.

Suzuki, David. 2001. "The Salmon Forest." *The Nature of Things,* Canadian Broadcasting Corporation, Vancouver, BC. <video>

Swanton, John R. 1905a. "Contributions to the Ethnology of the Haida." Vol. 5, part 1 of *The Jesup North Pacific Expedition.* New York: G.E. Stechert.

———. 1905b. *Haida Texts and Myths: Skidegate Dialect.* Smithsonian Institution

Bureau of American Ethnology, Bulletin 29, Government Printing Office, Washington, DC.

Swezey, Sean L., and Robert F. Heizer. 1993. "Ritual Management of Salmonid Fish Resources." In *Before the Wilderness: Environmental Management by Native Californians,* ed. Thomas C. Blackburn and Kat Anderson. Menlo Park, CA: Ballena Press, pp. 299–327.

Swoboda, Leo John. 1971. *Lillooet Phonology, Texts and Dictionary.* M.A. thesis, Department of Linguistics, University of British Columbia, Vancouver, BC.

Szczawinski, Adam F., and A.S. Harrison. 1972. *Flora of the Saanich Peninsula: Annotated List of Vascular Plants.* Occasional paper No. 16. British Columbia Provincial Museum, Victoria, BC.

Teit, James A. n.d. Unpublished ethnographic Field Notes. Originals held with the American Philosophical Society Library, Philadelphia, PA. Copy courtesy Provincial Archives of British Columbia (now British Columbia Archives, Royal British Columbia Museum), Victoria, BC.

———. 1898. *Traditions of the Thompson River Indians of British Columbia.* American Folk-lore Society. New York: Houghton, Mifflin & Co.

———. 1900. *The Thompson Indians.* Memoir of the American Museum of Natural History, Vol. 1, part 4, New York.

———. 1906. *The Lillooet Indians.* Memoir of the American Museum of Natural History, No. 4, part 7, New York.

———. 1909. *The Shuswap.* Memoir of the American Museum of Natural History, Vol. 4, part 4, New York.

———. 1912. *Mythology of the Thompson Indians.* Vol. 7, part 2. In *The Jesup North Pacific Expedition,* ed. Franz Boas. Memoir of the American Museum of Natural History. New York: G.E. Stechert.

Thomas, Mary. 1996. *Birch Bark Baskets: A Film.* Mary Thomas and Family, Neskonlith Band, Salmon Arm, BC. <video>

———. 1998. Keynote speaker. "Helping the Land Heal" conference. Ecological Restoration in British Columbia. Restoration of Natural Systems Program, University of Victoria, BC.

———. 2002. *The Wisdom of Dr. Mary Thomas,* ed. N. Turner, A. Garibaldi, R. Hood and J. Infanti. School of Environmental Studies, University of Victoria, Victoria, BC.

Thomas, Mary, Nancy J. Turner and Ann Garibaldi. In prep. " 'Everything Is Deteriorating': Environmental and Cultural Loss in Secwepemc Territory." In *Secwepemc People and Plants: Research Papers in Shuswap Ethnobotany,* K.P. Bannister, N. Turner and M.B. Ignace, ed. Secwepemc Cultural Education Society,

Kamloops. Submitted to Western Geographic Series, University of Victoria, Victoria, BC.

Thompson, Stith. 1965. "The Star Husband Tale." In *The Study of Folklore,* ed. Alan Dundes. Englewood Cliffs, NJ: Prentice-Hall, Inc., pp. 414–59.

Trosper, Ron. 1998. "Incentive Systems that Support Sustainability: A First Nations Example." Available online in *Conservation Ecology* 2(2), December 1998, www.consecol.org/vol2/iss2/art11.

———2003. "Resilience in Pre-contact Pacific Northwest Social Ecological Systems." *Conservation Ecology* 7(3): 6 March 2003, www.cansecol.org/vol7/iss3/art6.

Turner, Nancy J. 1973. "The Ethnobotany of the Bella Coola Indians of British Columbia." *Syesis* 6:193–220.

———. 1974. "Plant Taxonomic Systems and Ethnobotany of Three Contemporary Indian Groups of the Pacific Northwest (Haida, Bella Coola, and Lillooet)." *Syesis* 7: Supplement 1.

———. 1981. "Indian Use of *Shepherdia canadensis,* Soapberry, in Western North America." *Davidsonia* 12(1):1–14.

———. 1984. "Counter-irritant and Other Medicinal Uses of Plants in Ranunculaceae by Native Peoples in British Columbia and Neighbouring Areas." *Journal of Ethnopharmacology* 11:181–201.

———. 1988. "Ethnobotany of Coniferous Trees in Thompson and Lillooet Interior Salish of British Columbia." *Economic Botany* 42(2):177–94.

———. 1992. "Plant Resources of the Stl'atl'imx (Fraser River Lillooet) People: A Window into the Past." In *Complex Cultures of the British Columbia Plateau: Traditional Stl'atl'imx Resource Use,* ed. Brian Hayden. Vancouver, BC: UBC Press, pp. 405–69.

———. 1995. *Food Plants of Coastal First Peoples.* Royal British Columbia Museum Handbook. Victoria, BC: University of British Columbia Press.

———. 1997a. *Food Plants of Interior First Peoples.* Vancouver, BC: University of British Columbia Press and Victoria, BC: Royal British Columbia Museum.

———. 1997b. " 'Le fruit de l'ours': Les rapports entre les plantes et les animaux dans les langues et les cultures amérindiennes de la Côte-Ouest" ('The Bear's Own Berry': Ethnobotanical Knowledge as a Reflection of Plant/Animal Interrelationships in Northwestern North America). In *Recherches amérindiennes au Québec* 27(3–4): 31–48. Special edition of *Des Plantes et des Animaux: Visions et Pratiques Autochtones,* ed. Pierre Beaucage. Montreal, QC: Université de Montréal.

———, ed. 1997c. *"Making It With Your Hands": Projects Using Indigenous Plant Materials from British Columbia,* by the students of Environmental Studies 416, Aboriginal Peoples and the Plant World, fall 1997 classes, School of Environmental Studies, University of Victoria, BC.

————. 1998. *Plant Technology of British Columbia First Peoples.* Vancouver, BC: University of British Columbia Press and Victoria, BC: Royal British Columbia Museum.

————. 1999. " 'Time to Burn': Traditional Use of Fire to Enhance Resource Production by Aboriginal Peoples in British Columbia." In *Indians, Fire and the Land in the Pacific Northwest,* ed. Robert Boyd. Corvallis, OR: Oregon State University Press, pp. 185–218.

————. 2004. *Plants of Haida Gwaii. X̱aadaa Gwaay gud gina k̲'aws (Skidegate), X̱aadaa Gwaayee guu giin k̲'aws (Massett).* Victoria, BC and Winlaw, BC: Sono Nis Press.

Turner, Nancy J., and E. Richard Atleo (Chief *Umeek*). 1998. "Pacific North American First Peoples and the Environment." In *Environment and Development Values in the Pacific,* ed. H. Coward. Albany, NY: Centre for Studies in Religion and Society, State University of New York, pp. 105–24.

Turner, Nancy J., and Marcus A.M. Bell. 1971. "The Ethnobotany of the Coast Salish Indians of Vancouver Island." *Economic Botany* 25(1):63–104.

Turner, Nancy J., Randy Bouchard and Dorothy I.D. Kennedy. 1980. *Ethnobotany of the Okanagan-Colville Indians of British Columbia and Washington.* B.C. Provincial Museum Occasional Paper, No. 21, Victoria, BC.

Turner, Nancy J., and Cecil H. Brown. 2004. "Grass, Hay, and Weedy Growth: Utility and Semantics of Interior Salish Botanical Terms." In *Studies in Salish Linguistics in Honor of M. Dale Kinkade,* ed. Donna B. Gerdts and Lisa Matthewson. Occasional papers in Linguistics No. 17, Missoula, MT: University of Montana, pp. 410–28.

Turner, N.J., I.J. Davidson-Hunt and M. O'Flaherty. 2003. "Living on the Edge: Ecological and Cultural Edges as Sources of Diversity for Social-ecological Resilience." *Human Ecology* 31(3):439–63.

Turner, Nancy J., Chief A. Dick (*Kwaxsistala*), D. Sewid-Smith (*Mayanilth*), K. Recalma-Clutesi (*Ogwilogwa*), and D. Deur. In press. " 'From the beginning of time': Indigenous Land Rights, Environment and Resources on the British Columbia Coast." In *Forests, Fields, and Fish: Politiciẓed Indigenous Landscapes,* ed. M. K. Steinberg. Austin, TX: University of Texas Press.

Turner, Nancy J., and Barbara S. Efrat. 1982. *Ethnobotany of the Hesquiat Indians of Vancouver Island.* British Columbia Provincial Museum. Cultural Recovery Paper No. 2, Victoria, BC.

Turner, Nancy J., Marianne B. Ignace and Ronald Ignace. 2000. "Traditional Ecological Knowledge and Wisdom of Aboriginal Peoples in British Columbia." *Ecological Applications* 10(5):181–93. Special issue, ed. Jesse Ford and Dennis Martinez.

Turner, Nancy J., and Sandra Peacock. In press. "Solving the Perennial Paradox: Ethnobotanical Evidence for Plant Resource Management on the Northwest Coast." In *"Keeping It Living": Indigenous Plant Management on the Northwest Coast*, ed. Douglas Deur and Nancy J. Turner. Seattle, WA: University of Washington Press.

Turner, Nancy J., Robin Y. Smith and James T. Jones. In press. " 'A fine line between two nations': Ownership Patterns for Plant Resources among Northwest Coast Indigenous Peoples—Implications for Plant Conservation and Management." In *"Keeping it Living": Indigenous Plant Management on the Northwest Coast*, eds. Douglas Deur and Nancy J. Turner. Seattle, WA: University of Washington Press.

Turner, Nancy J., and Adam F. Szczawinski. 1991. *Common Poisonous Plants and Mushrooms of North America*. Portland, OR: Timber Press.

Turner, Nancy J., John Thomas, Barry F. Carlson and Robert T. Ogilvie. 1983. *Ethnobotany of the Nitinaht Indians of Vancouver Island*. British Columbia Provincial Museum Occasional Paper No. 24, Victoria, BC.

Turner, Nancy J., Laurence C. Thompson, M. Terry Thompson and Annie Z. York. 1990. *Thompson Ethnobotany: Knowledge and Usage of Plants by the Thompson Indians of British Columbia*. Royal British Columbia Museum, Memoir No. 3, Victoria, BC.

Umeek (E. Richard Atleo). 2004. *Tsawalk: A Nuu-chah-nulth Worldview*. Vancouver, BC: UBC Press.

U'mista Cultural Society, Juanita Pasco and Brian D. Compton. 1998. *The Living World: Plants and Animals of the Kwakwaka'wakw*. Alert Bay, BC: U'Mista Cultural Society.

UNESCO. 2004. *Encyclopedia of Life Support Systems*. Paris, France: Division of Science Analysis and Policies and Oxford, UK: EOLSS Publishers Co. Ltd. Web site: www.eolss.net.

Vancouver, George. 1801. *A Voyage of Discovery to the North Pacific, and Round the World*. London, UK: Printed for John Stockdale.

VanDine, D.F. 1983. "Drynoch Landslide, British Columbia—A History." *Canadian Geotechnical Journal* 20:82–103.

Vila, B., F. Guibal and J.L. Martin. 2001. "Impact of Browsing on Forest Understory in Haida Gwaii: A Dendro-ecological Approach." *Laskeek Bay Research* 10:62–73.

Wachtel, Paul L. 1989. *The Poverty of Affluence: A Psychological Portrait of the American Way of Life*. Philadelphia, PA: New Society Publishers.

Walker, Deward E., ed. 1998. *Handbook of North American Indians*. Vol. 12, *Plateau* (William C. Sturtevant, gen. ed.). Washington, DC: Smithsonian Institution.

Wall, Steve. 1993. *Wisdom's Daughters: Conversations with Women Elders of Native America.* New York: HarperCollins.

Whitford, H.N., and R.D. Craig. 1918. *Forests of British Columbia.* Ottawa, ON: Commission of Conservation.

Wickwire, Wendy C. 1994. "To See Ourselves as the Other's Other: Nlaka'pamux Contact Narratives." *The Canadian Historical Review* 75:1–20.

———. 1998. " 'We Shall Drink from the Stream and So Shall You': James A. Teit and Native Resistance in British Columbia, 1908–22." *The Canadian Historical Review* 79(2):199–235.

York, Annie, Richard Daly and Chris Arnett. 1993. *They Write Their Dreams on the Rock Forever: Rock Writings in the Stein River Valley of British Columbia.* Vancouver, BC: Talonbooks.

Young, Elspeth, Helen Ross, J. Johnston and J. Kesteven. 1991. *Caring for Country: Aborigines and Land Management.* Canberra, Australia: Australian Government Publishing Service.

Index